T0284936

Also by Urvashi Vaid

Virtual Equality: The Mainstreaming of Gay & Lesbian Liberation

Creating Change: Public Policy, Sexuality and Civil Rights
(with John D'Emilio and William Turner)

IRRESISTIBLE REVOLUTION

CONFRONTING RACE, CLASS AND THE ASSUMPTIONS OF LESBIAN, GAY, BISEXUAL, AND TRANSGENDER POLITICS

URVASHI VAID

MAGNUS
BOOKS

First Magnus Edition 2012

Edited by: Don Weise
Design: © Emerson, Wajdowicz Studios/www.DesignEWS.com
Photography: ©Jurek Wajdowicz

ISBN: 978-1-936833-29-0

www.magnusbooks.com

For Kate Clinton

TABLE OF CONTENTS

INTRODUCTION

"The responsibility of a writer representing an oppressed people is to make revolution irresistible."[1]
—Toni Cade Bambara

As I write this introduction, a dizzying array of events seem to suggest that the ultimate victory of the lesbian, gay, bisexual, and transgender (LGBT) movement is not only inevitable, but also irresistible. A sweeping decision by the 9th Circuit Court of Appeals condemns the unconstitutionality of Proposition 8, the anti-marriage amendment passed by California voters in 2008, holding that the measure "serves no purpose, and has no effect, other than to lessen the status and human dignity of gays and lesbians in California, and to officially reclassify their relationships and families as inferior to those of opposite-sex couples."[2] The Washington State Legislature passed, and its Governor signed, a law making marriage available to same-sex couples.[3] A week later, the New Jersey Legislature passed a same-sex marriage law, only to have its Governor veto the measure. The fight to overturn that veto has already begun.[4] Maryland just became the 8th state to offer marriage equality, although proponents must now defend the measure at the ballot in the fall.[5] On the global level, a grassroots campaign generated more than 70,000 letters of protest and resulted in the reversal of a Swedish government policy that required transgender persons to undergo sterilization in order to secure legal gender recognition.[6] These major achievements accompany literally dozens of other less-heralded gains made on nearly a daily basis by a vigorous and multi-faceted LGBT movement that operates at the local, statewide, national level in the U.S., in countries around the world, and increasingly at the transnational level. This is a uniquely gratifying and exciting moment in which to be part of the LGBT movement.

Despite the rather personal pride I feel as a movement veteran in the achievements being won, I find myself more cautious than euphoric. This is a mixed moment for LGBT liberation. We are making progress, and experiencing frustrating setbacks (such as having to defend many legislative gains against ballot initiatives aimed at their rescission). We are more visible than ever, and yet even today, large numbers of our people remain closeted, silent, and uninvolved. Support for LGBT nondiscrimination laws is high, but the national election campaign of 2012 is rife with anti-gay rhetoric and policy promises, freely expressed and cheered on by major political candidates. Cultural visibility is also strong, social tolerance rising, yet family homophobia remains a pervasive reality for millions of LGBT people. Internal divisions based on ideology, racial difference, economic disparity, disagreements about the prominence that gender and transgender issues should have on the LGBT political agenda, continue to influence the strategies and choices the movement makes. And the opponents of LGBT freedom remain intransigent, crafty, and militant in their refusal of demands for justice.

The LGBT movement's confidence and complexity were both in evidence at the 2012 Creating Change Conference, the largest national gathering of supporters of LGBT rights in the U.S., sponsored annually by the National Gay and Lesbian Task Force (NGLTF). More than 3,000 people who work in the grassroots movement participated in Creating Change, and their optimism about the future was energizing. The scope of the aspirations of the attendees was exciting to witness throughout the gathering, as advocates discussed projects to strengthen the life chances and political power of queer communities less powerful (homeless youth, working people, prisoners, for example) and to increase attention to issues less prioritized (disability, poverty, racial justice, immigration reform, to name three). The creative work of these activists informs my perspective on the state of the LGBT movement. This book joins a lively, ongoing and decades-old conversation about the agenda, composition, and imagination of the LGBT movement.

Several concerns motivate the essays in this book, and they set the context for my argument that an innovative LGBT movement must move beyond seeking the reform of laws to maximizing the life-chances, freedom, and self-determination of all LGBT people. First, is the ever-clearer truth that the battle for the full acceptance of queer people is cultural, or a struggle about the values that guide the societies in which we live, as much as it is a political struggle for the reform of laws. California and Uganda teach the same lesson: LGBT people will continue to lose at the polls and will face outrageous attempts to deprive us of full citizenship, to criminalize our relationships, and even to institute the death penalty against us, if we do not contest the denigration of our lives by religious and political leaders who appoint themselves arbiters of the great moral codes and traditions developed by humankind. As the 9th Circuit Court noted in its February 2012 decision to strike down the anti-gay Proposition 8, "Tradition is a legitimate consideration in policymaking, of course, but it cannot be an end unto itself."[7] This simple recognition, in a sense, drives a small group of innovators around the world who seek fundamental change on matters concerning sexuality and gender through an articulation of inclusive and ethical values. This work is taking place both inside religious traditions and outside them, in the public sphere, for example, in efforts to draft new constitutions and give practical meaning to human rights treaties and codes.

Second, although the LGBT movement sits within a global, plural, and multiracial world, its leadership still remains predominantly white, male, and economically priviledged. Hard-earned experience with life and death struggles against HIV/AIDS, violence, state repression, religious fundamentalisms, and political demagoguery teaches us of the need to expand the movement's leadership, broaden its agenda and programs to reflect the lives of people of color in the U.S. and non-Western countries, and to develop new organizing strategies and messages. Change in the nature and content of the LGBT movement's leadership is both possible and necessary for the continued success of this movement.

Third, it is clear that resistance to gender equality is a profound obstacle not just for women, but also for transgender persons, bisexual people, gay men, and lesbians. The brilliant leadership of transgender activists around the world has moved gender variance, nonconformity, and identities into the public consciousness to an unprecedented degree. The implications of new understandings of gender variance are still emerging and must be supported vigilantly to insure vulnerable people are protected and majority views of gender changed through education and policy change. But another, and even older, type of gender-challenge remains ahead for the LGBT movement: the challenge of transforming the vileness of the current landscape for women. At a moment in which women's power is still curtailed in many parts of the world and her earning power still fractional to that of a man; when women are seen primarily and still through their relationships with men; when women are not allowed to be agents in control of their own wombs, much less their own sexual pleasure; when women are still genitally mutilated in the name of tradition; when women individually are raped and abused in massive numbers in every culture and country in the world, violence for which women as a class pay the price; and, when there is still no penalty that men as a class bear for these violations, we must concede that we have not at all achieved the feminist goals of women's liberation and men's transformation.

Serious obstacles to ending misogyny and securing women's freedom come from the resistance of social and political institutions to change (religion, family, law, media, and government, among them). The global LGBT and feminist movements present a direct challenge to these institutions and the ways in which they reproduce and enforce traditions of order, family structure, gender-based power and autonomy, the stigmatization of femaleness, and the privileging of heterosexuality. The progress made to advance the human rights of LGBT people is undermined by the astonishing retreat of the mainstream LGBT movement from active engagement with projects that aim to challenge misogyny and end patriarchal bias.

I have long believed that what made the LGBT movement "irresistible" was its honesty. Truth may be unpleasant, unpopular, and sometimes unbearable to speak, but its power is undeniable. The LGBT movement changed attitudes, laws, cultural possibilities, sexual ideas, and family forms in revolutionary ways by telling truths about desire and gender, by showing the power of intimacy beyond reproduction, and by being able to bridge—with difficulty it is true, but also with success—across a wide range of social fissures: ideological, racial, gendered, and economic. Telling the truth about desire was and still remains revolutionary in a world built upon its control and repression.

Yet, lately, I have come to a more cynical conclusion: perhaps it is our cooptation that has made queer progress possible and so irresistible to the non-gay establishment. We have invested heavily in making sure that the heterosexist world sees us as no threat to its norms and traditions. Thus, women's reproductive freedom and choice, once a core value of LGBT liberation, are now absent from the mainstream gay rights movement; racial justice is still not a core goal of the mainstream movement, despite four decades of calls for such leadership; transgender politics and equality are paid lip service, but with the exception of the NGLTF, the mainstream movement's commitment to these remains thin and unreliable; and an agenda that addresses poverty is still absent from the mainstream, while an uncritical embrace of corporations and corporate values is touted as a norm.

The LGBT movement has been coopted by the very institutions it once sought to transform. Heterosexuality, the nuclear family, the monogamous couple-form are our new normal. In place of activism and mobilization, with a handful of notable exceptions, LGBT mainstream organizations have become a passive society of spectators, following the lead of donors and pollsters rather than advocating on behalf of sectors of the community that are less economically powerful and politically popular. The movement today does not question economic priorities and hierarchies, it seems willing to reconstitute gender inequality in queer drag, and to many it even insists we were "born this way," ignoring the actual lived experience of millions of women and men, and of bisexual people, and acting as if genetics ought to be the basis of political freedom. Lost long ago in the military fight against the anti-gay "Don't Ask, Don't Tell" policy was a decades-old critique of the military itself. It has been replaced by our acceptance of the inevitability, and the class politics, of war. A movement that once fought to expand definitions of family, to extend health benefits to all, to widen legal protection and recognition for forms of families not defined by marital status or parental status, now fights primarily for inclusion into heterosexual forms of intimacy and traditions of family structure that have proved incompatible with today's economic and cultural realities. Today's mainstream movement primarily seeks admission to existing regimes of intimacy, work, community, and governance that are riddled with inequality and violence. The power it once derived from the queer experience of otherness has long been replaced by the pleasure it takes in a queering of belonging.

The talks on which this book is based are, in a sense, interventions aimed at the silences and gaps that threaten to undercut the gains made by the mainstream LGBT movement in the U.S., namely, the mainstream movement's resistance to incorporating issues of economic, racial, and gender justice. The issues they engage reflect only a fraction of the challenges facing LGBT people today, and this book makes no claims to being comprehensive, much less adequately representative of the complex communities of which it speaks.

Lectures and public talks are a particular form of voice and engagement in the public sphere. They attest to a faith in ideas and optimism about one's audience. Public talks are intimate and unique events. They take place in a particular place and time, and they are given before people who have chosen to come because they are curious or want to argue, to question or to be inspired, or perhaps even because they must, as students assigned to attend a dreary lecture. The format of a public lecture (or speech) challenges both speaker and audience to pay attention to the moment in which they occur, to be relevant, and to be accessible. I have given speeches for decades and learned a great deal from the process. I like the immediacy of an audience. I like the unknown they represent—one never knows what questions will arise after, whether the ideas that animate you are at all interesting to a group you have never met. I like the conversational nature of a talk, and the freedom it provides to make any argument one wants to attempt. All the problems of the world are not solved in a talk, but many can be posed.

The essays in this volume speak about the mainstream LGBT movement in the U.S. in which I have worked and, as such, they are a form of self-criticism. This book is informed, and some might say limited, by this experience—a more than three-decade involvement in LGBT political practice that has involved me in efforts to change law and public policy, change attitudes and culture, engage religious tradition, expand the notion of family, increase resources for LGBT organizing and communities, as well as with the practicalities of building institutions, coalitions, multi-issue movements, and campaigns. These essays clearly reflect my ambivalence about the movement: frustration at its blinders, coupled with a persistent confidence that the many people within the LGBT community committed to challenging race, class, and gender exclusion are critical to its future.

The talks on which this book is based were delivered before various audiences, noted at the start of each essay—from colleges to conferences, from rallies to large forums. I have left their original arguments intact and attempted in the editing to trim outdated or redundant information and update data points where possible. Seven of the essays in this book grew out of talks written and given over the past two years; two talks were originally written in the late 1990s. The first four essays consider in different ways the dominant equality politics of the mainstream LGBT movement from the perspective of race, class, and progressive values. These talks reflect a longstanding question with which I have been concerned: namely, for whom does the movement work, and who benefits from its avoidance of poverty and economic justice. The next three essays explore the connection between feminism and LGBT politics, starting with some historical reflection and ending with a conception of what dykes stand for politically. The final two essays consider the values and strategies queer politics needs in order to move forward.

The talks collected in this book grow out of a queer politics that questions compliance and bristles at control. Such a politics seeks new forms of community, solidarity, and democratic possibility. The continued success of the LGBT liberation movement lies in its willingness to embrace otherness and a radical kind of love expressed in our boundless compassion for the broader communities from which we come. In a supposedly post-civil rights era, which claims as its legacy a social consciousness about human rights that is global and universal, an argument that calls attention to age-old identities like race, class, and even the idea of woman itself, may well be dismissed by some. But the experiences that inform this book caution against such glib and ideological denial. Racial and ethnic differences in power, the enforcement of class-privilege and economic inequality, the suppression of women's cultural and political freedom, and the fears triggered by sexual rights and gender expression are the main forces that motivate struggles for social change, as well as the main elements that undergird systems of control that resist social change movements around the world.

For me, an irresistible revolution is one in which the LGBT movement deploys the power it has gained to challenge and change traditions of ignorance, violence, poverty, and authoritarian control that continue to dominate the world. This moment calls for a renewed progressive and feminist politics defined not by narrowing but by expansion. It calls on us to answer the question posed by the Indian gay advocate and lawyer, Arvind Narrain: "Is the imagination of queer politics merely about access to rights for queer citizens or also about questioning structures which limit the very potential of human freedom?"[8]

Urvashi Vaid
May 2012
New York City

STILL AIN'T SATISFIED

Equality and the Limits
of LGBT Politics[9]

In 1977, as the anti-gay Christian singer and spokesperson for the Florida Orange Grower's Association, Anita Bryant, waged a public relations and electoral campaign against gay rights, the lesbian-record company, Olivia, produced an album called Lesbian Concentrate. Featuring a stylized frozen orange juice can on its cover, the vinyl LP was at the forefront of a cultural and politically-organized lesbian and feminist movement that grew out of a tradition of labor, civil rights, and anti-war protest music. I started my queer organizing in this early lesbian feminist, cultural movement, and learned much from its analysis of power, its humor, and insistence on politicizing everything.

During this time, I came across the song "Still Ain't Satisfied," an intervention aimed at the cooptation of liberal progress, by the Red Star Singers. The song is available online with its lyrics: "Well they've got women on TV, but I still ain't satisfied; 'Cause cooptation's all I see, but I still ain't satisfied; They call me Ms., they sell me blue jeans; They call it women's lib, they make it sound obscene; And I still ain't; Woa they lied…And I still ain't satisfied."[10]

When I sat down to write this talk in early 2011, I had this song and the question of cooptation of the LGBT movement in my head. Cooptation is the appropriation or taking over of an idea or faction by another in a manner that defuses the threat posed by the idea assimilated. It is a concept more troubling than compromise because it implies a selling out of the original goal. I was concerned that our movement had cheapened the word equality into a brand, not a meaningful goal measured in the lived experience of queer people. Influenced by critical race theory and its critique of civil rights law, by transgender activists and their challenge to the queer mainstream, and by the questions posed by queer theoreticians to the racism of the LGBT mainstream's failure to address the surveillance and criminalization of queers of color, I decided to try to answer why I thought equality politics was limited and what could be done to redeem it. The occasion for this talk was an invitation by the newly formed Center for Lesbian, Gay, Bisexual and Transgender Public Policy at the Roosevelt Institute for Public Policy at Hunter College. The Center invited me to be its inaugural speaker, and the talk was held in the beautiful lecture hall of the Roosevelt Institute, on the site of a renovated house in New York's Upper East Side, where Eleanor and Franklin Roosevelt lived in a building adjacent to the home of Franklin's mother. The audience was a mix of grassroots activists, college students, faculty, and administrators from Hunter and other area schools.

An acquaintance baited me with a question at a dinner party not too long ago. "So, is the movement over?" she asked loudly, displaying in her tone her contempt for the LGBT movement.

I was surprised by the hostility behind the question. We were at a good friend's house, and my interrogator was someone from whom I had not expected that derision. Because I was not interested in embarrassing my hostesses, I demurred, "Gosh, what do you mean over? Not in my mind."

"You know, now that we have won marriage," she taunted, "it's over, done, right?"

We were dining in Massachusetts, so she was marginally correct about marriage. But it was a hostile question, posed by an African American lesbian whose civil rights credentials are unimpeachable and who, while not an active participant in the LGBT movement, had long been an ally. It was a revealing moment.

I smiled and said it was far from over, as she well knew, and no one around the dinner table was going to stop working till we won it all—and that meant racial, economic, social, and gender justice. Ultimately, her girlfriend told her to stop being so rude and the conversation moved on.

But as we moved on, I had to admit that while my answer was true to the views of my dining mates that particular night in Provincetown, the question of "when is it over" would be answered very differently at other queer dining tables. LGBT people differ in their views about the society they are fighting to achieve, about the forces arrayed against the full acceptance of LGBT people, and, therefore, about when the movement will in fact be successful. In the months since this conversation, her skepticism about the mainstream movement's commitment to anything but a narrow version of equal rights has been confirmed in scores of conversations.

Equality as a Goal is Not Enough

In my book *Virtual Equality*, written over seventeen years ago, I argued that if the LGBT movement ignored the broader dynamics of racism, economic exploitation, gender inequity, and cultural freedom, it would achieve what other civil rights movements in America have won—a partial, conditional simulacrum called equal rights, a state of *virtual equality* that would grant legal and formal equal rights to LGBT people, but that would not ultimately transform the institutions of society that repress, denigrate, and immobilize sexual and gender minorities. I still believe that diagnosis.

The formal, largely legal, and very liberal forms of equality that the LGBT movement has pursued over these past two decades have become far less substantive than the demands the movement made in the 1970s or even the 1980s. From a demand that LGBT people be able to live a public life in a world in which queer sexualities were not only tolerated but also celebrated, the LGBT movement now seeks the much narrower right to live an undisturbed private life. From an exploration of LGBT difference, the movement has turned into a cheerleading squad for LGBT sameness. And from an LGBT movement that was deeply engaged in the big arguments and fights of its day, the movement has become an island onto itself. In my lifetime, LGBT organizations have moved away from actively working for reproductive justice (both lesbians and progressive gay men fought for these rights throughout the 1970s and 1980s); challenging racism, which was a central plank at its first national March on Washington in 1979; working for economic justice— reflected in the pro-union coalition building done by Harvey Milk and activists in the late 1970s in the Coors beer boycott and the queer alliance with the United Farm Workers. No longer would we find a nationally organized queer presence at a major anti-war rally as there was at the 1981 demonstration in D.C. against the war in El Salvador, or the 1982 anti-nuclear demonstration in New York, or the Women's Pentagon Action. No longer are there many LGBT organizational voices engaged in the articulation of new urban policy, seeking a more effective response to homelessness and poverty, pressing their clout in the service of universal health care. Rather, today's mainstream LGBT movement is strangely silent on the broader social justice challenges facing the world, oddly complacent in its acceptance of race, gender and economic inequalities, and vocal only in its challenge to the conditions facing a de-raced and middle class conception of the "status queer."

This impoverishment of ambition and idealism in the movement is a strategic error. It misunderstands the challenge queer people pose to the status quo. It shamefully avoids the responsibility that a queer movement must take for all segments of LGBT communities. And it is deluded in its belief that legal, deeply symbolic, acts of recognition and mainstream integration, such as admission into traditional institutions like marriage, or grants of formal equal rights within the current form of capitalism, are actually acts of transformation that will end the rejection and marginalization of LGBT people. Without a more substantive definition of equality, without a commitment to its extension to all LGBT people, without deeper and more honest appraisals of the limits of the traditions to which LGBT people seek admission, without a willingness to risk gains made for the opportunity to create a world that truly affirms the intrinsic moral and human worth of people's sexual, racial, and gender difference, the LGBT politics currently pursued will yield only conditional equality, a simulation of freedom contingent upon "good behavior."

What Has Been Achieved?

There is a heady optimism within the mainstream of the U.S. LGBT movement born out of its recent successes and its remarkable ability to turn even defeat to rededication and advancement. This optimism is grounded in real change. Five gains fuel this optimism.

First, policy wins for LGBT equal rights in the U.S. have been dramatic and significant in the past few years. The U.S. military's "Don't Ask, Don't Tell" (DADT) policy was repealed, overcoming decades of deep resistance. New state and local non-discrimination ordinances were enacted, defended, and expanded, despite organized resistance at every step. Advances in court cases on marriage equality and the win in the New York State Legislature guaranteeing that right in the largest state to make the change so far were further bolstered by the Justice Department's decision not to defend the federal Defense of Marriage Act (DOMA).

Second, public opinion has shifted strongly in favor of LGBT human rights, across all issues. Support for same-sex marriage is now the marker most identified with these positive shifts in opinion, and has moved dramatically toward tolerance in recent years. A national survey by the Pew Research Center for the People & the Press, conducted from February 22, 2011 to March 1, 2011 among 1,504 adults, found that about as many adults (45%) now favor as oppose (46%) allowing gays and lesbians to marry legally. The Pew poll found that "opposition to same-sex marriage has declined by 19 percentage points since 1996, when 65% opposed gay marriage and only 27% were in favor...As has been the case since 1996, there is a wide partisan division on the question of same-sex marriage. Currently, 57% of Democrats favor making marriage legal, while only 23% of Republicans agrees."[11] An ABC News/*Washington Post* poll released in March of 2011 found that support for same-sex marriage increased "From a low of 32% in a 2004 survey of registered voters...to 53% today. Forty-four percent are opposed, down 18% from that 2004 survey." The poll found that support was highest among younger Americans and lower among conservatives, Republicans, and evangelicals, but attitudes towards tolerance increased among every category.[12]

Third, a growing number of governments around the world now take strong stances toward LGBT rights and incorporate issues of sexual orientation and gender identity (SOGI) into their national and international policy frameworks. In the past two years alone, the international community has called for an end to criminal laws and penalties based on SOGI, through a major new report issued by the United Nations Office of the High Commissioner for Human Rights (OHCHR).[13] The report followed the passage in June of 2011 of the first-ever resolution by the Human Rights Council of the U.N. condemning human rights violations based on SOGI.[14] Belatedly, but boldly, the U.S. stepped up its public advocacy for the inclusion of SOGI in human rights; Secretary of State Hillary Clinton's extraordinary speech at the Human Rights Council on December 6, 2011 set a new high-water mark for U.S. foreign policy.[15] Shifts made by U.S. State Department under the Obama Administration have been strong and especially helpful—from support for LGBT rights through embassies around the world, to strong leadership at the U.N., to pressure brought on countries to forestall new and repressive policies, to commitments to fund LGBT rights and development through U.S. foreign assistance.

Fourth, religious-based opposition to LGBT human rights has long stymied progress around the world, but faces new challenge from inside faith traditions. Pro-LGBT allies are more vocal and better organized. This emergence is reflected in the widening support for LGBT equality from all parts of the religious and ideological spectrum, from the 2009 fights in the Episcopal Church to allow openly LGBT clergy to serve, to growing support among lay Catholics in the U.S. for same-sex marriage, to the greater organizing by evangelical leaders who are pro-LGBT faith. Even the Holy See and deeply anti-gay religious leaders have publicly come out against violence based on SOGI.

Finally, demographic changes favor greater acceptance. Younger people are on the rise as a population in the U.S. and globally, and their attitudes towards LGBT issues are more open. Recent data on Latino attitudes suggests that LGBT advocates might also benefit from more tolerance from these communities than had previously been expected.[16] Data on shifts in Catholic public opinion are even more dramatic, revealing that large majorities support equal marriage rights for LGBT people.[17] However, some data have shown that attitudes of young African Americans are not as positive towards LGBT people as the attitudes of their white or Latino counterparts.[18]

The LGBT movement has made huge strides and will continue to make progress toward formal legal equality. This progress is an amazing story, and one to which I have dedicated thirty years, so far. Nothing in this argument should be heard as deriding or minimizing the importance of formal legal equality—it is a necessary first step, but it is not enough. Winning these battles for equal rights is not the same as winning the new world—which once was and should again be the LGBT movement's objective.

The Trouble with Equal

The word equality has many expressions in the movement— some groups work for "immigration equality," "marriage equality," "workplace equality," others fight for equal access to social services and public systems or equal treatment and equal protection under the law. Many organizations have the word equality in their names—Out and Equal, Equality Florida, Equality California, Mass Equality, American Foundation for Equal Rights, and the well-branded logo of the largest LGBT political organization has queered the equal sign itself.

But what is the content of this often-used word? For the LGBT movement today, equality means the formal recognition of LGBT people in all legal codes, equal access to all institutions and systems in society, and equal protection under one standard of law. Formal legal equality is represented in the goals of nondiscrimination and integration of sexual orientation and gender identity or expression into all frameworks of law, policy and public institutions. The LGBT movement pursues a strategy tested and proved by other civil rights movements (especially the black civil rights movement and the women's movement) of arguing for equal protection under state and federal Constitutions, promoting inclusion in all legislative frameworks of LGBT people, and seeking an end to forms of public and private discrimination based on sexual orientation and gender identity.

In recent years, LGBT advocates have added a new dimension to the legal conceptualization of equality rights. To address the fact that LGBT oppression lies deeper than legal resistance alone, and expresses itself as a condemnation of queerness as immoral or sinful, the term moral equality was coined. It creates a goal-oriented framework for the culture-shifting work that must be done within and beyond faith-based institutions, and through media, popular culture, art, and educational strategies. Moral equality contests the denigration of homosexuality and gender variance as sinful, immoral, and unnatural. Its impact can be documented in the changes in denominational policies towards LGBT people—a direct result of the organizing done by pro-LGBT people working inside Episcopal, Methodist, Unitarian Universalist, Presbyterian, Lutheran, Reform and Conservative Judaism, and even Catholic churches. The continuing challenge of achieving moral equality can also be tracked in the data points of the annual General Social Survey (GSS) or Gallup polls that continue to show that large numbers of people still consider same-sex sexual relations morally wrong. In 2004, 56% answered, "sexual relations between two adults of the same-sex are always wrong," but by 2010, that number had dropped to 44%. Tom Smith from the National Opinion Research Center (NORC) at the University of Chicago notes the significant generational divide in how people answer this question, as only 26% of people under 30 felt homosexuality was always wrong, while more than 63% of people over 70 thought the same.[19]

As social movements that have come before the LGBT struggle have clearly shown, formal equality—and even progress towards greater cultural recognition of one's humanity—can be achieved while leaving larger structural manifestations of inequality and deeper cultural prejudice intact. Thus, after the passage of the 1964 Voting Rights Act and 1965 Civil Rights Acts, the civil rights movement leader A. Phillip Randolph observed that the black civil rights movement suffered from the "curse of victory" where equal rights had been achieved but "blacks still were not equal in fact."[20] The civil rights movement was split on the way forward, with Dr. King proposing a focus on economic rights, and Bayard Rustin pursuing a focus on building a progressive electoral coalition of which the black vote would be an anchor. But the civil rights movement's leadership acknowledged then what is painfully evident today— that formal, equal rights were a crucial first step from which the struggle for black empowerment, freedom, and respect had to enter another stage. The achievement of civil rights made the gap between formal and substantive equality even more clear.

Similarly, the women's movement by the late 1980s had achieved many of the formal legal gains it sought, despite the failure of the passage of the federal Equal Rights Amendment (ERA). These achievements changed opportunities for women and over time they changed many cultural attitudes. However, thirty-plus years later, formal legal equality for women did not end the glass ceiling for women in top jobs. It did not produce equal pay for equal work—overall men still earn $1.20 to every dollar a woman earns.[21] And, it did not transform women's role in families, nor end violence against women by producing a new consciousness of respect for women among men.

Equal rights and equal protection are claims for access to the protection afforded by law and governmental regulations. But they can be granted without disturbing any of the hierarchies, institutions, and traditions that perpetuate the idea that LGBT difference is unnatural, wrong, or harmful to society. The current LGBT mainstream, in effect, asks no more than the right to be equal to the average straight person trapped within a structurally unfair, racist, and heterosexist system.

At a minimum, the first concern about the limits of equality politics that queer activists must heed is that winning equality ought not to be seen as the end-point of any struggle for liberty. Equality as the LGBT movement pursues it, within the constitutional framework of civil and political rights and equal protection law, is essential. It will win LGBT people the right to fight back against invidious discrimination. It has and will win LGBT the right to be regarded as people entitled to equal protection, equal opportunity, fair treatment, and access to all parts of our society. But these forms of access and opportunity will not disturb the hierarchies of privilege, prejudice, and power that condemn LGBT people because we are gender or sexually non-compliant. That requires a more disturbing goal, one that challenges the institutions, norms, and traditions to which we so desperately seek admission.

There is an uneasy relationship between most social justice movements and notions of tradition—be they embodied in traditional culture, traditional family, sacred tradition, or inherited teaching that is accepted as the natural order of things. We stand against traditions, yet we stand inside of them. We argue for new worlds, radical new possibilities even as we pursue accommodation and renovation of the status quo to make ourselves more comfortable. Constitutional notions of equality embody an acceptance of tradition—here defined as transmission of order, of the way things should be, and its acceptance by the person to whom that order is transmitted— that will not protect LGBT people in the long run, but add to their protection in the short run. A more substantive view of equality would reintroduce into LGBT politics a set of aspirations that have dropped off its agenda.

This brings me to a second concern about the kind of equality politics the LGBT movement pursues. It is a politics that has been emptied of the redistributive aspirations it once advocated. Equality as it is currently articulated in the LGBT movement represents a politics of compliance with liberalism/ capitalism rather than a critique of the exclusions these systems perpetuate. The queer historian Lisa Duggan notes in her excellent book, *The Twilight of Equality*, "the false promise of the 'equality' on offer through liberal reform [is that of an] equality disarticulated from material life and class politics."[22] Duggan suggests that the LGBT movement has settled for "a model of a narrowly constrained public life cordoned off from the private control and vast inequalities of economic life."[23] The fact that equal rights and profound inequality in resource distribution, material opportunities, and life chances exist for

LGBT people is evident in the growing amount of data that show the great economic range of experiences to be found within LGBT communities. These data show that as civil rights (like nondiscrimination protections) are achieved, they do not necessarily impact the economic or political context in which LGBT people live. This context of low wage jobs, widening income and wealth disparities, unavailability of affordable health care, among other key markers of economic hardship, in turn affects the ability of LGBT people to assert these newly enacted rights, to engage in political mobilization, and have true opportunity to experience the "freedom" that has been won.

In a ground-breaking analysis released in 2009 titled "Poverty in the Lesbian, Gay and Bisexual (LGB) Community," the Williams Institute at the University of California, Los Angeles (UCLA) reviewed three existing data sets to find information about the actual economic situation of LGB people (the data sets they used contained too little or no information on transgender persons, a significant gap in knowledge that transgender organizers have moved forward to address). The Williams Institute found that poverty in the LGB community is "at least as common" as poverty in the broader world, and like that broader world has a racial dimension as well. Since then, additional data from the National Gay and Lesbian Task Force (NGLTF) National Transgender Survey have added more information about the economic hardships facing transgender people. Additional data analysis by the U.S. Census of the American Community Survey (ACS), the Current Population Survey, and other national data sets has added significantly to our knowledge. These various data reveal unexpected facts, such as the following:

- Less than half of unmarried same-sex couples in the 2010 American Community Survey (ACS) data set had a B.A. level college degree.[24]
- More than 16% of respondents to the ACS reported less than $35,000 in household income, and another 10% reported income from $35,000-$50,000.[25]

- Gay and lesbian couple families are significantly more likely to be poor than are heterosexual married couple families. ("Using national data from the National Survey of Family Growth, we find that 25% of lesbians and bisexual women are poor, compared with only 19% of heterosexual women. At 15%, gay men and bisexual men have poverty rates equal to those of heterosexual men (13%)").[26]
- "Lesbians who are 65 [years old] or older are twice as likely to be poor as heterosexual married couples."[27]
- Children in gay and lesbian couple households have poverty rates twice those of children in heterosexual married couple households. ("One out of every five children under eighteen years old living in a same-sex couple family is poor compared to almost one in ten (9.4%) children in different-sex married couple families").[28]
- "Within the LGB population, several groups are much more likely to be poor than others. African American people in same-sex couples and same-sex couples who live in rural areas are much more likely to be poor than are white or urban same-sex couples."[29]
- About 17% of female same-sex couples and 11% of male same-sex couples had income more than 200% below the poverty line.[30]

In light of such information, an LGBT equality politics that ignores the economic context is in the end a politics of exclusion. If the goal of achieving equal rights is to be seen by mainstream LGBT organizations as the endpoint, rather than as a necessary way station to the ultimate goal of social justice, then those groups should come out and admit that they are choosing to ignore the needs of thousands, indeed millions, of members of LGBT communities in favor of a smaller subset of middle to upper middle class people. To my knowledge, no queer organization would admit to such a limitation; therefore, they must be held accountable for a greater degree of representation than they currently provide.

Redistribution is, in fact, contained in every LGBT policy aspiration. Social services are urgently needed for every LGBT population that is not wealthy, from elders to parents to LGBT youth to young people in college to middle-aged people accessing social service programs like drug and alcohol treatment, mental health counseling, HIV services, and much more. Yet, queer leadership is silent and absent on the tax and fiscal debates in Washington, D.C., and in most state legislatures—despite the fact that the destruction of the safety net, the defunding, and the ever-growing privatization of the state will have severe consequences on LGBT civil society. Queer leadership has not yet used its political clout to fight back against the right wing's growth, concerned as it is with reaching across the aisle for legislative compromises. Even though a huge number of LGBT people get health care through Medicaid—and the LGBT elderly will need a strong system of Medicare—no LGBT organization has yet offered an analysis of the potential impact of proposed Republican budget and deficit reduction schemes, much less an analysis of the two-deficit reduction commissions and their recommendations. While queer labor activists have been on the front lines in Wisconsin or in other fights to squash unions, the LGBT movement has not mobilized, spoken out, or used its political clout to help union allies—sending a press release out or giving an award to a union leader at a dinner is not the same as fighting for unions every day in state and national legislatures or in the media.

Some may say, "What about the political diversity of LGBT people?" The LGBT movement cannot be about much more than formal equality, they argue, because it would not represent conservative people. Well, it is true that not all queers are progressive, and that anywhere from 25%-33% of our vote has gone to Republican candidates in national elections over the past twenty years. But this data point also suggests why conservative politics should not dominate the far more numerous progressive mainstream of the LGBT movement. Let us admit a truth: beyond a shared basic rights agenda, there is no political unity between progressives and conservatives in the LGBT community. LGBT conservatives may work for the same basic rights as LGBT progressives, but they stand for a very different social, economic, and political order. We are not in the same movement with each other. Rather, we are in an effective and strong coalition with each other to win equal rights.

A third problem with LGBT equality politics as it is currently practiced is that race drops out of the LGBT political and policy agenda again and again. The way the LGBT movement pursues identity-based equality easily excludes race because the movement can win equal rights to systems (like economy, family, government, society) without touching the structure of racism built into the social contract. This is so because this narrow form of equality politics is itself predicated upon an unexamined racial and gender assumption—the default of the definition of community from which the mainstream LGBT movement speaks is white and most often male.

Let me say this again—there is a racial and gender assumption within the mainstream LGBT movement that needs to be acknowledged. The definition of "gay," "lesbian," "bisexual," or "transgender" that the mainstream LGBT movement operates from, the definition of who it represents that it holds in its mind when it speaks of the community, is unconsciously (and at times consciously) limited to white LGBT people. More often than not, it takes positions that reference the needs and interests of gay men, not lesbians, bisexual, or transgender people. How else can one explain the LGBT movement's silence on issues that have a clear and disproportionate impact on LGBT people of color? How else can one explain the movement's refusal to address issues of race? And how else can we explain the silence of most mainstream LGBT groups on policy fights on reproductive justice, violence against women, police abuse, and criminal justice systems abuses?

In another essay in this book, I outline some reasons why race may be "dropping out" of the LGBT agenda. The essay considers a number of factors that inhibit inclusion of racism into LGBT organizational goals and also impact how the movement identifies, promotes, and supports its leaders. Chief among these is the fact that there are so few leaders of color among the LGBT movement's top ranks; it is appalling that many large LGBT organizations do not have any significant representation of people of color on their senior staffs and boards—their lack of accountability around race comes from a decision to keep race out of the central mission of LGBT work. I've often been told that fighting racism is the job of another movement not ours—that race is important, but we need to focus on LGBT issues alone (ignoring the central point that it intersects with sexuality in the lives of people of color), that adding race would make our agenda too big, that we've done our outreach and "she" is here. Today, it is time to stop making excuses and change practices. Race must be addressed in the mainstream of the LGBT agenda because race matters in the lived experience of all people in America—both within and outside the LGBT community. A social justice framework that explicitly includes a commitment to racial justice is a better resource for LGBT movement organizations than a neoliberal politics of equal rights that pretends color (and class and gender and other human difference) somehow do not affect ones life chances as long as "everyone starts at the same line in the race."

A final reason for concern with the mainstream movement's exclusive reliance on an equality framework is how obsessively it focuses on recognition. Naming and managing the inclusion or exclusion of LGBT identities becomes a primary preoccupation of many LGBT activists, and symbolic wins are a measure of progress. The assertion, calibration, and celebration of identities become an end in itself rather than the means to the larger end of living a full and rich and powerful life. In the context of a general collapse of democratic possibilities, the right to form an LGBT family is important, but is an incomplete marker for security and happiness. Eliminating a major barrier to citizenship, like the denial of out service members in the military, was important. But the right to die for this country does not mean that that one cannot contest and resist its chauvinism, racism, sexism, or even the dangerous and violent tendencies that lie behind the promotion of nationalist ideologies.

Identity assertion is important, and this critique of it comes out of a deep respect for the power of culture, community, and identity to address the stigma, shame, and derision that LGBT people still face. LGBT people do need to hear and believe that "we are alright," that "it gets better," that queer spaces exist and will care for LGBT people when other institutions abandon that responsibility. But forming and celebrating queer identity is not and never was the progressive queer movement's destination. That destination instead was the space to live openly LGBT lives in a transformed, wider world. Identity assertion is a means to a greater end, namely the creation of a self-determined life, and through that life, the creation of a more socially just and inclusive society overall.

What is interesting about identity-based culture and politics is the ways it bolsters consumer capitalism. We become the niche, happily marketed to by corporations that get a free pass on all sorts of horrible practices because of their (paltry) support for LGBT organizations. Identity focuses us on the individual and the personal rather than the social or the community level. Sociologist Zygmunt Bauman's essay "Happiness in a Society of Individuals" captures the appeal of identity in LGBT politics and communities, as well as in the larger world, and it warrants an extensive quote.

> *The predictions of the "end of ideology" that were rife and widely accepted twenty to thirty years ago do not seem to have come true. What we are witnessing, rather, is a curious twist*

in the idea of "ideology:" in defiance of a long tradition, there is now a widespread ideological belief that thinking about the "totality," and composing visions of a "good society," is a waste of time, since it is irrelevant to individual happiness and a successful life.

This new–type ideology is not a privatized ideology… This is, rather, an ideology of privatization. The call to "work more and earn more," a call addressed to individual use, is chasing away and replacing past calls to "think of society" and "care for society" (for a community, a nation, a church, a cause). [31]

This is a new ideology for a new individualized society: as Ulrich Beck has written, individual men and women are now expected pushed and pulled to seek and find individual solutions to socially created problems, and to implement such solutions individually, with the help of individual skills and resources. This ideology proclaims the futility (indeed, counter–productivity) of solidarity: of joining forces and subordinating individual actions to a "common cause." It derides the principle of communal responsibility for the wellbeing of its members, decrying it as a recipe for a debilitating "nanny state," and warning against care-for-the-other on the grounds that it leads to abhorrent and detestable "dependency." [32]

Bauman concisely defines how the importance of individual identity rises as the valuation of collective identities, or social solutions, decreases. The displacement he suggests is a hallmark of neoliberalism and advanced technological societies. Sociologists like Bauman or even Anthony Elliott (whose work on a new individualism is in many ways much more understanding and positive about this shift from collective to individual identities)[33] sound an alarm the LGBT movement should heed. Social movements built upon identity development and expression must be mindful of cooptation through the pacification that individual progress, individual resolution of homophobia, individual skill, and networks can provide. In this context it is not only the narrowing of broad social goals—like making sure that every family is financially secure—into narrow and personal ones—like making sure I am in a relationship—that are problematic in their individual solution. It is also the tacit acceptance that the private life is primary beneficiary of our social movement. A critical perspective on identity enables the movement to notice that personal objectives—fulfillment in a relationship, marriage equality as the marker for liberation, a narrow sense of family—may in the end reproduce the isolation and abandonment many LGBT people experienced from their families of origin. Not everyone is in a couple or will be or wants to be; not everyone has children or wants to have them. Identities are at once individual and multiple, but interest group politics requires them to be homogenous.

In a brilliant new book, the transgender activist and legal scholar Dean Spade explains why the above limitations are structurally inevitable in a politics focused on a pursuit of legal equality. In *Normal Life: Administrative Violence, Critical Trans Politics, and the Limits of Law*, Spade argues that declarations of legal equality by the state "leave in place the conditions that actually produce the disproportionate poverty, criminalization, imprisonment, deportation and violence trans people face while papering it over with a veneer of fairness."[34] Spade suggests that this is an outgrowth of the limited view of state power upon which civil rights era nondiscrimination strategies are based: a perpetrator/victim paradigm underlies legal remedies for civil wrongs. This paradigm focuses on individual or particular perpetrators, on particular harms, and ignores other forms of power (governmental, cultural, economic, religious, for example), which cause harm as well. "Systems of meaning and control that maldistribute life chance, such as racism, ableism, transphobia, xenophobia, and sexism, among others, operate in ways more complicated, diverse and structural than the perpetrator/victim model allows."[35] For transgender and LGB people, Spade suggests, two other forms of power operate even more ruthlessly: disciplinary power, which enforces "norms of behavior and ways of being," and "population management power," which "distributes life chances." Spade writes, "The kinds of harm that occur through both of these modes of power are especially difficult to reach through law reform efforts, and understanding these operations of power helps us to understand why, even when certain law reforms are won, conditions do not improve."[36] Spade's book calls for a shift in practice and focus for advocates concerned about populations within the LGBT communities not yet being served by the mainstream movement's approach. This persuasive rationale and constructive power analysis can guide the LGBT movement to produce lasting change in the lives of the diverse communities it represents.

What Would a Justice-Based Movement Look Like?

There are at least three domains in which a justice-focused movement would differ from the current version. First, it would differ in its policy and political objectives. Second, it would differ in its organizational forms and their operations (from the form of organizations, to their mission, to how they engage with constituencies and how they set their agendas, and to whom they see themselves accountable). And third, it would differ in its political operations, for one being more global, for another working in the administrative and regulatory arena as much as in the legal and legislative, working through new progressive coalitions, and operating less and less as a lone-issue, single-identity focused social movement. Let me speak briefly to these ideas.

Policy and Political Objectives

A re-formed LGBT movement focused upon social justice would commit itself to one truth: that not all LGBT people are wealthy or of one racial background. It might consider committing itself to the principle "No Queer Left Behind." LGBT liberation stands for a change in the lived experience of all LGBT people, not just the advancement of rights for some. This principle would not only commit donors and institutions to fulfilling equality for those most vulnerable in our communities, but would commit the resources that are going to be needed to do the implementation of equality once it is achieved. This means LGBT organizations would have to broaden the definition of what they see as a "gay" issue.

An LGBT movement focused on a more substantive notion of equality would fight for the broadest and most inclusive possible parameters of the issues on which it campaigns and not the narrowest or safest. So marriage activism would fight fiercely for full recognition of the freedom to marry, but it would also support the right to domestic partnership and civil unions for straight and gay people alike. The movement would not avoid fighting for the right of all people to have health insurance regardless of marital status. It would press for each of our freedom to choose the form of family in which we live, without being harmed by that choice. It could support a family policy agenda that recognizes and strengthens services that benefit parents (of all kinds), and enable people to make care-giving choices for each other that are not limited to gay versions of the nuclear family.

Similarly, a movement focused on LGBT youth might take on more than a narrow focus on the bullied child in school. It might tackle the question of racial bias in the administration of school discipline; or address how gender variance is handled; it might become a major voice campaigning against sexual abuse and how it harms all young people; it might tackle the violence of budgetary cutbacks as an attack on young people; it might resist the right wing's attack on Planned Parenthood and defend an organization that provides urgent primary health care to many poor women and kids; it might defend the freedom of young people to organize and speak out inside schools and communities. It might mount a serious challenge to familial homophobia, the biggest site of violence and bullying against LGBT youth—after all these years, Parents, Families and Friends of Lesbians and Gays (PFLAG) remains a tiny organization struggling for funding each year and really is the only intervention we have created here in more than thirty years.

Mission and Operations of LGBT Organizations

The organizational structures and forms of LGBT movements must also change to move from a narrow equality framework to one that engages more substantive ideals of justice and equality. The mission statements of organizations must be broadened; mechanisms for more democratic and inclusive methods of participation must be put in place; and non-donor-driven mechanisms of setting organizational priorities and movement agendas must be developed.

The need to transform mission statements seems a simple task, but its impact and complexity were brought home to me through a recent experience with Lambda Legal's Cultural Diversity Committee. Lambda invited diverse activists to engage with its staff and key partners about how its work could better address racism and racial justice. To prepare for that conversation, I looked at Lambda's mission, its programs, its diversity statement, and its engagement with issues involving race. What I saw reflected back was a wonderful organization, doing brave and heroic work, with a talented and devoted staff that had the willingness to be more inclusive, but not the structure or institutional support to do this new work. Lambda's organizational mission statement differed significantly from its much broader and more ambitious diversity statement. The mission was too small for the stated ambitions of diversity and inclusion, like trying to jam a size-fourteen foot of a diversity statement into a size-seven shoe (the narrow mission).

This is a common problem among national mainstream

LGBT organizations. Each of the national LGBT organizations would argue that they are committed to racial justice and to a more equitable society for all people. But hardly any of them express that aspiration in their mission statements: the words "racial justice" or "social justice" are absent from their organizational missions, no explicit commitments to racial parity on staff or to a race–conscious approach to program development are made: indeed there are rarely programs within mainstream LGBT groups built to address racial justice or to serve LGBT communities of color. Not surprisingly, the groups that have these words in their missions are those organizations that most consistently speak out on race, gender, economic justice, and that work on a broader set of policy issues. An organization's mission statement matters. It drives the goals and outlook of an institution. A change of mission is imperative to move beyond equality.

A second change that mainstream LGBT groups must make towards a more inclusive politics of justice is captured in the question of whom national LGBT institutions actually represent and how they secure input from the communities they serve. Very few and very limited mechanisms exist for individual members to participate in or contribute to the operations, direction, agenda, or leadership level decision-making bodies of national LGBT organizations beyond writing a check, attending an event, or filling out a survey. Boards are not elected by organizational members, but choose themselves. Policy decisions are not taken by deliberative input, but made top down and told to the communities represented. There are no annual conventions at which members can bring resolutions or introduce new ideas. This structure of nonprofit governance is a problem for both the accountability and the representativeness of LGBT institutions. For one, it leads institutions to act in ways that ignore less financially or politically connected parts of our communities, while being overly solicitous of others. For another, these structures privilege the voice and influence of large donors to the exclusion of the concerns of smaller donors.

Two short examples of recent actions by LGBT organizations illustrate the first impact of the absence of deliberative processes to set the movement's priorities. In the first, which unfolded in 2011, the New York City LGBT Community Center voted to ban a pro-Palestinian organization from meeting at the Center because of its disagreement with the political perspective of that group. It was not the first such ban of a group at the Center, but it was a rare occurrence. The board of the New York LGBT Center banned the pro-Palestinian group from meeting there because some donors and board members disagreed with the content of what they were expressing. Explanations were offered for the ban: the group was not gay enough, the content of what the group focused on was not core to the Center's mission, and the banned group made some people feel unsafe at the Center.

The Center hosted an open meeting at which a strong desire was expressed by a majority of attendees for an inclusive meeting policy, one that would allow the Center to be a space where unpopular and politically dissonant ideas could be expressed. The Center promised to create a new policy on meetings, informed by an open drafting committee that would work on this policy. It promised to remain a space for all parts of the community. In the end, months later, nothing "new" was issued—the decision to ban was maintained, and a critical space for progressive dissent closed itself from parts of the community it felt were disposable, in this case pro–Palestinian queers and their allies. The Center's action was a case study in subjectivity and bias—the voices of some donors were weighted far more strongly than the voices of others; the conservative politics of some board members prevailed over the pro-debate, pro-Palestinian, and pro-dissent politics of others, including longstanding supporters and volunteers of the Center.

The outcome would have felt different to me had the Center been engaged in a truly consultative process, a process that was public, transparent, and accessible. If after a series of public discussions, a policy had been issued and a vote invited; if board meetings had been opened up to the public and all Center members and donors; if people who used the facility (organizationally) had been polled and the results been made known; if any number of deliberative strategies had been employed, shared, and the findings publicly discussed, perhaps the impact of the whole experience would have been more positive. Instead of engaging in a truly deliberative process, the Center hired a consultant to "facilitate" a process whose outcome was pre-determined in private. It used the traditional model of nonprofit board authority, in effect hiding behind the undemocratic vehicle of corporate board governance that is the practice of all LGBT organizations.

A more than decade-old decision by the national lobby, the Human Rights Campaign (HRC), to endorse the Republican Alfonse D'Amato over Charles Schumer in 1998 operated from a similar closed-loop process. It is old history in a movement as dynamic as the LGBT movement, but it still resonates with veteran activists across New York State because they felt so disempowered. For HRC, the endorsement was a tough call because they try to be bipartisan and because they felt they needed Al D'Amato's vote at the national level. But for local leaders it was not a tough call at all, because they had a particular agenda they were promoting and they expected their national LGBT organizations to defer to their positions in political decisions that affected their state and communities. HRC ignored local political leadership in favor of its own objectives; and it did so without consultation or input from these leaders—much less its own rank and file.

Both of these examples also illustrate the power of donors in the positions taken by LGBT mainstream organizations. Individual and even institutional membership to national organizations is virtually meaningless when it comes to influencing positions taken by groups. The individual is merely a seat-filler at a dinner, a body count at a press conference, and a check writer. The individual member to any LGBT organization has no voice in electing its board, no formal role to play in the setting of organizational platforms, priorities and policy agendas, and is generally not convened through an annual convention nor consulted through an irregular town meeting. As a result, the positions the national movement takes are not and cannot be said to be representative of the views of the members of those organizations, much less of the diverse and far larger community that is not a part of the formally organized LGBT infrastructure.

Lisa Duggan notes the privatization of participation and control. "No longer representative of a broad based progressive movement, many of the dominant national lesbian and gay civil rights organizations have become the lobbying, legal and public relations firms for an increasingly narrow gay, moneyed elite."[37] This is the dirty little secret of LGBT movement organizations. Leaders will privately tell you that while they are certainly driven by concerns about how to win those not reached by LGBT messages, and that while they care and pay attention to what our opponents might do to undermine and defeat us, the fact is that they spend most of their time courting, listening to, and worrying about people from whom they are generating resources for their organizational budgets. As a result, knowing what their major donors and foundation funders think, what *they* care about and whether *they* are alienated or offended assumes a higher priority than determining what the average gay person or the non-major donor member of the organization thinks.

In the past few years alone, I have been a participant in a small, sit-down dinners with six sitting Democratic governors; informal meetings with several other political leaders; formal and informal meetings with high level officials in the Obama Administration; meetings with high-level politicians across the country; and had invitations to meet with scores of others, if I produced enough money to have that privilege. None of this access has been based on my representation of a constituency—

it has been either about my access to people with funds who are major political donors or about my own minor status as a political donor. The issues I remember being raised in these conversations were marriage equality, the Employment Non-Discrimination Act (ENDA), the military ban, and violence. Issues not at the forefront were about job creation, ending the war and redeploying funding for social services, school bullying and youth suicide, HIV funding, immigration reform, homelessness, or health issues facing LGBT people.

The overvaluation of people with resources by LGBT organizations has accelerated over the past fifteen years, as the budgets of LGBT organizations have grown and their needs for new resources have increased. What is amazing is how few individuals these major donors actually represent—the data confirm the view that the treatment received by major donor overvalues certain life experiences and viewpoints. Currently fewer than four percent of LGBT people actually give any funding to LGBT organizations. Of an estimated 8.73 million LGBT people, fewer than 250,000 gave $35 or more to any of the forty national organizations surveyed by the Movement Advancement Project (MAP), a national think tank that studies the LGBT movement; fewer than 12,500 people gave more than $1,000 to any of these groups in 2010.[38] Because such a small number of people donate to LGBT organizations, those who give a large amount have a hugely disproportionate impact on LGBT institutional leaders. The attention they are given, the ways that the frameworks the donors promote through foundations set and limit the agenda and dreams of LGBT organizations, the ways in short that wealth influences the politics and goals of our social movement are all aspects of the today's equality politics that warrant much closer attention.

The influence of donors is not necessarily negative; certainly the major donors—of whom I am one—will tell you that. Why should we not be listened to as donors if we are investing significant funds and time into a project? What is wrong with having an expectation of some returns on an investment? Are foundations so far off the mark in the priorities they set that they warrant skepticism? The matter of concern is not whether a donor ought to be able to campaign for their ideas, ideologies, and priorities—they should. The problem is instead the absence of any additional mechanisms to gather a broader set of inputs into organizational policies and decisions. Technology allows us to ascertain what a broader subset of the community might actually want. But few organizations have the practices in place to actually solicit input and then be accountable to the input they receive.

We need to create new structures for democratic participation and agenda setting within LGBT communities that do not depend entirely upon the boards and formal structures of nonprofits, and that do not require money from people for their participation And frankly, we need to re–engineer the existing national political organizations.

A Justice-based LGBT Movement Would Be Global, Policy-Oriented, and Electoral

This essay has been domestically focused and in that it mirrors the limitations of the larger mainstream movement about which it is concerned. This decade brings an explosion of energy and growth among advocates for sexual orientation and gender identity globally. Global bodies like the U.N. and the World Bank are beginning to grapple with the ways that SOGI is integral to human rights and to development. Grassroots movements around the world tackle harsh violence, state and police repression, poverty and health crises, and cultural resistance derived from ideas of tradition and norms. The arguments and frameworks used by advocates for SOGI in the global South differ from those used by legal reform-based advocates in the U.S. But there remain few opportunities for cross movement engagement as well as a sense that the U.S. model or the European Union model for LGBT rights can be superimposed upon other countries. It would transform the domestic movement to incorporate the ways that our cousins in South Africa or Nepal, for example, are creating space for visibly transgender and queer lives, and to understand the deep resistance to women's freedom is so linked to the violence perpetrated against lesbians, bisexuals, transgender people and gay men.

Similarly, a shift in focus from legal recognition alone to the broader context of the administration of governmental power might enable the movement to focus on broader policy frameworks such as national security and immigration, crime and punishment, government's role in the funding and delivery of social services. As the transgender legal scholar Dean Spade argues, "The aim of getting the law to declare a group equal through anti-discrimination and hate crime legislation recedes and we become interested in the legal systems that distribute security and vulnerability at the population level and sort the population into those whose lives are cultivated and those who are abandoned, imprisoned or extinguished."[39] Shifting the arenas where we concentrate—from courts to executive and administrative agencies, for example—and then also shifting how we consider the goal of our work there, from mere recognition or naming in a regulatory scheme to a consideration of how it does or does not help the lives and life chances of our communities, offers a practical path forward.

Finally, a fascinating aspect of the growing tide of data about LGBT demographics lies in the ways it challenges certain myths America cherishes about itself. Gary Gates' recent compilation of several U.S. and international sexual attraction, behavior, and identity survey questions is revealing in this regard.[40] The data summarized there reveal that according to the National Survey of Family Growth, more than 11% (or 25.6 million people) of the U.S. population acknowledges they have had same-gender attraction. About 8.2% say (or 19 million people) say they have actually engaged in same-sex behavior. About 3.8% identify as lesbian, gay, bisexual, or transgender (with 1.8% claiming bisexual identity; 1.7% claiming lesbian or gay identity; and .3% identifying as transgender). That is a lot of people (almost nine million people), of whom only a small fraction are formally participating in the LGBT movement.[41]

The potential for this untapped resource is vast. LGBT activism could lead and actually direct the formation of a new political coalition and this awakening could be one of the most exciting projects that lie ahead for any who are interested. Sure, the challenge of organizing any new coalition is daunting. But these times cry out for a new unity among those who are being kicked around and set aside, a renewed alliance among those who represent a threat to the traditional order and privileges in existing society—the women, queers, people of color, working class, immigrant, and good hearted and socially responsible capitalists. The time is now for our own LGBT-party—a party whose planks for social justice, human rights, and environmental sustainability could truly transform the future.

Conclusion

In 2011, at a conference titled "Gay Rights are Human Rights" held at the Carr Center for Human Rights at Harvard University's Kennedy School of Government, the facilitator of my panel asked whether we believed that the LGBT movement today stands at some new "tipping point" in the LGBT struggle. All the panelists did the dance of equivocation. Yes, we said, we are at a tipping point in some ways, but none of us liked that frame, because there is no one point at which the magical "It" tips over and gay nirvana emerges. As we gave our answers, I remembered a number of times throughout the '70s, the '80s, the '90s, and the early 2000s when I had been asked the very same question.

Like many people, I have lived through a number of game-changing moments, where everything feels like it is going to shift in a dramatic manner, and sometimes it even does:

the 1970s and the rise of the Moral Majority; the 1980s and Reagan's election; the rise of AIDS; the explosion of LGBT activism at the local level after the 1987 March on Washington; the legal wins of the past decade—*Lawrence v. Texas*[42] in 2003— the various same-sex marriage cases in Massachusetts and other courts; the election of Barack Obama. Each of these moments— and so many more we could discuss—were moments in which LGBT activists moved a new notion of freedom forward against incredible odds.

But the history of social movements is not about tipping points—that is too passive a concept. History is made by actions taken, choices made. Social movement history is about turning points—moments that present new challenges, offer new choices or open up possibilities that hard work or some fortuitous and unplanned action created.

Such a turning point moment faces the LGBT movement. It presents an opportunity to turn away from an ever-narrowing understanding of LGBT freedom and an isolationist form of LGBT politics. It presents the chance to avoid missteps by other social movements that have journeyed to a dead end of equal rights in an ever more unjust world.

This turning point presents a choice to LGBT activists to renew a focus on a safer and saner world for all, on contributing solutions to the big problems facing in the world—the problems of economic justice under the current form of capitalism, environmental degradation, structural racism, gender rigidity and its consequence, and undemocratic power. It is the choice to challenge the status quo at its deepest roots that will protect LGBT people the most.

WHAT CAN BROWN DO FOR YOU?
Race and the Future of the LGBT Movement[43]

For many reasons, it was a challenge to write this talk, chief among these was my reticence to speak personally. I live in a strange world— often the only brown person in a roomful of mostly white lesbian, gay, bisexual and transgender (LGBT) leaders, or one of a few black and brown people in rooms of white progressives. While I have always worked actively against racism, I have also worked primarily in non-race specific organizations. This experience has been scarring, frustrating, and rewarding. The scars come from the ignorance of colleagues about racial justice, the frustration from saying things again and again while finding little progress, while the rewards come from being part of a stronger queer people of color and grassroots progressive movement than existed twenty years ago. Like many LGBT people of color, I have pushed, prodded, cajoled, challenged, and pushed yet again. I have made arguments that led to larger resources being given to grassroots racial justice groups in the progressive world and to LGBT people of color groups and projects in the queer universe. And I have benefitted from the exceptional friendship, challenge, and support of colleagues who "lead with race." Racism is something I started out thinking of as only in black and white, but have seen expressed in every shade.

The occasion for this talk was my selection for the Kessler Award, an annual honor presented by the board of the Center for Lesbian and Gay Studies (CLAGS) at the City University of New York to a "scholar who has, over a number of years, produced a substantive body of work that has had a significant influence on the field of GLBTQ Studies."[44] The Kessler Award is accompanied by an invitation to give the annual Kessler Lecture, which I did on November 18, 2010.

I've written at least four different talks before arriving at the one I am actually giving tonight. The first version was so angry it prompted my partner, Kate, to suggest that I start a version of the "It Gets Better" viral campaign called "I Get Bitter." In the second version I tried autobiography, but I bored even myself. Then my inner wonk came out and I wrote a term paper on racism in America. Finally, I started to say things that reflect the praxis-based politics to which I tend to gravitate. What I learned along the way is there are many ways to talk about race, sexuality, and the future of LGBT politics. What follows is just one. Tonight, I want to start with some broad and frank observations about three things—first, the state of the LGBT movement overall, and the state of racial justice, racial equity and racial privilege within the mainstream of that movement. Second, I want to consider why mainstream LGBT politics remains so absent on racial justice—what makes it so difficult for the LGBT movement to face race? Third, I'd like to suggest some principles that could orient a new and more productive course in addressing racial equity within and outside our communities.

State of the Mainstream Movement

As the 2010 midterm elections came and went I found myself thinking of the memorable opening paragraph from Dickens' *A Tale of Two Cities*.

"It was the best of times, it was the worst of times, it was the age of wisdom, it was the age of foolishness, it was the epoch of belief, it was the epoch of incredulity, it was the season of Light, it was the season of Darkness, it was the spring of hope, it was the winter of despair, we had everything before us, we had nothing before us, we were all going direct to Heaven, we were all going direct the other way…"[45]

This passage describes the perplexing dualism of the present moment—an age of remarkable technological change and human possibility, in which more wealth exists than ever before yet objectives like ending hunger and poverty seem unreachable. We live in an "epoch of belief"—millions upon millions of people fervently embrace their faith traditions filled with absolute certainty that they are on the righteous path. At the same time, we live in an "epoch of incredulity," in which millions of others are so disillusioned and alienated by corruption or fear that they are apathetic. So, in the recent 2010-midterm elections, white Protestant and Catholic voters increased their turnout and voted overwhelmingly for Republicans.[46] Yet overall only 42% of eligible voters came to the polls. In 2010, only 20.9% of eligible youth ages eighteen to twenty-nine voted, a sharp drop from the 25% of youth who voted in the 2006-midterm elections.[47]

It seemed we had everything before us in 2008 when President Obama won. I remember feeling that way in 1992 with Bill Clinton as well, or even in 1968, only to watch that hope turn sour in 2010, as it did in 1994, or in 1968 when Bobby Kennedy was killed. The merry-go-round of political promises keeps us bobbing up and down with excitement at each revolution, but our enjoyment and engagement in the process leaves us sad at the end of the ride, awake to the fact that we have only gone around in a circle.

A similar dualism—of growth and inertia, progress and stagnation, optimism, and frustration—exists today in the LGBT movement. The scale and size of the mainstream movement remains significant. Recently, the Movement Advancement Project (MAP), a national think tank on the LGBT movement, analyzed the most recent returns of all LGBT-identified nonprofit organizations found on the Guidestar database.[48] In its review, MAP identified 506 LGBT organizations focused on LGBT issues in eight broad categories: community centers, arts and culture, social/recreational, service provision, research, advocacy, issue-based, and legal organizations. These organizations had combined expenses of $500 million dollars.[49] Of this total, more than $225 million was spent on four strategies: advocacy, legal, issue-based, and research-focused groups. For several years, MAP has surveyed forty of the largest LGBT groups and in 2011, MAP documented the combined budgets of these groups to total more than $143 million, while their actual 2010 revenue was nearly $127 million.[50] These forty organizations employed 879 paid staff and had 704 board members.[51] The mainstream movement is a large infrastructure indeed.

Yet, the LGBT political agenda at the national level, especially before Congress, is stalled. The largest LGBT advocacy organization, the Human Rights Campaign (HRC), which in its fiscal 2011 year had a budget of approximately $38 million and a staff of 179 people,[52] managed to secure full passage and implementation of only one LGBT rights bill in Congress over the past twenty years—the Shepard/Byrd Hate Crime Act, passed in October of 2009. The second largest national LGBT political organization, the National Gay and Lesbian Task Force (NGLTF), with a 2010 budget of $8.3 million and a staff of more than fifty people, seems great at process (managing coalitions, producing trainings and conferences, conducting research, and policy analysis) but unable to turn those into muscular leadership for results. The mainstream gay rights legal movement, still the most successful strategy in the LGBT movement, remains an island onto itself—making its own decisions in small conclaves, rarely consulting in a meaningful way with grassroots activists, limiting participation in key strategic meetings to those who agree with the strategies underway,[53] and rarely coordinating its efforts with political advocates so that a powerful media, educational, and organizing push could be made alongside each major new direction in litigation.[54]

The anti-gay military policy was repealed, but barriers to transgender participation in the armed forces remain in place, and the military's epidemic levels of violence and sexual harassment of women (and also of significant numbers of men) remains unchallenged by the LGBT mainstream movement.[55] The Employment Non-Discrimination Act is not moving, leading some to assert that it will advance if gender identity is removed. It will not, because that obstacle is simply a pretext for a deeper lack of political support in Congress for LGBT equality. Immigration equality is also stalled, and with the election of an anti-immigrant Tea Party minority, the chances for comprehensive immigration reform are minimal. The appointments of talented, openly LGBT leaders to key positions by a friendly Administration continue to be stymied by hostile and vigorous opposition.[56]

The gains made during the Obama years have come about for the same reasons as they did during the much more hostile Reagan, Bush I, and Bush II years, through the efforts of a small group of people lobbying behind the scenes within the Executive branch—making quiet and significant changes in agency-led actions and regulations at places like the State Department, the Department of Health and Human Services, and the Department of Labor.

Even this is not a complete picture. Because of the inability of the existing larger infrastructures to represent the diverse constituencies and issues that LGBT people face, the movement has spawned a number of even more specialized, single issue-focused organizations at the national level over the past ten years, each focused on a particular subject or constituency (freedom to marry, health, immigration, military, transgender, family policy, youth, community centers, and even two Republican organizations—because the first was deemed too liberal by the second).

Indeed, it could be argued that there are at least two movements fighting for LGBT equality and freedom today: one explicitly anti-racist and the other doggedly single-issue. One that is progressive and one that is center-right. One that consists of locally-based grassroots advocacy, organizing, and service-oriented groups (Queers for Economic Justice, Audre Lorde Project, Sylvia Rivera Law Project, FIERCE, Southerners on New Ground, the Community Center movement, the HIV/AIDS organizations, the youth groups, and key public community foundations like Astraea) supported at the national level by the NGLTF, and the other, which consists of larger, more national organizations (HRC, ACLU, Lambda Legal, Gay and Lesbian Alliance Against Defamation (GLAAD), National Center for Lesbian Rights (NCLR), the Gay and Lesbian Victory Fund (GLVF) to name a few, as well as the mainstream corporate and largely private philanthropic institutions that support them. These movements share a common history, they often share institutional origins, they overlap, they coexist, they cooperate, and they compete. But they are not coterminous: their endpoint differs dramatically. And their power to determine the course of queer politics varies as well.

It is my contention, however, that neither the grassroots (race-inclusive) nor mainstream (liberal) parts of the LGBT movements have yet meaningfully tackled structural racism and racial privilege. Neither has made more than a superficial dent in the way racial separation exists in our communities. Neither has convinced the majority of LGBT people who are active in the movement that race is and must be "our" issue. Indeed, advocates of racial justice in the LGBT movement still find ourselves having to make the case again and again, year after year, about why race matters to the achievement of

LGBT equality. Here, for example, is a summary of the "What Can Brown Do for You?" speech, which I have given for two decades.[57] The LGBT movement should work on racial justice, I've argued:

- Because it is a matter of justice and we are about a fairer society.
- Because we need to reciprocate—so when we ask communities of color to support us around sexuality, we need to show up on issues of race.
- Because there are LGBT people of color in our communities and racism affects us, so our movement must deal with it.
- Because dealing with race is in the mainstream gay community's self-interest and brown will help us win at the ballot box.

Not only am I tired of having to make this speech, it saddens me that while most of the audiences to whom I have spoken have no problem hearing the argument framed in those terms, they resist the reverse proposition that the LGBT movement must make racial justice one of its core commitments. The existence of LGBT people of color is simply not deemed important enough to warrant what many white gay and lesbian people see as a "diversion" of the LGBT agenda to address race. As a result, race in our movement is seen largely as something that affects a "subset" of LGBT people. When addressed at all, it is done primarily under the rubric of diversity or outreach, occasionally as a matter of equity that it is the movement's business to pursue, but extremely rarely as a substantive matter, integral to the goals of LGBT rights and central to its success or failure.

The key structural reason why neither branch of the LGBT movements has operationalized its stated intersectional politics is quite simple: the default definition for what "gay" means has been set by, and remains dominated by, the ideas and experiences of those in our communities who are white, and this fact has really not changed in more than fifty years. We have not changed this definition in the policy agendas we promote, in the language the movement uses, and in the representation of our communities at the leadership levels of our organizations. Issues, identities, problems that are not "purely" gay, read as affecting white gay men and women, are always defined outside the scope of "our" LGBT movement. They are dismissed as "non-gay" issues, raising them is interpreted as an act of divisiveness, and the issues are marginalized as the business of some "other movement," not ours. We have our hands full, we are told. We need to single-mindedly focus on one thing: equality based on sexual orientation (and some would add gender identity). This is an argument that many LGBT liberationists and gay equality-focused activists have bought wholesale for decade—without malice, without prejudice—just because there has been an unquestioned assumption that this narrow focus works, that we are getting results because we are making a "gay rights" argument, that this is smart and successful political strategy.

I contend that this narrow and limited focus is the problem. The gay rights focus was historically needed but is a vestigial burden we need to shed. It leads to failure at the polls, is bad political strategy, narrows our imagination, does not serve large numbers of our own people, and feeds the perception that we are generally privileged and powerful. It not only leads us to abandon or ignore large parts of our own communities, but it is also causes us to stall in our progress towards formal equality.

Single-issue gay rights politics rooted in the interest group approach adopted by many political movements once provided coherence, helped us build infrastructure and visibility, and certainly helped us achieve progress; but it has done so at the expense of people of color, transgender people, the working class, youth, and those who are less empowered in our communities. And its success has reached a limit.

From a broad liberationist agenda, in which lesbians led the peace movement and the anti-nuclear movement, in which LGBT people spoke out passionately in support of black civil rights and against racist drug and sentencing laws, in which we demanded that government save our lives and that we get our fair share from it, we have become an ever narrower, individual rights movement, where the "freedom" to assert our individual right to marry is argued by some to be the most radical thing we could ever seek. Issues of reproductive freedom, sexuality and birth control, challenging the patriarchal nuclear family, support for working families, ending violence against women, prison reform, poverty, redistribution—all once critical parts of our LGBT liberation movement's agenda have disappeared in the national LGBT movement discourse. As these issues have receded in our movement, we have lost our past alliance with the feminist movement, with the peace movement, with anti-poverty movements, with the environmental movement, and even with the labor movement. We never had much of an alliance with the civil rights movement.[58] Because we cannot win on our own, weak alliances are a critical obstacle to our movement's ability to enact pro-LGBT policies at every level of government.

The absence of racial justice, economic justice, and gender justice from our national movement's objectives results in the LGBT movement being wrongly seen, even by our allies and certainly by most straight people, as a relatively small, very narrowly-focused, largely white, mostly male, and deeply self-interested group of people. Frankly, the LGBT movement rarely, if ever, expends political or financial capital to support so-called "non-gay" issues. As a result, we are not regarded as valuable partners to our allies in any coalition that we join; we offer them very little positive help, and we generate powerful anti-gay opposition to boot. It is a measure of their principles that key LGBT allies have not abandoned us despite our absence from their fights, and despite the pressure they sometimes face from constituencies they serve. So, for example, in the late 1980s the Hate Crime Coalition working for passage of the Hate Crime Statistics Act was repeatedly pressured by members of

Congress to dump the gay community and move a bill without the provision requiring data collection on sexual orientation. The Coalition resisted, and the Hate Crime Statistics Act passed in 1989. In the past year, the immigrant rights coalition working on Comprehensive Immigration Reform has resisted strong pressure from the Catholic Church to exclude the Uniting American Families Act from the comprehensive immigration reform agenda.

Across the country, LGBT rights initiatives have failed precisely because we have not organized to meaningfully engage racial and immigrant communities, nor made our case effectively to working mothers of all colors. We lost Proposition 8 in part because the campaign for our rights did not know how best to organize the people of color communities in California; we simply did not mount an effective organizing campaign in black and brown communities. We also lost Prop 8 because we did not organize seriously within progressive religious communities. We lost the judicial election in Iowa because we mounted no broad defense of the notion of an independent and non-politicized judiciary, a principle bigger than the pro-marriage equality vote of the judges who adhered to it.

Yet, the mainstream of the LGBT movement today still does not question the value of the single-issue approach it has taken. The time is now for these questions to be asked. It is this broad context of national LGBT movement weakness, of significant recent failure, and of an increased attention to racial and economic disparities caused by our social and economic policies, that challenges the mainstream LGBT movement and its grassroots counterparts to look more closely at why the LGBT mainstream has such difficulty claiming racial justice as a central and core concern.

What Are the Obstacles to the LGBT Movement Facing Race?

While I will talk specifically about the resistance to the inclusion of racial equity as a core mainstream LGBT movement demand, and the impact this resistance has on our movement, it is important to acknowledge that parts of the LGBT movement are working for racial justice. These efforts are largely the work of the queer people of color or progressive LGBT groups I've mentioned already, as well as a handful of non-gay progressive groups (Applied Research Center, Center for American Progress, Highlander Center, Opportunity Agenda). Groundbreaking work is being done by grassroots progressive groups in arenas like criminal justice and prison systems reform, welfare organizing, homelessness, housing, youth development and leadership, immigrant rights, detention of immigrants, and public schools. Creative work is also underway to strengthen investment in LGBT people of color organizations (Funders for Lesbian and Gay Issues' Campaign for Racial Equity)[59] and to build people of color leadership (the Pipeline Project). Fascinating potential exists in the global LGBT movement for linkages across national boundaries, linkages that might illuminate ways that the U.S. movement's framing of identity is more limited than that of activists in, for example, Africa.

This second movement was in evidence in late 2011 at a conference titled "The Bold Gathering," which was subtitled "A Queer and Trans People of Color Gathering to Support our Own Liberation and Self-Determination." The conference, held over December 2- 4, 2011 in Minneapolis, MN, assembled over 200 grassroots queer people of color leaders to strategize about a set of policy objectives, and a set of communities, that are rarely mentioned inside the black-tie dinners and deal making rooms of moneyed parts of our movement. The press release for the gathering noted that while more than $100 million was given from private and public foundations to LGBT causes in 2008, less than 12% went to people of color organizations, and less than 20% of all funders supported LGBT people of color projects.[60]

I have been a part of this second movement for decades, learning from its leaders and developing my own approach to

LGBT politics from its vantage point. When I was appointed head of NGLTF in 1989, a prominent donor called the Task Force offices and said to a development director there that he could not believe the Task Force board had hired that radical woman who was "practically a nigger." More than once, I have had people question my claim of being a person of color, as one colleague noted, I was "practically white." Brown is an intermediate state that occupies a different place in the American racial consciousness—but after September 11, 2001 and the past decade of anti-immigrant bashing, brown and black are both more stigmatized than I thought they would be in my lifetime.

Over the years, I have experienced the visceral awkwardness and discomfort of some male donors because I am a woman; an awkwardness that increases when I do anything that reminds them I am also foreign. My girlfriend, for example, always wants me to wear kurta pajamas or even a sari to LGBT formal dress events, but my experience in them is uncomfortable—not just because I am more used to wearing suits, but because I already feel highly conspicuous in the largely white and largely male gatherings I attend regularly, and wearing Indian clothes makes me feel even more so. My discomfort has been confirmed on more than one occasion, when well-meaning colleagues have joked that I am "going native" or "putting on the Kente cloth" on those occasions when I have worn Indian clothes.

Throughout my time in the movement, I have raised issues of racism (and sexism), economic equality, and privilege—with very mixed response. Sometimes I have succeeded in creating innovative new programs to impact racial disparities in our communities, at other times, I have had my suggestions ignored, and ideas marginalized. While some doors were opened to me because I am a woman of color and the movement wanted that tokenized "representation," others were not opened far enough, or simply never pointed out. Yet I have succeeded—in large measure because of the class privilege that my education gives me, and the social capital that I have cultivated and gained from jobs in law, philanthropy, and the nonprofit sector, a capital built on access and relationships that come from being economically successful and being backed by people with money and resources.

But I never deluded myself into believing that my success proved anything more than the exception to the general experience of most of my colleagues—which is that because so many major donors are most comfortable giving to people like themselves, that women and people of color have a hard time raising funds in our community of donors. Every honest Executive Director or Board Chair will tell you that they try to hire at least one cute white guy to help out with their development departments, that making people in the middle, upper-middle, and wealthy classes in the LGBT movement comfortable is critical to one's success as a leader. The funder community is not organized or actively supportive of innovative leaders, of people of color leaders, or of folks who come from backgrounds outside of Ivy League or professional schools.

In a 2010 report titled "Better Together,"[61] the Applied Research Center (ARC), a think tank focused on race and social justice issues, studied the relationship between racial justice organizations and LGBT communities. The report throws more doubt on the notion of the allegedly unsurpassable homophobia in communities of color when it details that the majority of groups and leaders surveyed in the racial justice movement reported working for LGBT rights. The report identifies three key obstacles cited by racial justice organizations to their work on LGBT issues. The biggest barrier identified was a perception pervasive in racial justice organizations that most LGBT people are white and not interested in race. The low visibility and weakness of LGBT people of color leaders, and the limited agendas of the organizations we have created, fuels this perception and informs ARC's recommendations to funders: a call for greater investment in people of color organizations working on both sexuality and race, increased investment in the development of LGBT people of color leaders, and increased investment in media and other outlets that can engage people in communities of color on sexuality.

A second barrier identified by ARC is a lack of understanding about how to apply a sexuality lens to racial justice issues. Allies still need to understand that LGBT people are parts of various communities, and that LGBT people are affected in particular ways by issues seen primarily through a racial lens (e.g., police violence, homelessness, immigration, prison and incarceration, schools and harassment to name a few).

A third barrier identified was the fear of community resistance (both actual and perceived) from within communities of color. Interviewees cited fear of religious organizations' reaction to working on LGBT issues, fear of causing internal divisions in racial communities, and a lack of demand for work on LGBT rights coming from inside communities of color.

All of the above-named challenges reveal additional and possible work for the LGBT movement, but there is a threshold question that the data begs: what explains the resistance of the mainstream movement to a deeper incorporation of racial justice into the LGBT agenda? In an excellent two-part series on the racism of liberals and progressives, author and white anti-racist activist Tim Wise provides helpful insights to answer this question. Wise discusses several mechanisms he believes allow liberals and progressives to avoid taking up racial justice and allow them to "reinforce the notion that persons of color are less important, their concerns less central to the larger justice cause, and that ultimately they are to be viewed as inferior junior partners in the movement for social change."[62] Each of these mechanisms of avoidance is one I have experienced within the LGBT movement. They are 1) *colorblindness*, 2) *color muteness*, 3) *white privilege*. Wise also identifies a fourth mechanism he calls *class reductionism*,[63] or the notion that it is economics more than racism that needs to be addressed. In the LGBT movement, this operates primarily as *class denial*—we act as if all of our people are upper middle class. Let me talk in turn about these challenges.

Not Seeing Race

The post-racial concept known as "colorblindness" has been promoted by neo-conservatives as representing Dr. King's ultimate dream. Certainly Dr. King envisioned a day when color would not matter, but merit would. However, to claim that color does not matter in this moment is to ignore how racially biased outcomes arise out of the structure of our social, economic, and daily lives—not just as a result of intentional and malicious racial prejudice. Tim Wise describes the "well-intentioned but destructive colorblindness" as one of the mechanisms by which the progressive left marginalizes racial justice and fails to address race.

There is a perverse way in which the election of a black man as President has made the expression of racism even more permissible—assertions rooted in age-old bias are now simply and hotly defended as not racist, but just comments on the President as a leader. The very people who do and say the most white supremacist things—like Glen Beck or Rush Limbaugh or Karl Rove—vigorously deny the charge of racism. Race-based prejudice is all over the Tea Party and the Republican Party's skillful exploitation of lies, like the assertion that Barack Obama is a Muslim, Obama is un-American, Obama was not born in the U.S., Obama takes care of his own (read: black people), Obama does not get or care about ordinary (read: white) Americans, he is secretly other than what he claims. Yet, these undercurrents, even when repeated by candidates for office, are treated by the media as if they were fringe elements, instead of shown for what they are—an effective tool deployed by Rove and other Republican tacticians to undermine the President's support among independents. What after all does a writer like Peggy Noonan mean when she says, "That at the heart of... [President Obama's] descent [in recent polls] was the inability of the President to understand how the majority of Americans were thinking."[64] The word "white" before the term Americans is simply understood.

President Obama was elected despite the country's racism, not because we had transcended it. Indeed, an Associated Press poll in September of 2008 found that "More than a third of all white Democrats and independents...agreed with at least one negative adjective about blacks"[65]—adjectives like violent, boastful, complaining, lazy, and irresponsible. Surprisingly, race and racism have become the hate that dare not speak its name, while sexuality and homophobia has become the love shouted from every media outlet, championed by corporations, and the new cause célèbre among liberals. The pretense of "colorblindness" in our communities allows for these and other forms of conscious and unconscious racism to be asserted and actually operates to maintain racial exclusivity in our spaces.

A clear example of how "colorblind" policies can lead to colorful outcomes is evident in a look at the racial composition of the leadership of the national LGBT movement's key organizations. When I started organizing in the movement, the staffs of LGBT organizations were small and generally not diverse. But within them, there was a lot of conversation about the urgent need for racial representation. Most feminist and LGBT groups had specific targets they set for the number of people of color they wanted on their boards. The National LGBT Rights Marches on Washington in 1979, 1987, and 1993 set high targets for racial representation (and these were soundly derided at the time as bad quotas by the gay right wing). As a result of this critique, national organizations have backed away from setting formal targets or prioritization for representation that they give to people of color on boards and staffs. The data speak for themselves. Board and staff representation of women and people of color remains low. So, for example, MAP's 2011 National Movement Report detailed that 32% of staff of national advocacy organizations and 25% of board members were people of color, while 48% of staff and 40% of board members were women; 3% of staff and 2% board were reported to be transgender.[66] Within LGBT Community Centers (of sixty-five centers surveyed) 47% of staff and 16% of the boards were people of color.[67] Board representation of people of color within LGBT movement groups appears to be slightly better than board diversity within nonprofits in general: a large 2007 study of nonprofits by the Urban Institute found 14% of boards to be non-white.[68] While it would appear that numerically, the racial diversity on the staffs of LGBT organizations in general is good, it is hard to know how many of the queer and transgender people of color in these organizations have management or senior leadership roles. Certainly very few queer and transgender leaders of color are the heads of non-race-based or non-trans-based organizations in the mainstream movement. Of the forty national LGBT movement advocacy organizations surveyed by MAP in 2011, only two had CEOs who were people of color, and both ran queer race-focused groups.

What should we make of this weak diversity at the board and CEO level? Outside the LGBT movement, after all, there are strong and brilliant leaders of color who are LGBT, running multimillion-dollar organizations. There are powerful and successful professionals, lawyers, business people, academics, and political figures, artists—all of whom could be tapped to be board members. Yet, every organization will tell you it is having a hard time doing its "outreach." I think the reason has everything to do with a lack of specific commitment to racial inclusion, with the lack of focus of LGBT organizations on issues that matter to people of color, and with the low comfort level of existing board members, donors, influencers, and decision-makers in our movement with a racially diverse group of peers. It is my experience that many leaders in our communities are not as comfortable with the voice, leadership, and political orientation of LGBT leaders of color, and even less so when those individuals come from anything but the middle or upper middle class. I can see this in my own experience, and I can see this in the experience of other strong queer and transgender leaders of color, like Garciela Sanchez, Sharon Day, Joo Hyun Kang, Rikki Manzanala, Carmen Vazquez, or the amazing Phill Wilson. Strong leaders of color are generally found running racial and economic justice-focused groups. We are not often given opportunities to step out of these roles and be seen as broad leaders—capable of representing an entire movement.

Leadership is promoted through networks—through social capital or relationships as well as through the influence of economic capital. LGBT people of color do not have social capital with existing board members of many of our institutions because we live in racially and generationally segregated social worlds. This is why I think it is very difficult for persons of color to be selected as CEO's for a non-racially focused organization—it generally requires a campaign to convince a board that the candidate can raise money from and command the respect of the less diverse donor and member base of our organizations. I would not have become the head of NGTF in 1989 without such a campaign. I banked on the social capital and leverage of a vast network of grassroots allies and colleagues in the movement who lobbied the NGLTF board on my behalf through phone calls and letters.

Not Talking About Race

A second mechanism to perpetuate avoidance of race identified by the writer Tim Wise is defined by him as "a tendency among many on the white liberal-left to neither see nor give voice to race and racism as central issues in our communities and the institutions where we operate…"[69] He calls this color-muteness. The LGBT movement's muteness with regard to race is made shocking not only by the significant number of people in our own communities who are queer and transgender people of color, but also by the pervasive and overwhelming evidence of race-based disparities which show the U.S. to be a deeply divided society, in which race, gender and class operate to produce starkly different options for similarly situated people.

Structural racism operates, even where "individual" racism is less vivid.[70] The media and education-oriented think tank, the Opportunity Agenda, releases many useful reports on the state of economic and cultural justice based on race, gender, and economic status, including an annual *State of Opportunity Report*,[71] which synthesizes a wide set of data to show the status of progress toward fair treatment and equal opportunity in a wide range of arenas in life (income, housing, education, criminal justice, and civic participation, among others). The data show significant race, gender, and ethnicity gaps in these areas.

- The gender wage gap for women remained high, with women earning 76.8% of what men earned. The numbers by race are worse: 67.4% for African American women and 57.4% for Latinas.[72] The wage gaps between African Americans and whites and between Latinos and whites overall increased.
- The dropout rate for African Americans was 1.6% higher than the rate for whites in 2007.[73]
- African Americans experienced a poverty rate of 24.7% as of 2009 and the Latino rate was 23.3%, while the white poverty rate was 8.6%.[74]
- Immigrant incarceration increased by 11% between 2006 and 2007.[75]
- African American male incarceration claims one in three black men; by one measure more than 60% of all African American men born after 1965 have spent time in prison.[76]
- Disparities in sentencing lead to an overwhelmingly high representation of people of color on death row—of the 3,220 prisoners on death row, 42% are African American and 12% are Latino.[77]

Widespread racial disparities exist in every arena—health care access, infant mortality, educational access and completion, criminal justice prosecution and sentencing, homeownership, college completion, wages, and many other objective measures of equal opportunity. And economic disparities are widening—with the middle class of all colors shrinking and being hurt most by the policies of the past thirty years (post-Reagan).

Willful silence about the interrelationship of race and racism to all of the issues on the LGBT agenda is pervasive, even when the connections are so clear. So, for example, during the Clinton years, the NGLTF Policy Institute and grassroots people of color-led groups, like Southerners on New Ground (SONG) and the Audre Lorde Project (ALP), were among the few LGBT organizations to engage with the welfare reform fight, arguing against the destructive impact of these so-called reforms on poor women and children, and pointing out the blatant heterosexism of the policies. In the present marriage battle, few if any connections are made to the way that a focus on marriage equality has dramatically narrowed a larger and more diverse family policy agenda that once was an LGBT movement staple, an agenda that would also benefit a large number of people of color who do not live in "traditional families. These critiques have been made by scholars like Dean Spade, Kenyon Farrow, the late Paula Ettelbrick, Roderick Ferguson, David Eng, Jasbir Puar, Nancy Polikoff, among others, and by a number of progressive grassroots organizations like AgainstEquality.org and Queers for Economic Justice.[78] These writers have all urged the movement not to rely solely on marriage equality as the index for family protection in the LGBT community, not to tie the receipt of benefits to marital status, and to instead build a family protection agenda that includes a larger number of diverse families (for example, an estimated 5.7 million grandparents live with their grandchildren and at least 2.4 million are primary providers for their grandkids).[79] Despite these critiques, the

LGBT mainstream movement's family recognition agenda has narrowed drastically since the 1990s.

National LGBT organizations also do not prioritize issues that queer and transgender people of color identify as vital. Until 1997, when the Policy Institute of NGLTF started its Racial and Economic Justice Initiative (REJI) under my direction, there was no dedicated, full-time, substantive project on racial and economic justice at any LGBT national organization that was not focused on racial justice as its primary objective. Today, there are still very few.

MAP's detailed review of the forty largest LGBT organizations revealed that although several of the sixteen advocacy groups it surveyed named "Issues Affecting People of Color" as part of their program priorities, the actual content of these efforts primarily involved "outreach" to include or diversify the membership of the organizations themselves. These national groups reported little substantive or programmatic work on racial justice issues.[80] Similarly, although the Center for American Progress (CAP) recently documented LGBT health disparities by race in a report released in December of 2009,[81] these issues were not among the top priorities of the mainstream LGBT organizations.

A number of recent surveys have shown that LGBT people of color prioritize policy issues differently than the LGBT movement's mainstream, but queer and transgender people of color have not had the power to elevate their priorities onto the policy agendas of the mainstream movement. For example, over 2007-2008, HRC conducted a survey of 727 LGBT people of color, and also convened nine focus groups to research the priorities and experiences of LGBT people of color who were interacting with the LGBT movement. The overall issues that these respondents identified as most important to them were, in order: affordable health care (89%), jobs and the economy (84%), equality for people of all races and ethnicities (83%), prevention and treatment of HIV (80%), and equality for LGBT people (79%). The first three of these issues are not the top priorities of HRC, or any mainstream LGBT organization. In response to survey questions about the priorities that should be given to existing LGBT issues, violence and job discrimination were ranked most important (80%); civil unions ranked third (70%); adoption was fourth (66%); and marriage and military inclusion were cited by 60% of respondents as very important.[82] The Arcus Foundation also funded national research on African American attitudes toward LGBT issues and white LGBT attitudes towards African Americans.[83] These data reveal issues of common and overlapping concern, including access to jobs, health care access, and education. Zuna Institute's survey of black lesbians[84] found a high percentage of respondents had concerns about jobs and financial security, health care, and education—above and often before civil rights issues like marriage and partner protection.

Yet, generating jobs and financial security, health care reform, the reduction of violence or HIV are not the top four issues for any of the major national LGBT organizations. Instead, we have developed a system of issue-specific LGBT groups that exist to pick up the slack for particular communities—on immigration, on the military, on family, on health, on HIV/AIDS. While these issue-focused groups are more receptive to applying a racial and class lens, they have also struggled to take the lead and to make links. The point here is that a key reason for our willful silence on color is the absence of leadership that champions race, and not merely a lack of information, data, or connection to the broad set of policy arenas in which the LGBT movement works. The critical challenge is to build leadership in the mainstream LGBT movement to champion race.

White Privilege

This lack of leadership is tied to the third mechanism Tim Wise names: white privilege. Wise describes the concept as the process by which "in our activities, issue framing, outreach and analysis: specifically, the favoring of white perspectives over those of people of color, the cooptation of black and brown suffering to score political points, and the unwillingness to engage race and racism even when they are central to the issue being addressed."[85] Frustration with the unexamined and unquestioned, if well intentioned, white privilege within our LGBT movement is what prompted me to attempt this talk. The privileging of white LGBT experience shows up again and again, in ways small and large, visible and hidden. From the wrong analysis of the defeat of Prop 8, which blamed it on African American voters (instead of white Protestants, for example, who were a larger share of the electorate), to the naming of the Shepard/Byrd Hate Crime Act, to which James Byrd was added late, and only after pressure from our civil rights allies, to the absence of women of color from the leadership of the military fight despite the fact that they have been discharged in disproportionate numbers—one can see a racial privileging of certain experiences over others.

While no firm data are available about the racial composition of LGBT movement donors, we can hypothesize based on experience that an overwhelming majority of these individuals are white, a significant majority are male, and the age cohort is generally older. This is also the case of a substantial majority of donors at almost all LGBT gay fundraising events that cost more than $25. The generosity of these individuals has helped to build a multi-faceted movement and it is to be applauded. Yet, the donors to our movement bear significant responsibility for the lack of focus on racial justice by our research, organizing, and legal and advocacy organization.

There are very few champions of funding for LGBT people of color: the H. Van Ameringen Foundation is one of very few that has long invested in LGBT people of color organizations; the Astraea Lesbian Foundation for Justice is another; and the Arcus Foundation, which started its racial justice funding program in 2006, has been another leader. Despite these efforts, the philanthropic research organization Funders for Lesbian and Gay Issues (FLGI) found that only $7.8 million of foundation funding for LGBT issues went to organizations and projects serving LGBT people of color in 2007. This number increased to $12.6 million in 2008. But less than one-half of all autonomous people of color organizations received foundation funding in 2007, and 75% of these had budgets under $100,000.[86] Groups focused on racial justice face steep challenges in persuading a majority white donor base to move beyond its racially-limited world view, because it depends for its funding on a constituency whose privilege it is questioning. Donors often actually discourage organizations from working on racial justice issues. For example, leaders of NGLTF have been told by some of the organization's individual donors that they were not interested in funding work on race (like affirmative action or immigration reform). National LGBT organizations that took a stand against the death penalty after the Matthew Shepard murder trial lost donors and board members over their position. The relative lack of investment in LGBT organizations by mainstream foundations that work on social and economic justice issues, like the Atlantic Philanthropies and Marguerite Casey Foundation, also harms the ability of queer and transgender people of color to get support for their policy advocacy and projects.

Class Reductionism

A fourth mechanism that Tim Wise identifies as an obstacle to the left's engagement with issues of structural racism is what he terms "class reductionism"—or the argument that class more than race is the most important thing to focus on. Wise notes that this is an argument that ignores the truth that racial prejudice among the white working class is a key reason why class-focused remedies and movements have failed in the U.S. Saying that "it's class more than race" is a very interesting response because it is certainly true that class and race are linked at times and that economic justice remedies—such as insuring that people make living wages or that communities of color have access to a great and affordable local health clinic—might actually result in some positive impact regarding racial disparities in wages or health. But, as Wise notes, "racism affects the lives of people of color quite apart from the class system. Black and brown folks who are not poor or working class; indeed, those who are upper middle class and affluent are still subjected to discrimination regularly, whether in the housing market, on the part of police, in schools, in the health care delivery system, and on the job." [87]

Within the LGBT community, we have very little dialogue or analysis of class—it seems we live less in class reductionism than in a form of class denial. Inside the LGBT movement we have not developed a policy agenda that comes out of the needs of low-income much less poor LGBT people. Indeed, there is a significant part of the LGBT community that votes its endorsement of an economic agenda that dramatically favors wealthy people and is extremely antagonistic to the needs of low and middle-income people (a full 29%, if we are to believe national exit polls for those LGB people who said they voted Republican in 2010).[88]

Until very recently few data sets have existed to enable us to develop a fuller picture of LGBT communities. The Williams Institute's analysis of U.S. Census data allows us to suggest that at least 25% of the LGBT community consists of people of color, comprised in roughly the same proportion as the representation of people of color in the broader society. LGBT people of all colors can be found within this broader picture of income and race-based disparity.[89] These and other data gathered by Queers for Economic Justice (QEJ), NGLTF, and the Zuna Institute provide a more robust and interesting picture of LGBT communities. Among fascinating data points:

- LGBT youth comprise a large percentage of homeless, poor, and foster care populations. LGBT youth, large numbers of them kids of color, comprise from a significant 4-10% of the juvenile justice system population in New York State.[90]

- There were more than three million investigations of child abuse done by state welfare agencies in 2004. An estimated 500,000 children live in foster care, and gay and lesbian parents are raising 3% of them. Nationwide a disproportionate number of foster children are kids of color.[91]

- Over 20% of homeless youth are LGBT, according to several different studies. In New York, more than 40% of homeless youth are estimated to be LGBT.[92]

- Analysis of U.S. census data reveals that same-sex couples raising children are more diverse by race than heterosexual couples.[93]

- A detailed analysis of the 2000 U.S. census in California shows that at least 52,000 same-gender couples were raising at least 70,000 children. More than half of all lesbian, gay and bisexual (LGB) African American, Asian/Pacific Islander and Latino couples between the ages of twenty-five and fifty-five were raising their own kids (43%, 45% and 62% respectively) versus 18% of white same-gender couples. Across all the racial categories, California's same-gender couples with kids earned less than different-gender married couples with kids ($13,000 less per household).[94]

- When it comes to adoption, gay and lesbian couples are raising 4% of all adopted children in the United States. Indeed, researchers from the Urban Institute and the Williams Institute who collaborated on this study noted that LGB couples are adopting at a higher rate than single heterosexuals.[95] Yet, the Evan Donaldson Adoption Institute did a survey of 307 adoption agencies nationwide in 1999 and 2000

and found that more than one-third would reject a
gay or lesbian applicant.[96]

QEJ also summarize data in two excellent publications.[97]
These reports make clear that there is a significant population
of LGBT people of all colors who receive social services, depend
on public assistance, and would benefit from an expansion of
education and advocacy on their behalf before a wide range of
non-gay and LGBT institutions.

There are many unaddressed class issues among people of
color, within and beyond the LGBT community. There are
differences in power and privilege by virtue of educational
background and financial status. The fact that graduate
credentials are often required for jobs inside foundations and
nonprofits eliminates as institutional leaders those whose
expertise comes out of organizing and practice as well as
formal school environments. An extensive literature exists on
the challenges faced by women who strive to be leaders; it is
logical to assume that queer and transgender people of color
will encounter comparable challenges. Language barriers,
cultural differences, and assumptions about what constitutes
proper behavior and appropriate language are often markers
for standards of white, middle class propriety. These class
issues produce tension, between African Americans and Asians,
between Latino immigrants and African Americans, and within
the black community itself there is a longstanding tension
around the black bourgeoisie and its "politics of respectability,"
as Melissa Harris-Perry labeled it at the Facing Race Conference
in 2010.[98]

To what extent is the secondary marginalization of LGBT
people within communities of color itself a byproduct of class?
Are upper class LGBT people of color more accepted by the
mainstream inside these communities? How does the class
allegiance of people like me who have skipped several class

levels in my lifetime change my politics as we move on up? These and a hundred other questions are yet under-discussed and would be provocative to raise inside the relatively narrow circles of the colored elites of the LGBT movement. My point here is that we cannot see race as a problem entirely of the white parts of the LGBT movement. To what extent are those of us who are people of color contributing to the failure to address racial justice and how does class facilitate or inhibit that effort?

Action Steps to Set a New Course

The poet June Jordan in a speech in 1997 to the National Black Gay and Lesbian Conference said, "I wanted to say political unity based upon sexuality will never achieve lasting profound victories related to the enlargement of freedom and the broadening of equality of entitlement unless political unity based upon sexuality will become a political unity based upon *principles* of freedom and *principles* of equality."[99] Ultimately, this is what an LGBT politics for the future must articulate with regard to race: our shared "principles of freedom and principles of equality."

In this talk I have hinted at three such principles that we must make explicit in the work ahead. The first is the movement must work for the freedom of everyone who is part of the LGBT community. LGBT liberation stands for a change in the lived experience of all LGBT people, not just the advancement of rights for some. We must explicitly commit to not leave anyone behind when partial equality is won for some of us. The fact is that the class and racial division in who has power in the LGBT mainstream movement results in a deficit of Democratic accountability. This deficit arises out of the very success of the political elite in our community as donors to mainstream politics. As a result, a "loose affiliation of millionaires and billionaires"[100] and high-income professionals like me have become the ones who serve as the gateway to our communities for almost all politicians, corporate elites and media elites. There are no mechanisms in place for the clients of GMHC, say, or the clients of social service agencies like community centers, to register what they would want to say to political leaders in their communities. The access that donors have—and the fact that most of the major donors and their representatives in our movement are largely white and often men—is significant because our philanthropic and political donors carry with them issues closest to their hearts. If the overall movement's agenda can become more broad and inclusive, a wider range of issues will be carried into policy-making rooms than are presently raised.

Another consequence of this democracy deficit was raised to me quite thoughtfully by long-time activist Kevin Jennings in a lunch we had several months ago. He said what worried him was the potential disconnect within the LGBT movement between those who think that with marriage equality being achieved, they can see an end point to our movement's work. He worried that gains won by our movement benefit some of us more than others and leave large numbers of our own communities behind. As the privileged parts of our communities—of all colors—win the freedom to live out and queer lives, will they declare victory and stop investing in the movement, he asked? What would happen to other, less economically and culturally powerful, members of our communities who still need a movement to fight to get them access to rights, access to services, and access to support? They could be left behind to fend for themselves, without the resources to continue the struggle.

Why do I believe this scenario is possible? The experiences of other social movements show us that the achievement of formal equality—though essential and urgently necessary—produces mixed results because of the differences in people's economic and social status. For one, equality is not evenly distributed; its realization is affected by ones economic status, race, geographic location, religion, and many other factors. In our own history, we saw what happened in the HIV epidemic when some parts of our community, namely the well insured, secured access to life-extending drugs: leading voices declared the "Twilight of AIDS" (in the *Wall Street Journal*[101] and the *New York Times*).[102] Donations to HIV and AIDS service groups dropped dramatically, as did volunteer support. Government support also dropped as constituency pressure decreased (it had primarily been secured because of that pressure). Fourteen years later, the epidemic still continues and spreads, uncontrollable and far from over for the poor, the disempowered, and the weakest among us. In an echo of their stance on AIDS, the same neoconservative commentators claim today that when the LGBT movement wins measures like marriage equality, ENDA, military service and other examples of formal legal rights, our movement can declare an end. I find this view troubling and indefensible and, for this reason, would urge the movement to adopt the clear principle that our movement is not "over" until the weakest among us has seen the benefits of freedom.

The second principle it is time to adopt is that racial justice is a core LGBT issue. We need to simply commit to this truth by putting it in the mission statements of our organizations and on the policy agenda of our legal and advocacy movement. This means that once and for all, LGBT organizations must broaden the definition of who comprises the "gay" community and what constitutes a "gay" issue. Our limited definition is itself a byproduct not merely of ideological differences, but even more directly of pragmatic fears about overextending the LGBT agenda. As our success in making legal gains and political access continues, the argument about over-extension seems less relevant: we are not entering an era where the task of the movement must shift from winning formal equality to ensuring that people of color within LGBT communities also benefit from the gains made.

Further, the avoidance of racial justice also minimizes the extent to which economic realities affect all LGBT people and how the economic policies of leading parties impact every aspiration on the LGBT agenda. Job security is among the top issues of concern raised by LGBT people in poll after poll. Economic anxiety is the legacy that the Baby Boomers have left its successors, and our communities are no different in their concerns than the larger society in which we live. Within this context, nondiscrimination is an important but inadequate goal to address the concerns of all classes and races of LGBT people. And given our understanding of how race and gender affect economic opportunity, it is imperative that issues of economic equity rise to the top of LGBT agendas. So, support by LGBT organizations at the state, local, and national level to extend unemployment benefits, expand workforce development for low-wage workers, support ex-offenders to get training and jobs, support passage of living wage laws, develop microfinance strategies to help U.S.-based low income entrepreneurs—all are examples of policies that could increase economic security for working LGBT people, and could express the commitment of an LGBT movement built to achieve social justice and not just equal rights.

Choice and reproductive health, access to health care, and ending health care disparities are critical issues for LGBT women and men of all colors, as is adequate resourcing of the ongoing HIV/AIDS epidemic. These issues must be restored to prominence on the LGBT agenda. Similarly, reducing the over-criminalization of certain communities, sentencing reform, support for better treatment of prisoners, working for an end to rape inside prison affect many LGBT people, and disproportionately affect people of color.

Defending a robust role for the state in securing economic prosperity for all is a meaningful LGBT issue. It has always been a myth perpetuated by those with privilege that success is possible "on one's own" and that the people getting "handouts" from government are undeserving, lazy, poor people who are largely black or undocumented immigrants. Despite the evidence of massive government supports that helped create the white middle class—the GI Bill, Social Security, Medicaid, free education through high school, subsidized public colleges and universities—this myth persists. You can hear it at Tea Party rallies as they claim how tired they are of carrying freeloaders and that these "other" people, namely the poor and most vulnerable, should take care of themselves. The tax cut mania of the moment has never been more than a thinly disguised attempt to shrink the size and social-democratic role of the state.

A critical part of adding race to our agenda requires of LGBT politics a confrontation with this era's anti-government sentiment; we are ironically a community that needs much more government investment to address many of our biggest challenges. Yet we are a community rightly skeptical of state power, having experienced its abuses. How do we reconcile this complex historical relationship with the state? What new ideas can we introduce to the polarized debates that emerge from our experience of being regulated, managed, and negated by state power? How do we conceptualize services that state funding enables, such as elder care, youth services, school curriculum teaching tolerance, alternatives to incarceration, affordable housing, mental health services, drug and alcohol programs, HIV prevention, treatment, and care, support for people facing life-threatening illnesses? How can we engage with government in ways that do not expand its police power to target parts of our communities?

The third principle to which we must commit is to increase the representation and to enhance the leadership voice for LGBT people of color at decision-making tables. LGBT institutions and leadership in our movement must reflect the racial and gender composition of our communities. Data from MAP reported the demographic composition of boards and staffs of the forty largest organizations in 2011. Racially, staff were identified as 68% white, 12% African American, 13% Latino/a, 6% API and 1% Native American. However boards were less diverse. Boards were 75% white, 12% African

American, 7 % Latino/a, 4% API and 2% Native. Boards were also majority male (58% male, 40% female and 2% identified as gender/queer or other; 6% identified as transgender).[103]

The LGBT movement's organizations should set voluntary goals for people of color representation on boards and staff senior teams, and be accountable through annual reviews for their performance towards meeting these targets. LGBT board members and major donors need to have space to have frank conversations with each other about the reasons why they have had difficulty supporting and nurturing leaders of color. There is a critical need to invest in and provide resources to grassroots organizations and LGBT people of color-oriented programs that are trying to network, nurture, and strengthen leaders who come from under-represented communities—the Rockwood Leadership Institute, the Center for Progressive Leadership, the Pipeline Project are three examples of such programs. We need programs that reach out to corporate, philanthropic, and academic sites to recruit out and diverse LGBT leaders who might be willing to lead a board or a staff.

Principles are the guidelines that can help set our future course. But action must also be taken. For the LGBT movement to work in a meaningful way on race, some propose that we need to truly reconfigure the definition of which allies we work with, what we work for, and how we work for LGBT freedom. I agree. I also believe that we need significant consolidation and restructuring in our national movement organizations. And we need to take up some new campaigns that actually put into practice our long-held theories that sexuality, race, economic status, disability status, gender, gender identity and expression are all interconnected. So, at the U.S. Social Forum, the Queer Caucus, led by FIERCE, ALP, and SONG led hundreds of LGBT people attending in a participatory process to determine if they would be willing to join forces in non-gay campaigns working to achieve specific policy change in education, criminal justice, or health care policies. Queer and trans groups came together to create the Roots Coalition, "a national network of Queer and Trans People of Color (QTPOC) led organizations and collectives engaged in cutting edge multi-issue organizing across progressive movements which has been meeting ever since."[104] Grassroots innovations like the Roots Coalition, as well as other local and state experiments in projects striving to meet community needs, hold the key to breaking through the impasse of present racial justice politics. Let me propose three additional examples of experiments that illustrate ways that race could be readily incorporated into existing forms of LGBT organizing.

At the outset, it would be interesting to see the queer and transgender movement consciously and significantly support Latino, African American, or Asian candidates of color who are pro-LGBT at the national level and local levels. Could we meaningfully mobilize the rather significant LGBT vote in mid-sized cities not known for the coherence of such a vote, in support of pro-LGBT people of color leaders at the state and local level, especially in the South and the Midwest? Cities I would pick would include, Milwaukee, WI, St. Paul, MN, Grand Rapids, MI, Columbus, OH, Lexington, KY, Asheville, NC, and Charleston, SC. The goal here would be three fold: 1) to develop new methods of voter mobilization and engagement in cities where the LGBT movement is less developed and visible; 2) to create deeper relationships of trust and reciprocity between a local LGBT community and a local community of color; and 3) to demonstrate that by working together, communities of color and LGBT people can win, even in difficult contexts.

A second set of experiments might commit the movement to invest queer money and talent to race-based ballot initiatives in order to mobilize a significant and serious vote to defeat them. This would not only serve as a meaningful statement of queer commitment to align our political interests with those of communities of color, but such actions could also build the electoral base for the LGBT-specific electoral repeals the movement must win in the decades ahead (to rollback the more than thirty-six anti-gay, state level, defense of marriage bills, that exist, for example; or to preserve the basic LGBT equal rights gains made thus far). Such ballot measures could involve affirmative action initiatives, voting rights restrictions, immigrant rights initiatives, criminal justice initiatives that seek to expand police power, or public schools initiatives. Experience in places like Oregon and Maine shows that electoral efforts to bridge LGBT and non-gay voters can strengthen ties between constituencies and build a more cohesive progressive electorate in the long run.

A final set of interventions could involve the queer movement in making the case for LGBT equality to a wider set of audiences in a particular community. Electoral strategies that aim for wins are not necessarily hearts and minds strategies that can secure those wins.[105] It would be valuable to explore whether public education messages could meaningfully shift public opinion in a particular constituency within a particular city (or two). We have gathered significant data on the attitudes of various segments of each community, including women, old people, young people, African Americans, and Latinos. Can we take the stories and lives of queer people, our families and relationships, out of the context of the reactive anti-gay campaigns that our opponents thrust upon us, and instead plan and pursue a pro-LGBT educational campaign to build more allies and support in particular communities? Within the LGBT movement, there is much talk about public education campaigns about homophobia aimed at either the general public or at segments of that public within majority white communities. There has been very little investment in educational organizing campaigns that frame the challenges that LGBT people of color, and economically challenged parts of our communities confront. Such campaigns could be considered as mechanisms to build deeper understanding within populations that the LGBT movement has not yet engaged—including, for example, communities of color, low-income white voters, single women, small-town and rural residents.

Conclusion

The poet June Jordan wrote:

What is the moral meaning of who we are?
What do we take personally?
How do perceived issues propel or diffuse our political commitments?
I think these questions can only be answered again and again with difficulty.[106]

These are questions we face in this moment of partial fulfillment of LGBT formal equality. The moral meaning of who we are will be determined by our actions: by what we stand for and by whom we stand with.

LGBT identities are mutating, and LGBT politics must as well. The LGBT politics of the future—LGBT politics 3.0—must be a more inclusive, democratically determined, decentralized and multi-issue politics. It must be an LGBT politics willing to provide leadership to a wider progressive movement that is desperate for new voices and new energy.

To succeed, it must be a politics that speaks to critical issues like racial and economic equity, gender inequality and justice, the role and value of government in our society, the role and value of the market and economic sector when it is harnessed for socially responsible and sustainable ends, for global justice, and the need to end racial and tribal hatreds and nationalist mindsets arising from a purity-based politics of ethnic superiority.

We need an LGBT politics of the future that seeks respect instead of pity, affinity instead of tolerance, connection instead of isolation, and full citizenship on queer terms. A politics that does not need crutches like the biological argument—we were born this way, so don't hate us—to assert our moral integrity and win our civil equality; a politics whose goal is to deliver equality and social justice, and access to the "good life," to all people; and a politics within which we are free to be as diverse, nonconforming, and inside or outside of heterosexual structures as we each desire.

ASSUME THE POSITION
Class and the LGBT Movement[107]

It seemed appropriate to talk about economic inequality and class when I got the invitation to speak at my alma mater, Vassar College. The talk keynoted a queer conference reflecting on LGBT life at the college on the occasion of Vassar's 150ᵗʰ anniversary. I attended Vassar on generous scholarships. It was my first close encounter with both wealth and privilege. Economic privilege, its affects and its effects, was part of the DNA of the college. Not surprisingly, I became a feminist and a socialist there.

Although we have been together nearly twenty-five years, my partner, Kate Clinton, had never come with me to the college, although she had performed there once. Before this keynote, we walked the campus and I pointed out the highlights. She quickly dubbed it the "slutwalk" and marveled at the difference in our educational experiences. She lived at home in the late 1960s, while attending Le Moyne College, a Jesuit college in Syracuse, sleeping in her childhood bedroom under the crucifix that adorned her wall. The chapel figured prominently in my life at Vassar, but only as the site of demonstrations I organized, and the Patti Smith concert that my friends and I stuffed the student activities ballot box to secure.

The talk below was created as the Occupy Wall Street protests ignited across the country. Predictably, those who benefit from the current system had little sympathy for the protests. My neighbor, an investment banker, when asked by her kids to explain what people were protesting at Wall Street, answered, "Success." Rich and powerful people seemed annoyed and angry that anyone would question their privilege. Many worked hard to get where they had arrived; they had an absolute right to exert political influence, and lead. Being successful financially was the reward for working harder, being smarter, being more innovative, and being tougher than the competition. What was wrong with success? The failure of the Left lies in its inability to convince people that shared success and social prosperity, structured through systems that provide for and care for the common welfare, is as critical to the existence and continuation of individual wealth and privilege as cherished notions of hard work and being smart.

The LGBT movement operates within and is deeply affected by this era's economic transformation. Curiously, while the external progressive world is increasingly skeptical of corporate power, critical about the increase in police control and surveillance on poor, brown and immigrant people, and alarmed by the collapse of political power into the hands of fewer and wealthier people, the LGBT movement embraces each of these arenas. We are refugees desperate for shelter. The alliances we make are opportunistic and not strategic: they reflect a short-term focus on the rights of only parts of our communities. The following talk explores the way class allegiances inform the politics of the mainstream LGBT movement.

What stands out for me as I reflect on being back at Vassar College for this queer conference marking 150 years in the college's history is the persistence of queer uneasiness and alienation on campus. I suspected Vassar would still have encounters with prejudice, but I am surprised to find the discomforting persistence of narratives of isolation, harassment and ridicule, the continued sense of longing and not belonging that was expressed in the narratives of graduates of Vassar in other eras, collected in the book *Wolf Girls at Vassar*,[108] and especially surprised by the dearth of attention to the amazing contributions queer activists from this college have made to every single movement for social, economic, gender, racial and sexual justice. Why? Because despite the atmosphere of defiant individualism and expression that is the hallmark of the Vassar experience, despite the blatant or latent evidence of queerness found in every era of the college's existence, Vassar (like the heterosexist world in which it exists) plays the trick of graying out our flaming, pink lives.

The norm is a construction, a superimposition of certain forms of being over others, a generalization made out of a particular experience that at once universalizes that experience and averages it out. The neutering of difference is an aspect of collective belonging. To the college as well as to each of us, we individually are a collectivity–Vassar graduates, above and beyond our being "queer" Vassar graduates. Even the idea of queer is but another norm, albeit a newer one, and one that bristles at self-limitation.

Homophobia is perhaps an incomplete term for this still uneasy and unequal experience of being queer. Blatant manifestations of prejudice based on sexual orientation or gender identity certainly still exist—in legal barriers still to be overcome, in the many institutional policies that have not yet been changed to accommodate the emergence of LGBT people and our families, and in various social practices and attitudes that refuse the fundamental moral equivalence of queer people and practices. Yet today, the queer experience of injustice is determined as much by a subtler silencing of lives, a silencing in which LGBT people and the institutions to which queer people strive to belong both participate. It may seem anachronistic for me to recall the idea of silence, an early and richly mined trope in the LGBT liberation movement of the 1960s or 1970s; queer theory might label it as multiple subjectivities rather than some totalizing form of silencing. But I am interested in silences.

The poet Muriel Rukeyser, who was both bisexual and a Vassar graduate, wrote, "Pay attention to what they tell you to forget."[109] This admonition has always rung in my ears as an activist. And with it in mind I have focused this talk on what LGBT activism must attend to, not what it can congratulate itself on having achieved; on what we keep forgetting, rather than what we valorize about our histories.

My talk today covers three dimensions—first, some observations about economic class and privilege; second, some thoughts on the ways that assumptions about privilege and economic security made by the mainstream LGBT movement's leadership affect the agenda and strategies of this movement; and finally, what it would look like if we imagined a movement centered on the lives and concerns of queer folks of all colors who are poor, those who are less powerful, those who are transgender, those who are people of color, or otherwise deviant from the hetero-normative mainstream that the movement currently represents.

My favorite Patti Smith song has long been "Privilege/Set Me Free" from the *Easter*[110] album, in which Patti intercuts the Lord's Prayer with an existential cry to God to set her free from her seeking, her desire, her youth, her angst. The song has served me as an anthem, rallying me again and again to rebound when I feel defeated by privileges that I cannot access, or trapped in my own heady melodramas within the privileges I occupy.

The irony of my discovery of Patti's song while studying at Vassar College is obvious. The common element in the diverse experiences of all who graduated from Vassar is that we attended and benefitted from one of the most elite institutions in this country, an institution built upon economic privilege and dedicated to its continuance, an institution inaccessible to most people, and one of the critical institutions that operates in overt and informal ways to maintain, prepare people for, or otherwise keep people in, certain social and economic class positions. The fact that so many of us who attended Vassar found within it a world of amazing ideas, people, knowledge, and a questioning and even at times radical spirit of expression does not change the structural reality of Vassar's impact on our lives: by virtue of our attendance here, we each assumed, and have been assumed into, an upper middle class position.

I was not to the manor born, yet over the years since I graduated from Vassar, I found, and in many instances deliberately placed, myself in positions to work inside and sometimes even to run the manor. Vassar changed my socio-economic class status forever—from immigrant working class to upwardly mobile and securely middle class. Attending Northeastern Law School changed it again—to the professionally employable and credentialed managerial class. Working at the Ford Foundation changed it once more—giving me a truly comfortable upper middle class life, for the first time in my adult life, including the first pension plan I ever had. And working to help a billionaire build his foundation changed my status yet again—from comfortably upper middle class to a platinum card-carrying member of the small group of people that staffs, supports, and serves the ruling elites in this country.

My friend Henry, who is a prominent philanthropist in his early eighties, once observed to me dryly, "For a socialist you certainly are surrounded by a lot of money." I answered Henry that as a socialist my job was to redistribute the wealth so I needed to be surrounded by lots of money. But the underlying and cynical truth of his critical observation is not lost upon me. When one ascends to a certain economic class position, by virtue of education, labor, or inheritance, one assumes a certain position in the social order—of being a statistical member of the economically most privileged in this country, the elite few; of going along and getting along in the system; of a certain subservience to those whom the system benefits—all these positions are assumed.

Many tangible forms of power accompany the opportunity that comes with economic status, greater educational access, and social privilege. These include, most practically, the power to live comfortably and securely, the material "opportunity" to fulfill wants, the ability to provide for one's loved ones, the ability to access health care and social services with greater ease, the ability to be heard in ways that people without money are not heard, and the promise, even if it proves to be a form of false consciousness, of being able to achieve "the good life." Specifically, being part of, or a servant to, the ruling class brings with it three forms of power: the power to see and be seen, the power to want and have those wants met, and the power to transform ones identity and experience in very material ways.

Class positions embody and generate *a way of seeing and being seen*—and like all observation and experience, this way of seeing is raced and gendered. Socio-economic class affects whom or what you notice, with whom you affiliate; to whom you pay attention; with whom you see yourself belonging; it shapes what you see and to what you remain oblivious; it determines whom you must please and whom you can disregard. Class-based seeing is aspirational; it is fantasy-based. So, we see people richer than ourselves and identify with them much more than we see and affiliate with our own class peer group, or those poorer than us. Poor, working, and middle class people have a lot of anxiety and shame about not being better off. People with higher incomes spend more than they can afford to be seen as "belonging" to the class they aspire to become. Class also affects who notices you. I've always wondered, for example, why the horrific murder of Matthew Shepard struck such a strong chord with so many LGBT and non-queer folks. The outcry against the attack was enormous and critical to an increased political commitment to challenge violence. It certainly set the stage for a decade of new work around LGBT rights. The same year his murder took place, dozens of queer, lesbian and trans people of all colors were also killed; grassroots organizations at the local level launched a number of campaigns to seek justice for these murders. Yet, in my thirty years of work in the LGBT movement

I can remember no comparable nationwide mobilization around the murder of a poor, nonwhite, queer person.

Class is *a way of wanting*. It informs our desires, what we aspire to seek, not to mention whether we can meet our own aspirations. Class-based wants for most people include the desire for various forms of material comfort and security—a job, a home that we own or affordable rent, a stereo, the ability to take a vacation, the ability to afford transportation, to provide for a better life for their kids. Wanting is about our imaginations and fantasy life as well—and class colonizes our creativity. Those of us who lived through the emergence of HIV/AIDS in our communities in the 1980s remember the many battles fought against the right wing for attention to this epidemic. But equally bitter battles were fought within the LGBT movement—over what we wanted, over our political imaginings. Did we want treatment or prevention (or both)? Did we want to push the FDA or push for health care reform (or both)? Did we want to insure that funding for HIV went to poor African American and Latino intravenous drug users or primarily to gay men (or both)? Did we want to fight for Medicaid reform overall or make the AIDS specific fix that would take care of HIV-positive people (or both)? These were class-based fights, and while the way the lines got drawn and who sided with what position was not determined by class positions, the battles we waged certainly revealed them!

Money and educational class privilege are forms *that allow transformation*, they bring about the magic of migration, of transition, even erasure—one can literally move from one neighborhood to a better one, become less marginal, and be seen as race-less by virtue of access to wealth. Money can transform one's race or gender in a way that appears to transcend ordinary race or ordinary gender-based exclusion—but that on closer examination does not change the structural barriers and exclusions that apply to those without that same access to money. So Sean Combs (or P. Diddy) is a fixture on East Hampton's social circuit, but I suspect even he still finds himself excluded from certain enclaves in that world. Or Meg Whitman and Cheryl Sandberg rise to the top in business, but their success does not negate the structural fact that women number fewer than twenty percent of the members of corporate boards or that they earn less than men performing the same jobs. Wealth and educational privilege, it would seem, transform race and gender for the individual beneficiary, not for the class from which they come. Still, the transformational power of money and a higher socio-economic class is what drives us to earn more, to change our lot, to provide a better life for our families than we had for ourselves.

These three intangible yet material impacts of class status, on seeing, wanting, and transforming operate in stark ways in the LGBT movement. I want to spend some time on an example of a fundraiser for marriage equality to explore the operation of class in our movement further. Hosted by prominent philanthropists and co-chaired by Republican Mayor Michael Bloomberg, the fundraiser involved Republican and Democratic major donors and was held on October 13, 2011 in New York City to support the four Republican members of the New York State Senate who voted for marriage equality earlier in 2011, and who had, as a result of their support, been targeted for defeat by the National Organization for Marriage. The fundraiser reportedly raised $1.2 million dollars. *The Advocate* reported that co-hosts included Tea Party Founder David Koch, hedge fund managers Paul Singer and Daniel Loeb, and prominent gay political activists, both Democrat and Republican.[111]

Those of us with memory and history had to shake our heads—what a difference thirteen years makes in political bedfellows! You might recall that in October of 1998, The Human Rights Campaign (HRC) endorsed the conservative Republican Senate Incumbent Al D'Amato for U.S. Senate from New York State over Chuck Schumer—the community was in an uproar. Local activists denounced HRC and vowed not to work with them. Irate, board members of HRC resigned and decried "sleeping with the enemy."[112] By contrast, the October 13 fundraiser for anti-choice Republicans drew nary a peep from most queer New Yorkers.

It is neither logical, nor valid, to argue against the strategy of bipartisan politics: moderate Republican and at times conservative votes are needed to advance LGBT rights (and civil rights) in all state and national legislatures. Nor is the idea of being a friend to get a friend offensive. Additionally, since so many conservative and liberal people have LGBT members of their families, it makes sense they, too, would support the LGBT equality agenda (Paul Singer has a gay son, David Koch is rumored to have some close gay relative). Nevertheless, the LGBT political movement's alliance with powerful conservative, and indeed reactionary, donors raises many troubling questions—about who our movement sees as part of "our" community and whom it sees as dispensable, about the broader vision the movement wants to achieve, and about what exactly movement leaders are seeking in this alliance with those who oppose other aspects of our queerness through their political actions. What values is the LGBT mainstream compromising through this act of collaboration? Should the LGBT movement only care about gay rights and not women's reproductive rights or immigrants rights to fair opportunities or labor's right to organize or people of color's right to not face disparities?

Gay conservatives, be they Democrat or Republican, have long argued that we are and should remain a single-issue movement. What they fail to accept is that such narrowing of an LGBT agenda is neither possible for many LGBT people who confront barriers beyond their sexual orientation, and that such alliances have a cost. At best, single-issue politics alienates LGBT people from longstanding allies with whose help we have advanced in the workplace, the courts, and the legislatures. At worst, taking the position that anyone who supports gay rights is our friend aligns us with political partners who promote policies that will maintain inequality and misery for large numbers of LGBT and straight people.

Writer and progressive gay organizer Kenyon Farrow asked in a blog in late June of 2011, "What does it mean when so-called progressives celebrate a victory in large part won by GOP-supporting hedge fund managers, Tea Party funders and corporate conglomerates—the oft-spoken enemies of progressive causes?"[113] Farrow wondered if this embrace of gay rights was in fact a GOP strategy to undercut the gay vote and siphon off some support for Republican candidates. It's an interesting point, because siphoning off votes was a conscious strategy that Ralph Reed once deployed towards the African American vote when he ran the Christian Coalition. Farrow asks if the mainstream movement is in effect "pink-washing" the Republican Party's homophobia with such a single-issue alliance. In fact, the embrace of Paul Singer, David Koch, or newly out Republican conservatives like Ken Mehlman reflects a class-based politics within the LGBT movement, an economic bias that the movement conveniently avoids behind a claim that such alliances are necessary and tactically smart. And such alliances highlight whose agendas and values dominate elite LGBT political strategy.

When the movement makes alliances with economic reactionaries, what message does it send to our own community members who are targeted by the campaigns these conservative donors have launched? Ken Mehlman, who was once chairman of the Republican National Committee and served as campaign manager for the 2004 election of George Bush, still lends his name to support some of the most viciously anti-gay politicians, like House Speaker John Boehner.[114] Koch, Singer, and other Republican mega-donors actively oppose President Obama, who is the most pro-LGBT president in American history. Their opposition seems more personal than fact-based, as Congressman Barney Frank noted recently about Wall Street,

"They're whining because Obama hurt their feelings...He did not interfere with their incomes."[115] Singer also reportedly funds the *American Spectator*, sits on the board of the Manhattan Institute (which has been vigorous in its opposition to health care reform of any kind), and vigorously opposes campaigns for corporate regulation.[116]

The right wing credentials of the Koch brothers (David and Charles) run deep.[117] They favor minimal social support for the poor; David Koch has campaigned for abolishing social security, and abolishing the Federal Reserve; they have funded campaigns to discredit claims that corporate pollution is contributing to climate change; they fund the anti-choice, anti-fair taxation, anti-immigrant movements; they fund work that is anti-judicial independence and against expanded civil liberties; and they have been widely credited with the massive funding infrastructure underlying the pro-business, anti-poor Tea Party movement. Such an alliance abandons the large numbers of LGBT people who are poor, jobless, economically struggling, people of color, women who might need an abortion, and queer people on Medicaid, Social Security or welfare—in short, middle-income and working class queer people who benefit from government supports in various ways.

By seeking the support of folks like David Koch, Paul Singer, and Ken Mehlman, the LGBT political movement prioritizes an alliance with conservative donors and politicians over alliances with those who have supported the LGBT movement for decades. It should be noted that thirty-six Democrats voted for the New York State marriage bill, but no comparable LGBT and straight allies' fundraising effort has been launched to defend their re-election. Unions invested heavily and lobbied hard for marriage equality in New York—but the LGBT movement's coalition with David Koch allies it with someone who defeated collective bargaining rights in Wisconsin, and who is identified with nationwide efforts to destroy union power.

The common argument for making these alliances with

conservative straight people is that their endorsement of LGBT rights will get more pro-corporate Republican and Democratic politicians to opportunistically support LGBT rights—that the politicians will follow the money. We are told this is smart politics, savvy in today's polarized political climate, necessary and the "reason why we are winning." I question these romantic rationalizations. They obscure the proven historic irrelevance of such an approach, and minimize the outright danger of such alliances. Gay alliances with right-wing donors and anti-choice candidates have had no impact on the tenor of Republican attacks on LGBT people. The Republican Party platform remains deeply hostile to LGBT equality, to reproductive choice, and to a wide range of issues of social, racial and gender justice. LGBT movement support for Republican candidates has been irrelevant to LGBT progress in the past twenty years; however, our targeting of anti-gay opponents for defeat (a strategy deployed in Massachusetts, Colorado, and New York, for example) has made a difference. Our advances have come under Democratic administrations, through the timid leadership of Bill Clinton and the more forceful, if at times frustrating, lead of Barack Obama. We won marriage equality in New York not merely because of four Republican votes, but because of the savvy political leadership of Democratic Governor Andrew Cuomo, and a decades-old grassroots educational and organizing effort to educate and advocate in Albany.

Partnering with the enemies of social justice is dangerous. It places the LGBT movement in a coalition with people who have funded and fought vigorously to re-criminalize, re-pathologize, and maintain discrimination against queer people and women. Dick Armey, Karl Rove, Haley Barbour, George Bush Sr. and Jr., Dick Cheney, Newt Gingrich, Rick Santorum, Steve Forbes, and their backers have not been the friends of LGBT folks when they had power.

I know from my own participation in elite lobbying strategies and political advocacy that an assumption made by elite donors in our movement is that we are acting in the best interests of the community. Participants in elite donor tables sincerely hold, and I trust that they act out of, this belief. We assume that our judgment, our views about issue priorities, and our norms about being LGBT are shared by the majority of our people. This false consciousness is an artifact of privilege—the experience of specialness reinforced when one is part of a dominant power group by virtue of money or race or gender or any other factor. The false premise that structures the operations of most LGBT organizations is that the experience of highly privileged and un-representative people who sit at decision-making tables is universal. But this is not in fact true. Unfortunately, good intentions do not always produce good results. When the HRC seriously explored passing ENDA without protections for gender identity, they put the economic interests of employed gay and lesbian queers above those of a much less powerful and poorer population of transgender people. Similarly, when prestigious gay donors ally with right wing elements in the Republican Party on marriage, they ally themselves with a set of moneyed interests whose agenda is overtly hostile to the needs of many differently situated LGBT folks. In so doing I think we once again universalize our own economic and social class interests in ways that harm the political power of poor LGBT people, LGBT immigrants, and others targeted by the policies of the right.

What exactly will the mainstream LGBT political movement transform in moderating its broader social justice aspirations to make new alliances with right wing elements? A few legislative wins may come sooner than they otherwise would were we to take the slower route of electing progressive candidates to legislatures to replace reactionary ones. But these short-term gains will not be secured for the long term until we actually change the power dynamics of legislatures and shift the reactive consciousness of our country towards human rights. In the end such alliances produce nothing deeper than a short-term advantage for those making them. In making alliances with the right, the male-dominated, mostly-white and white-acting, comfortably wealthy advocates (like me) who get to sit at or set up the tables of political decision-making merely get to assume the power position for a brief moment. We get to promote first and foremost our own acceptance, credibility, and respectability within existing systems of power. We reassure the wealthy and powerful that our admission to their club will not rock their privileges or their worldview; we demur that we are just like them, that we believe in what they believe. We are asked to prove our loyalty, and our adherence to broader elitist values, by being willing to sacrifice parts of our own souls, and our own people, in order to win short-term battles.

If economic class informs a way of seeing, a way of wanting, and seems to offer a path of transcendence from experiences of oppression, what are the ways these lenses affect the agenda and operations of the LGBT movement? Let us start by considering the socio-economic status of LGBT people. What do the data tell us about ourselves? How does the class composition and class orientation of the mainstream LGBT movement result in wealthy people dominating the movement's agenda and activities?

Class and the LGBT Experience

The limited data available on the demographics of LGBT populations reveal two truths: first, that significant percentages of LGBT people are low income and poor; and second, that a large number of members, as well as staff and board members of mainstream queer organizations, are middle to upper middle class. The class composition of the LGBT communities is quite different from that of many of the people who staff, fund, and lead our movement's mainstream institutions

The Williams Institute's groundbreaking report on "Poverty in the Lesbian, Gay and Bisexual Community," released in 2009, and the NCTE/NGLTF survey of transgender persons, released in 2011, document significant economic diversity within LGBT populations. Williams concludes that poverty is significant in lesbian, gay, and bisexual populations and at least as common as is found in the general population.[118] The NCTE/NGLTF-supported National Transgender Discrimination Survey gathered information from more than 6,500 transgender and gender nonconforming respondents, and revealed that transgender people are nearly four times more likely to live in poverty than the general population.[119] Transgender persons report extremely high incidence of discrimination in employment, housing, public accommodation, medical care, access to police and other emergency services, and a high impact from family rejection. Transgender people in general have twice the rate of unemployment as the national average, and people of color who are transgender people experience four times the national rate of unemployment. Discrimination is rampant, with 19% report being refused a home and 11% report being evicted.

Queer youth are also extremely vulnerable. The Center for American Progress estimates that more than 100,000 LGBT youth are homeless in the U.S. In New York City alone, a 2008 survey of homeless youth revealed at least 4,000 young people in need of housing, an estimated 1,600 of whom were LGBT; but homeless advocates note there are fewer than two hundred beds available for these LGBT youth.[120] Both the Williams Institute data and the 2011 Movement Advancement Project (MAP) report on LGBT Families (released in December of 2011) note that LGBT families experience more financial hardships than heterosexual families.[121] MAP reports that one in five LGBT families are raising kids in poverty, as opposed to one in ten heterosexual families. The Williams Institute reports that children in LGBT families have poverty rates twice of the general population and that 20% of kids growing up in same-sex households are being raised in households that meet the poverty threshold, this compares to 9.4% of kids being raised by heterosexual households that meet the poverty threshold (defined as $22,000 a year for a family of four; or in the case of extreme poverty $11,175 a year for a family of four).[122]

The pervasive myth of LGBT people being high-income earners is also dispelled by several online surveys that ask people to self-disclose their wages. Despite the tendency of such samples to over-represent higher earners, the data show that millions of LGBT people are low wage earners. For example, 27% respondents to the National Survey of Transgender Discrimination reported earning incomes of less than $20,000. And in the 2008 HRC/Hunter College poll of 768 randomly selected LGBT people, 33% reported incomes under $25,000 a year.[123]

A different archive was gathered by the Welfare Warriors Research Collaborative through the auspices of the Queers for Economic Justice (QEJ) in 2009, and published in 2010.[124] Unlike the above data, which were all largely gathered online or via government-funded research, the QEJ survey was based on research meetings and a self-reported survey completed by 171 low-income LGBT and gender nonconforming people in New York City. The participatory action research study found that 69% of the people surveyed reported being homeless at some point in their lives; 58% currently lived in a shelter.[125] Approximately 80% of respondents had used need-based public benefits (food stamps, public assistance, and housing assistance); more than 70% used health benefits like Medicaid, HIV/AIDS Services Administration benefits, SSI, and Social Security Disability.[126] Most participants reported very high levels of police harassment, violence, and harassment by government agencies.

A Movement of the Middle and Upper Middle Class

Social movement theorists have long documented the

middle class nature of most post-1960s social movements (peace, environmental, women's). While the "old" social movements were grounded in material interest (unions organizing for the rights of workers) the new social movements are often focused around claims for rights, assertions of identities, desires for community, and assertions of values. Frederick Rose notes, "By measures of occupation, education and income, membership in new social movement organizations is disproportionately upper middle class."[127] This is certainly borne out in the LGBT movement.

One marker for LGBT class interests can be found in the data on the LGB vote in national elections. Since the early 1990s, anywhere from 22% to 33% of the LGB vote (surveys have not yet tracked the transgender vote) has gone to Republican candidates in national Congressional and Presidential elections. This voting bloc migrates depending on the level of homophobia of the Republican Party candidates, reflecting the fact that queer voters are influenced most by what candidates say about LGBT rights.[128] But the long-term data are clear: there has been significant gay voter support for Republicans despite the hostility of that party to LGBT issues. One clear reason for this vote by LGBT folks is that some people prioritize their perceived economic class interests over their gay self-interest.

The class position of the people who staff and volunteer for mainstream LGBT organizations impacts the agenda of these organizations. This is clear from the programmatic priorities of LGBT mainstream organizations. Interestingly, the leadership of LGBT grassroots organizations is more economically diverse and derives more widely from people with poor and working class backgrounds. QEJ's fascinating report called "Poverty, Public Assistance, and Privatization: The Queer Case for a New Commitment to Economic Justice"[129] presents the personal and political perspectives of a number of leaders of the grassroots racial and economic justice wing of the queer movement. They share their experience with being on public assistance, coming from poor and low-income families, and the importance of this experience to their work as queer activists. The publication is striking in the cross-section of voices and backgrounds represented and in the very different political agenda, which these working class leaders are pursuing through their LGBT political work. The voices in the report work in ways that expand the mainstream rights agenda to include a defense of public assistance, government control versus privatization of basic social support services, support for public infrastructure and investment, and support for human needs (housing, food, health, education).

MAP's analysis of revenues sources for the mainstream LGBT movement is also interesting to review. The forty largest national LGBT organizations accounted for one-fourth of all revenue raised by the 506 LGBT-focused organizations identified by MAP as reporting to the IRS.[130] Sources of revenue included 35% raised from individuals, 20% from in-kind contributions, 18% from foundations and 11% from events, 4% from corporations, and only 2% from government sources. The remaining 10% was earned from bequests (4%) and other forms of earned revenue.[131] Data about the economic situation of individual donors to the LGBT movement is very limited as most organizations hold any such information quite proprietarily, but MAP notes that the average participant in the study receives "almost half (45%) of its revenue from its 10 largest contributors—including individual donors, foundations, and/or corporate donors." MAP notes that individual donors account for 35% of the income for the forty LGBT nonprofits it studied.[132] Finally, MAP tracks a high rate of donor turnover each year among these large LGBT organizations. Nearly one-half of all donors to gay organizations do not give again the following year. Most gay people are not members, not contributors, and not even connected to the work of the organizations that strive to speak, lobby, and campaign on their behalf.[133] These data reveal the extent to which LGBT organizations depend on a small number of individual donors, and why those donors could have such a disproportionate impact on the politics and stands of the mainstream movement.

A Mainstream Movement That is Silent on the Needs of Many LGBT People

The overall silence of mainstream LGBT policy, legal, and advocacy organizations on bread-and-butter economic justice and social welfare issues is noticeable and rather remarkable, especially in the post-2008 global economy. The avoidance of the pressing need for economic security by many parts of the mainstream LGBT movement ignores hard data that now show: queer youth are disproportionately homeless, therefore often out of schools and on track to low-wage or underground-economy jobs; large numbers of lesbians with children live in poverty (about 24% according to one estimate by the Williams Institute); gay men earn less than straight men because of workplace discrimination; lesbians, like all women, earn less than men for comparable positions; LGBT people are often passed over for promotions, raises, and other advancement because of their sexual orientation and gender identities; and that large numbers of LGBT people are employed in social services, in education, and the arts, generally lower paying sectors of the economy.[134] The fact that equal rights and profound inequality in resource distribution, material opportunities, and life chances exist for LGBT people is evident in the growing amount of data that show the economic range within LGBT communities. These data show that even as civil rights (like nondiscrimination protections) are achieved, they do not, on their own impact the economic or political context in which LGBT people exist. This context affects the ability of LGBT people to assert these newly enacted rights, to engage in political mobilization and have true opportunity to experience the "freedom" that has been won.

Over the past two decades, the grassroots LGBT economic and racial justice movement has championed a very different economic and policy agenda than the mainstream movement. It advocates for low-income people. It allies with a broader social justice community of advocates, but it remains dominated by the larger LGBT establishment. The divergence between this grassroots and the mainstream LGBT movement's advocacy becomes apparent upon consideration of nearly any of the LGBT movement's policy approaches in areas like health care, jobs and taxes.[135] While grassroots LGBT organizations (like Sylvia Rivera Law Project, QEJ, Audre Lorde Project, Critical Resistance) work on issues of criminal justice reform, police harassment and exploitation of those who are homeless, those who are transgender, and those who are working in underground economies (like prostitution), the mainstream LGBT movement is disengaged from these issues. Nearly all the work on criminal justice (from representation to advocacy) is being done by grassroots queers in transgender, immigrant, and progressive global justice-focused organizations. Similarly, immigrant rights activists are leading on issues ranging from detention and deportation, denial of visas, family reunification, employment sweeps that target undocumented people, access to education by immigrant young people, access to work and public support for people who have actually often paid into the system and are being denied, among other issues. While no mainstream LGBT organization has endorsed or joined the Occupy Wall Street (OWS) movement, to my knowledge, many poverty-focused and people of color LGBT grassroots groups have; indeed, the Audre Lorde Project held a forum on OWS to engage members of the LGBT community with the issues being raised.

A Mainstream Movement That Avoids Race

In another essay in this book, I address the consequence of the LGBT movement's avoidance of race. Here, it bears noting again that class informs that avoidance. An abiding myth about class status in America is that it is tied to merit—and not any more influenced by factors like race, gender, family background or place. But class is very linked to race, and class mobility has changed today for all races of people: the rich get richer, and their kids do, too, while poor people seem to just stay poor. When data on household net worth are analyzed, the sharp income disparities between whites, African Americans, Hispanics, and poor people without assets become starkly evident. Data clearly show that one's socio-economic class position is tied to assets and that these conditions are heavily impacted by race. The Economic Policy Institute's briefing paper titled "The State of Working America's Wealth, 2011" reveals that while the median net worth of white households in 2009 was $97,900, the median net worth of black households was $2,200. In 2009, one in four households had a negative net worth (up from 18.6% in 2007); for black households, that total was 40%.[136]

The queer mainstream does not foreground race in its agenda. It does not yet see the issues for which it lobbies through the lens of the different communities that comprise this movement. The parts of the queer movement that have internalized race as a central priority are again those whose agendas include: criminal justice system inequalities; the inequalities in health care access and health disparity; the ways that the educational system targets and stigmatizes youth of color; the challenge of homelessness and displacement in cities and towns and how that is to be addressed; the impact of race and class on aging; the experience of immigrants and the criminalization of certain ethnicities; the shrinking access to social safety net programs at the very moment that more people need them.

A Movement Motivated by a Politics of Access

One striking aspect of mainstream gay equality politics today is the extent to which more mass-based and elite-based, and largely private or hidden, forms of political lobbying and litigation have replaced public forms of political and cultural engagement. The structure of American politics requires

politicians to raise money and gives disproportionate influence
to people who are organized to give. Class-based access—and
providing it to people with money in the LGBT communities—
is the currency that makes the HRC the largest LGBT
organization in the national queer movement and the most
dominant mainstream LGBT movement entity in Washington.
Critiques of the effectiveness of the HRC are as ubiquitous as
its presence, but none can doubt the huge space that this entity
occupies, and the class orientation that it has thus far chosen
to represent. In 2010, HRC raised more than $29.7 million
and spent $27.8 million in educational, lobbying, and political
activities. It reported raising $5.2 million (more than 18% of
its income) from major donors belonging to its Federal Club
(individuals who give $1,200 to $5,000 a year); an additional
18% came from special events; and 48% ($14.2 million) came
from individual donors giving smaller amounts than the Federal
Club minimum.[137] With a network of dozens of city-based
dinners around the country, a mailing list that numbers several
hundred thousand, a large national staff, HRC is a giant, a very
successful organization built and supported by middle to upper
middle class people in the LGBT movement.

Should we take pride in the fact that we are now in the
back rooms where deals are being cut and politicians are being
lobbied? I've been in these rooms and I do not feel pride at the
evolution of a democratic and diverse movement into a moneyed
elite pressing for rights (largely for itself). Who has access to
tables of decision-making and power? In my experience, access
is available to those who have and have organized to bring
money to the table. Delivering bodies—or a constituency—can
also bring one access, but few queer organizations representing
poor and LGBT people of color are yet able to bring large
constituencies as their base.

Throughout the 1980s and 1990s, and long before the new
anti-globalization movement, LGBT national agendas were
articulated through more public and open-ended, accessible

processes of consultation—town meetings, endless processing and meetings to determine what the demands of national marches should be (this happened for the 1979, 1987 and 1993 LGBT National Marches), statewide conferences, local political club meetings on endorsements, ACT UP meetings at which everyone could (and often did) speak. These formats were unruly and imperfect.

Ironically, in the ensuing decade since the late 1990s, although the technologies exist to allow greater consultation and engagement than ever before, a narrower group of decision-makers is setting and controlling the LGBT agenda. So the 2000 Millennium March was simply declared by HRC (and was little more than a big street fair for that organization); and the 2009 National Equality March was called and declared by a handful of people, although it was mobilized using the new technologies and brought together more than 100,000 people. Decisions to bring major law suits that will have serious implications for the future of LGBT rights for all are made by a handful of privileged lawyers and advocates, who are also overwhelmingly white and majority male. Decisions on funding priorities and strategies are similarly made without broader input and consultation. It is "my money," we are told by donors; I'll do what I want.

The politics of access has long triumphed over democratic participation in agenda setting in the LGBT movement. And what this means is that certain people have replaced others as the key arbiters of what issue is foregrounded and what is placed on the back-burner; what arguments are made and what downplayed; who makes the case and who is left out of the room and the picture, and what is compromised on behalf of the community and what is deemed non-negotiable.

An LGBT Movement for Social and Economic Justice

In an Op-Ed column in the *New York Times*, Columbia University professor Alexander Stille noted the contradiction in the U.S. between increased equal rights and increased economic inequality: "It's a puzzle: one dispossessed group after another—blacks, women, Hispanics, and gays—has been gradually accepted in the United States, granted equal rights and brought into the mainstream. At the same time, in economic terms, the United States has gone from being a comparatively egalitarian society to one of the most unequal democracies in the world."[138] Progress on rights has coincided with the destruction of economic security for the middle class, and a consolidation of wealth and power by the most wealthy and powerful. U.S. social movements have generally pursued claims for equality of opportunity divorced from equality of condition. The existing power structure of neoliberal capitalism readily accommodates such demands for equal rights, equal protection, and equal opportunity. But even when made, demands for racial equity, economic support of poor and working people, and social justice—all of which require some form of redistribution (of power, taxes, assets)—are largely ignored or actively undermined. The article notes one key reason for such resistance; the rich have organized effectively to protect and advance their economic privileges. "One of the groups to become mobilized in response to the protest movements of the 1960s and early 1970s was the rich. Think tanks dedicated to defending the free–enterprise system—such as the Cato Institute and the Heritage Foundation—were born in this period."[139]

So, even as racial barriers in higher education, professional employment, and cultural recognition fall, even though a black President is elected, the actual economic status of black America is worse today than it has been in several decades.

So it is with LGBT equality. LGBT rights are advancing in a larger context of growing class inequality. The mainstream movement has paid very little attention to insuring that rights can be accessed by all parts of the community, and even less attention to policy goals that might secure greater equity for poor LGBT people. The movement puts forward the optimistic message that "it gets better" to young people to offer hope, in a context where the possibility of achieving the "good life" has shrunk for most people.

In her new book titled *Cruel Optimism*, critical theorist Lauren Berlant coins a term that might be well applied to the queer movement's attachment to the possibility of a "better life" without any commitment to transforming the current form of capitalism. Berlant is thinking about this very problem: "What happens to fantasies of the good life when the ordinary becomes a landfill for overwhelming and impending crises of life-building and expectations, whose sheer volume so threatens what it means to 'have a life' that adjustment seems like an accomplishment."[140] The book brilliantly explores how individuals, groups, even movements become trapped into expectations or experiences that are not serving them; and it asks why we remain in such unsustainable forms of political thinking, citizenship, and intimacy. Berlant sees our hopefulness as "cruel optimism" because it is cruel "when the object/scene that ignites a sense of possibility actually makes it impossible to attain the expansive transformation for which a person or a people risks striving; and...it is cruel insofar as the very pleasures of being inside a relation have become sustaining regardless of the content of that relation, such that a person or a world finds itself bound to a situation of profound threat that is, at the same time profoundly confirming."[141]

The fact is that for most ordinary people, the present economic order is profoundly threatening; it will not help us realize the economic dreams we have of a "good life." The system works for some, and fails most. Yet, social movements, like the LGBT movement, remain attached to defending a status quo that does not allow for the achievement of equality of condition. This talk has suggested some ways that the mainstream movement could change—in whom we see as belonging to our community, in whom the movement represents, in what agendas it carries out, and how it determines those priorities.

I'd like to conclude with three further ideas that could help the LGBT movement attend more vitally to class-based differences. The first shift is simply conceptual and involves a classing of what is meant by the word "we" when it is used to define LGBT community. The second shift is institutional, and involves the heretical idea of consolidating a wide range of currently separate organizational efforts into a more coherent force for economic justice and political power. The third idea is transformational and concerns how to change current forms of financing and agenda setting in the LGBT movement.

Having spent a lifetime pursuing it, I certainly agree that we need to win formal legal equality. And I would argue that we are a lot farther from that goal than the self-congratulating tone of today's LGBT movement acknowledges. But it is neither truthful nor historically justified to assert that equality of rights will trickle down to poor queer people. Equal rights once achieved are not equally accessed nor equally distributed. Without attention to economic justice, we risk abandoning significant segments of LGBT communities that experience profound levels of inequality to multiple systems of exclusions that they encounter. We need to class the "we" in the LGBT communities to include poor queer people and working class queer people and build a movement that strongly advocates for them.

Conceptually, the key question for the LGBT movement is what will winning look like and how do we define that possibility? A narrow view of winning frames it as the achievement of equality—defined as the achievement of legal and political nondiscrimination in all aspects of life and family recognition; in other words, the right to have the same rights as straight people. A broader view of winning would frame it as equal rights, accompanied by the power to enforce and experience them; equity and liberty are core elements of justice.[142] Framing our goals under the rubric of freedom or liberty rather than civil rights achieves three objectives; liberty re-engages the concern with freedom that early LGBT advocates raised, and does so in a moment in which freedom is being diminished; a focus on liberty allows the movement to engage the economic rhetoric of the right, which grants freedom to capital that it denies to a worker, a consumer, or a citizen; and the concept of liberty engages the ongoing resistance to sexual orientation and gender identity (SOGI) that arises out of tradition-bound notions of gender, sexual, and reproductive order. If the LGBT coalition of movements chooses to answer the question of what winning looks like narrowly, it will limit itself to the very narrow kinds of freedom that the current political order will grant—the freedom to belong to an exhausted and failing set of institutions.

As an interesting aside, it bears noting that the narrow view of equal rights ignores lessons from a study of right wing movements in the U.S. and around the world. Two recently released reports by Political Research Associates (PRA) and by the Association For Women's Rights in Development (AWID)[143] note an increase in the cultural and political influence of religious fundamentalists (not only the Christian right in the U.S., but also the Islamic right, the Hindu right, and the evangelical and Catholic and Mormon right globally). Among the recent diverse factors these reports say have contributed to the rise of religious fundamentalisms: neoliberal privatization, the corruption of political systems, and the failure of state institutions to provide economic opportunity and needed services rank high. Religious right movements at times set themselves up as alternatives to the state, as entities that can deliver things people urgently need (the promise of hope, jobs, help for the poor, schools, social services, health care). The complex reality of the political exploitation of religious movements by authoritarian regimes on one hand, and their mobilization against authoritarian regimes on the other, complicates the manifestation of religious fundamentalism around the world—its liberatory potential co-exists with its repressive possibilities. But the truth remains that if attention is not paid to economic inequality by the body politic, some other force will step into the vacuum.

A second shift the LGBT movement could make in order to address class is to consolidate the presently fractured infrastructure of progressive queer institutions. We need a new federation that unites groups working for racial, economic, sexual, and gender justice under a meaningful, common rubric. NGLTF should perhaps offer up its elimination and its rebirth as the umbrella to a new federation that is owned and controlled by grassroots groups and individual members. Diverse queer groups now working in the arena of social service delivery, criminal law, homelessness, immigrant rights, and racial justice should all come together in a new powerful federated network that works through one institution, as a new freedom-focused human rights and social justice organization, committed fully to civil, political, economic, social, and cultural rights, and the political power to win these objectives. What would this mean? That progressive queers could finally be part of creating a genuinely democratic, multi-faceted leadership organization that is comprised of organizational and individual members, that sets its national agenda through some more democratic method than the selection of a self-appointed board, and that is actively working—through lobbying, education, research, litigation, and grassroots organizing—to advance policies that will benefit poor, low-income, middle class, and progressive people of all kinds, including LGBT folks.

Social movement organizations matter to any movement— they serve as a focal point for activism and policy-oriented action. They provide a voice to a point of view. A federation structure can facilitate autonomy for existing groups, while enabling them to come together to claim a greater role in the movement agenda. Since many of the economic and racial justice groups that operate in the queer movement are local, service-focused, or quite small, a seriously organized and funded federation would enable the groups to actually have a greater influence on the national movement agenda. Absent such a joining of forces, there will not be a shift in the voice, politics, and aspirations of LGBT political leaders.

Finally, to achieve such a transformation, the LGBT progressive movement will need to find new ways to finance its work. Existing mechanisms of reliance on individual people with money and foundations are not sustainable for groups working for economic security and the rights of poor and economically vulnerable populations. Foundations are dominated by the values of high-income or wealthy people. They can do a lot of good funding, but they also extract a tacit commitment not to rock the boat too much. Dependence on philanthropy is the antithesis of progressive politics. It invariably requires conformity to ideas, values, and practices that are in the self-interest of the wealthy who fund and control these institutions. It also produces vulnerability as foundations shift on the changing fashions in vogue or the changing of the guard in their leaderships or the changing interests of their donors.

Earned revenue through benefits or social enterprise, low-cost internet-based donations, and reliance on foundations and major funders for investment capital rather than operating capital are some of the funding shifts needed for new and more politically brave forms of organization to come into being. Revenue for political work earned through events has anchored the growth of HRC. Can low-cost events, held across the country on campuses, around Prides, and in communities actually finance change? Similarly, social enterprise or social-benefit businesses are being explored around the world in the global development sphere. Can they be a resource to groups working with low-income LGBT and other populations? What services that we currently pay for—essential services—might a progressive entrepreneurial institution provide as a means for earning some of its costs?

Conclusion

The biggest form of silencing is external—in the assumption of heterosexuality that pervades most institutions and experiences, and how that assumption negates so many forms of queer being. But the queer internalization of the dream of belonging to what Adrienne Rich so aptly named "compulsory heterosexuality"[144] is part of our challenge as we go forward. The queer embrace of the heterosexual norm—and the adoption by LGBT people of its attendant forms of domesticity, family, and sexuality—have privatized many issues that once were part of our public demands upon society. This abandonment of previous critical discourses of sexual liberation, the way the movement has walked away from representing non-traditional families since the mid-1990s, the still-underdeveloped economic and racial justice are all examples of what Lisa Duggan has labeled "homonormativity" and what Jasbir Puar has named "homonationalism."[145] Homonormative framing of the LGBT agenda has grown in the movement because two external conditions—the emergence of the anti-LGBT right in the late 1970s and 1980s, and the emergence within the LGBT movement of a queer conservative movement (in the early 1990s). Responding to the right's reductionism of LGBT lives has led, sadly, to our own embrace of reductive logics. They say things like we want special rights; we counter with we want equal rights. They say being gay is a choice and we can be cured, we say no, we can't help ourselves, we were born this way. They say we are promiscuous and that the idea of legislating "families we choose" is dangerous to social life, we say then let us into the status of marriage so we can be monogamous—just like you (no irony intended). They say gay people are powerful and privileged and do not deserve rights, and we counter with a victimization discourse that emphasizes the facts of LGBT marginalization and discrimination but minimizes or omits race, class, and gender differences within queer experience.

But the unconscious or conscious promotion by the LGBT

movement of hetero-forms of family or white privileging-forms of community building or class-informed notions of the "gay agenda" can also be seen as internally driven and desired. As a movement, we are constituted by our constitutions; we express who we are and our desires and imagination themselves are grounded in these material experiences of being. In a white-dominated, couple-based, relationship-seeking, mainstream movement led by high-income and privileged people, and one that seeks affirmation, belonging, and benefits from the existing system, largely seeking membership in what we have inherited, the norm has replaced transformation in our political imagination.

The world to which we seek so desperately to belong is itself crumbling all around us. That sad irony is also lost in our hungry and urgent assertions of identity. It is much harder to explain queer diversity and deviance in a public forum, so we opt to tidy it up and downplay its divergence. Could it be in that by silencing ourselves, we foreclose the larger society's access to forms of intimacy and community that could actually offer sustenance to decaying institutions like government, the organization form, the family, and the couple-form? What do I mean? Queer practice—LGBT life in its widest range—builds curious and sometimes marvelous communities: subcultures that turn pain into caring; institutions that work to deliver services; resilience and humor instead of bitterness and violence; extended kinship structures that deliver emotional and material support but that are independent of blood ties; exceptional acts of generosity and affiliation with those who are social and political outcasts. Instead the LGBT movement tries to conform these creative forms of expression, to run from the freedom we have had to build unique lives, and submit ourselves to the confining forms that propriety, adherence to tradition, or legibility in this form of capitalism demands.

I look forward to a political praxis for the queer movement that does not limit itself to a politics of inclusion, which intends to leave the limitations of the status quo in place. I look forward to an emerging wave of liberation, to a multi-faceted movement whose dominant symbol is not an equal sign but perhaps the "greater than" sign, suggesting that we can be greater than the limits of the world in which find ourselves.

THE MEANING OF A PROGRESSIVE MOVEMENT [146]

This keynote speech came out of my interest in coalitions—in seeing if one could build common purpose and understanding through debate and dialogue across ideological difference. To some of the people I respect the most, this presentation to Log Cabin Republicans represented a betrayal at worst and a naïve miscalculation at best: two friends argued forcefully with me that I was mistakenly giving legitimacy to a group that deserved none, and that I was betraying the progressive movement that I claimed to represent.

The talk was given at the 1998 Annual Convention of the Log Cabin Republican Clubs, an organization formed in the early 1990s to give voice to gay conservatives. When these remarks were written, I was running the Policy Institute think tank of the National Gay and Lesbian Task Force. There I had initiated the organization's work on racial and economic justice; created an interfaith roundtable to promote faith-based organizing and religious coalition building, and launched a national roundtable to foster greater cooperation across all national policy-oriented LGBT groups, to name three key initiatives.

Log Cabin's executive director at the time, the charming, tireless, and effective Rich Tafel was someone I respected and trusted as a colleague, despite our significant ideological disagreements. We planned to write a piece together on how progressive and conservative supporters of gay rights could work together, but we were unable to complete it— perhaps because of the inherent inconsistency of the project. When he asked me to come talk to the convention about what I meant by the term progressive, I agreed. I was curious to see how an audience that harbored different values would receive progressive ideas. The talk was well received and a good discussion followed.

But in the succeeding years, the divergence between the Republican and neoliberal Democrat agenda on one hand, and a more progressive politics rooted in the needs of ordinary and poor people, has grown too sharp to be bridged. I still believe in the spirit of dialogue and respect that led to my invitation before Log Cabin Republicans convention, but I no longer believe that the kind of coalition of which I spoke in 1998 is possible. The past two decades have seen a rapid destruction of five key elements that have historically enabled American democracy: a domestic economy that delivers jobs and opportunities; public funding and popular support for socially-beneficial services like public schools, public health, social services for those in crisis or need, and basic infrastructure; a fair and accessible electoral system; an independent media; and restraints on police, intelligence and military power. These changes are the achievements of deliberate and ideologically rooted efforts of right-wing social movements and funders. As a result, corporations control all U.S. and global media. The wealthy control the outcomes of all national elections and their vassals pass laws to make it harder for those who might dissent to vote and participate. The economy is in the hands of oligarchs and financiers who operate shell games to create paper wealth but not actual jobs. The corporations that now run the U.S. military also control the intelligence apparatus, the prison system, and inform policing strategies; they work to erode the independent oversight of the judiciary, and their interests dominate the foreign policy options of the executive branch. In the late 1990s, this neoliberal economy was emerging, but its escalation of repression

*was less prevalent until the post-9/11 policies enacted by the Bush
Administration (which have been largely untouched by the Obama
Administration).*

*In this stark context, my call for a narrow, single-issue alliance with
gay Republicans seems hopelessly romantic. We are actually opponents
on most issues that matter in the broader political sphere, for example,
issues like social supports for poor and middle class people, a fair tax
system, greater freedom from the national security state, and increased
freedom for women from repressive regulation of reproduction.
Coalition in this context seems little more than collaboration. So I
include the talk to give a sense of the romance I have left behind, but
one that many in the LGBT mainstream still cherish.*

It is a bit counterintuitive to program an unabashedly
progressive voice into your solidly conservative conference.
Many of my friends do not understand why you invited me,
nor why accepted. I will tell you that I am here for two reasons.
First, because Log Cabin President Rich Tafel and I share an
interest in fostering dialogue across our differences. And second,
because I appreciate the work you are doing to challenge the
right wing within the Republican Party—that work is vital.
In just a few years, Log Cabin Republicans (LCR) has made a
significant place for itself in the LGBT movement's landscape.
I salute your determination and your perseverance. And I thank
you for being on the frontline against the destructive forces in
our country that were responsible for the violent rhetoric of the
1992 Republican convention.

I must tell you, though, that you almost lost me when I
learned several weeks after I had accepted this invitation that
Mayor Giuliani, whose policies I disagree with and even abhor,
would also be here. I am no fan of Mayor Rudy. His police
department policies overreach, violate civil liberties again and
again, are racially biased and deserve the criticism they have
gotten, and I am glad to be here to speak that message directly
to you. Indeed, I want to take a moment to urge you to take a

closer look at one conflict involving the Mayor, the New York
Police Department (NYPD), and LGBT people of color that is
currently raging. I refer to the conflict between LGBT people
of color communities and the New York Log Cabin Republican
Club that has grown out of the June gay Pride march in which
the Mayor and local Log Cabin leaders entered the march,
out of order, in the middle of the people of color contingent,
bisecting that contingent. Entering the march in the middle
of the people of color contingent in itself upset people who
would not have chosen to march with the Mayor because of
long-standing conflicts with his Administration, but the larger
issue was the reaction of the police escort for the Mayor. LGBT
people of color in the contingent were harassed, threatened with
arrest, and treated unprofessionally by the some police officers.
That is wrong. What is being asked for is an apology. And what
is needed is dialogue, a willingness to secure accountability a
shouldering of responsibility, and some healing. Just as many
of you have felt disrespected by progressives, a sentiment that
Rich has written eloquently about in his book, so now do many
LGBT people of color in this city feel disrespected by your
refusal to realize that communities of color in this city have a
great deal at stake.

It is these kinds of divides that operate to keep people like you
and people like me separated, even though there is significant
common ground on which we can stand as gay, lesbian, bisexual,
and transgender people. The desire to transcend the anger
and pain our disagreements produce and to replace them with
communication is why I appreciate this invitation.

I am here to speak to you about what progressives in our
movement have to offer and what we are doing. I want to speak
of how we can work together, and to acknowledge that there
will always be arenas in which we will work in opposition to
each other

Who Are Progressives?

Progressives are a diverse lot and you would gain a very different perspective in this conversation if you had invited someone from a more traditional left background than I have. What I share is a perspective that comes out of the lesbian feminist wing of the gay rights movement. It is a wing that has long pursued a broad agenda for economic and social justice, racial and gender equality, and of sexual freedom. It is a wing that is as interested in ending institutionalized racism, ending structural economic inequality, as it is in ending the heterosexism embedded in the economy, in the family, and in government.

Progressive politics is for many of us a politics of intersection, not identity affiliation alone. It is a politics that believes institutions more than individuals reproduce inequality and need to be transformed. It is a politics that believes that institutional racism and sexism are connected to institutional homophobia and to structural economic inequality.

Progressives are people who believe in enhancing democratic values and increasing civic participation. We are people who defend pluralism, the notion that there are many voices and views in civil society and the goal of government is to allow them to flourish without regulation. We are people who believe in social and economic justice for all, under one standard of secular law. We are people who believe that prosperity in a society should be shared through mechanisms like free education for all, universal health care, compassionate and focused strategies to assist working people to raise up their standard of living. We believe that hunger and homelessness do not need to exist in a world in which technological advances can allow us to feed and shelter all the people. We believe that the environment ought not to be abused in the interests of short-term bottom lines— and that a focus on sustainable development is both possible and profitable in the long run. We believe that human rights are vital, essential, and that they include racial justice, women's reproductive freedom, and sexual freedom, along with the basic rights to food, clothing, shelter, and other aspects of life articulated in the Universal Declaration of Human Rights.

I use the term progressive broadly to affirm a set of values and to claim my opposition to idealized notions of unfettered free-market capitalism. I believe deeply in the possibility, and necessity, of a socially responsible capitalism, and in a role for government in the care and security of its people.

My faith is not in a particular party or some decaying undemocratic government or some discredited centralized economy. It is in a set of principles and values or what might be called ideology. The past two-decade's triumph of conservative ideas confirms that this country has been hungering for ideology to go along with its over-glut of identity. It does not confirm that this is a post-ideological moment.

For several years, we have been at a place in the LGBT movement where our principal paradigm—of identity-formation, building community, and trying to define an LGBT specific politics—has needed to be refined and supplemented. Historians like John D'Emilio and political scientists like Cathy Cohen have pointed out that we have used an ethnic-based model of organizing—articulating ourselves as a minority, seeking access to the provisions in the Constitution and American democracy that protect minority voices and interests. This has been a productive model for our work. In addition to this identity-based model of political organizing, we have needed more ideological approaches. That is what you provide for conservatives. And that is what progressive groups like the National Gay and Lesbian Task Force (NGLTF) seek to provide for our side of the spectrum.

The disagreement between LGBT progressives and conservatives has to do with two major sets of issues: first, what we see as the goal of our movement, and second, what we see as the proper role of the public and private sector in our society.

Movement's Goals

Many LGBT progressives would define our goals as ending institutionalized homophobia, racial and gender inequality, and poverty. LGBT conservatives, like the eloquent writers on this panel, have defined their goal as ending public sector discrimination. There is a world of difference between these two different visions. No wonder we are baffled by each other! We are pursuing different ends!

In addition, conservatives and libertarians often say they see the goal of the LGBT movement as ending discrimination and prejudice against gay people, and pursuing gay and lesbian rights issues singularly.

Sometimes we disagree with each other on the extent of discrimination and prejudice, its sources, its roots, and its resolutions—but ending anti-gay prejudice is certainly a goal that progressives and conservatives share.

But for LGBT progressives, homophobia does not occur in a vacuum; it is affected for many gay people by their race, class, gender, age, and so on. We recognize that the experiences of homosexuality and homophobia are connected to ideas of maleness, or femaleness, to our gender identities, economic class, and racial background. We see homophobia as a weapon of sexism, used to enforce rigid gender roles, and to deny sexuality its natural value in human experience. And we believe, therefore, that it may not be possible to fix the "lesbian" piece of a public policy problem without fixing the "woman" piece.

It is in this aspect of our understanding that we—conservatives and progressives—disagree most fiercely. We argue with each other about whether LGBT organizations ought to take stands on affirmative action or other racial remedies. We argue about the death penalty and whether it has any place in "our" movement. We argue that women's right to control their reproductive lives is not "our" issue as the LGBT civil rights movement. Yet, at the same time as progressives are criticized for championing these "other" issues, you here at Log Cabin actively promote your support for your own "other" issues, like lower taxes, welfare reform, and opposition to affirmative action.

The progressives in the LGBT coalition work to build bridges between gay folks and those who might support us from other communities and other social justice movements like religious denominations, unions, professional associations, and more. We identify with our counterparts in the movements for racial justice. We often share with them an analysis of history, a set of values, an approach toward government, and a desire for equity—just as you who are conservatives share a set of values and try to build bridges with a broader conservative movement. The reason we disagree is that we do not share an understanding of intersectional politics.

It is unfair for gay conservatives to condemn gay leftists for attempting to forge connections between movements against homophobia, racism, and sexism when you yourselves work to make links with non-gay partners with whom you share a set of "non-gay" objectives. I find especially disturbing the targeting by some of you of lesbian-led progressive institutions like the Esperanza Peace and Justice Center in San Antonio, Texas. Why not allow that institution to operate? I do not spend my time trying to destabilize and defund the paltry public and private support received by gay-supportive institutions with which I politically disagree.

In my view, the question of what these "other" issues—of the death penalty, poverty, lack of minority representation in media, class bias in hiring, ageism, school voucher programs, or police brutality—have to do with LGBT politics is not a productive question to ask. We will not agree. To my way of thinking, these issues have as much to do with my gayness as the libertarian economic ideology to which you subscribe, as your Republicanism has to do with your gayness. They are not "other" issues to me, and I am tired of defining and defending the connections to you whose skepticism or ideology may never allow you to see any connection.

Instead of arguing whether these issues are appropriately gay or not, I am more interested in asking what answers LGBT people might bring to these vexing situations. Let us abandon the an argument about whether an issue is "gay" or not and turn instead to the question of ideas and insights, if any, our varying ideological vantage points might give us to solving the problems of racism or police brutality. Such a refocusing would certainly make for a more interesting and less polarized conversation across our differences.

Role of Government

Progressives, libertarians, and conservatives in the LGBT community also disagree on the role of government. The thoughtful gay rights and AIDS lobbyist Jeff Levi, formerly executive director of NGLTF, used to say that the LGBT movement went from wanting government out of our lives in the '50s and '60s to demanding our fair share of government in the 1970s to asking government to save our lives in the 1980s to wanting government to affirm our lives (through marriage) in the 1990s.

Today, our movement embodies many contradictory stances in our relationship towards government. We say we want less, but our community's health crises and social service agencies need more (youth suicide prevention programs, mental health programs, community centers, alcoholism programs, lesbian health services, AIDS programs, health clinics, job training, and counseling programs). We say we want to outlaw only public discrimination, yet we are a movement whose main gains have been in the achievement of private non-discrimination policies and private sector domestic partnership benefits policies. In a broader sense on this public/private issue, we are a movement that is engaged across the divide of ideology in changing the cultural devaluation of homosexual being: it is not just the public sector we care about, but reinventing the private.

We say we want our taxes dramatically lowered, yet we are often the very middle-class people who have benefitted most from the very programs that these taxes pay for: loans for college education, free public schools, housing projects for people with HIV and limited income, even recycling, cleanup of toxic waste, and much more. Nearly every piece of the LGBT civil rights agenda requires some form of government intervention.

Questions about the role we see government playing in our lives also require our movement to think through the role we see the private sector playing. A libertarian economic mentality pervades in our movement—the assumption underlying it is a tremendous faith in the market and the freedom and prosperity that capitalism has undeniably generated in the lives of so many people in this country. Ironically, it is these same libertarian values that most endanger our democracy today. Free-market capitalism is guided by a different set of values and a different code than representative and democratic government—the market decides based on the dictates of individual profit, the government decides based on the common good. Markets need governments; no less a capitalist than the billionaire financier George Soros has made this argument. In a recent book that I heartily recommend to you, two political theorists make this argument anew. Stephen Holmes and Cass Sunstein's *The Cost of Rights: Why Liberty Depends on Taxes* debunks the myth that no government is possible, much less desirable.

Many questions remain to be debated between us. If the market takes over services currently provided by non-profits or governments (such as public schools), will we necessarily be better off? If churches take over the functions that government agencies working on poverty or child welfare provide, how will LGBT people be treated? Will racial and gender and homophobic inequality be reduced or increased? Would a mixed economy, where certain functions are socialized, be a more equitable form of community than the polarized encampments of rich versus poor that we are headed towards at present? I think it is imperative that our movement—from whatever ideological vantage point we each sit inside it—discuss these kinds of questions. But let us be clear that progressives will answer them differently than you in this room might.

Progressives and Libertarians: An Unlikely Coalition

The final set of points I want to make is that it is necessary for us to face up to a simple truth—we are not all one movement or one kind of people pursuing one unitary set of objectives. We are in fact more of a coalition than a movement, even though I use the latter term far more than the former. Indeed, I am here to speak to you because I believe this is the central piece of the progressive movement's message. I believe strongly in coalition politics and I believe that it is possible for us to forge a coalition with each other on some issues, while accepting that we are not in the same movement on others.

This is not idle rhetoric because I am not talking about the insipid one-of-each tokenistic, symbolic coalition that is about feeling good and doing nothing; I am talking instead about the gritty, tense, unpleasantness of engagement in achieving a goal with people with whom one disagrees. In the real world of pragmatic coalition politics, we work for social change alongside people with whom we disagree on many matters of great importance. To paraphrase the cultural activist Bernice Johnson Reagon's classic talk on the necessity of coalitions, we have a choice with whom we choose to work, but the process of coalition work is not easy, simple, or necessarily happy.[147]

I believe we can form such a coalition to achieve several shared objectives. Before outlining the specific issues, on which we can coalesce, let me outline some points of surprising agreement between us.

Progressives, like Republicans, believe in liberty. We are passionately committed to democracy, to increasing civic participation, to defending pluralism, and to the freedom to dissent and organize. Many libertarians, like most progressives, are pro-choice. We are both civil libertarians—we believe in limiting the prosecutorial and police power of the state and in enhancing individual freedom. Many of us also agree on pursuing a practical set of civil rights objectives to secure the full equality of LGBT people. We agree on nondiscrimination, on reducing and ultimately ending hate violence, on equal marriage rights, on protecting LGBT families from discrimination, on eliminating criminal sanctions for private, adult consensual sexual behavior, on securing fair and equal treatment under one standard of law. That is a lot of agreement. It is true that when we get specific about remedies to handle the institutionalized discrimination that legacies of homophobia, racism, sexism, and poverty have left, that is where we begin to disagree.

What I think we can agree on—both libertarians and progressives—is that the devolution of government affords us some opportunities for working together in state legislatures and city councils to achieve the shared civil rights objectives I outlined above. In the 21st century, the principal battleground for gay, lesbian, bisexual, and transgender equality will be state legislatures and city councils. Whether the issue is marriage, family law, custody of children, adoption, Medicaid regulations to allow HIV-positive gay men to get funds to pay for life-saving drugs and care, safe-sex education, school curricula for youth, housing for low-income gay people, sodomy laws, hate crime bills, police standards and accountability—major parts of the issue will be decided locally. NGLTF tracks state lawmaking on LGBT and HIV/AIDS policy issues and has since 1996. Lawmaking on issues specifically affecting LGBT people has increased four-fold from one hundred and five bills overall (41 pro, 64 con) in 1995, to four hundred and seventy-two bills (255 favorable and 217 unfavorable) in 1999.

The message here is this: the devolution of power from federal to state and local government bodies presents opportunities for creative law making. LGBT progressives are focused on pushing and taking advantage of these opportunities.

Log Cabin chapters can partner with NGLTF and other activists working in state legislative arenas around a wide range of issues.

Another arena in which we can and must work more closely together is in defeating the right. You have been and must remain strong and forceful advocates against the right wing within the Republican Party. The press conference you did earlier this year, challenging Senator Trent Lott and others to leave the racist Conservative Citizens Council, was an example of gay Republican moderation and leadership at its finest. Engaging the right wing is something we can do powerfully together, in particular by working to defeat anti-gay ballot measures. We will confront several initiatives this fall and next year, and they require all sectors of our communities to come together to defeat the right in Dade County, FL, Spokane, WA, California, Maine, and New Mexico, among other places.

Let me conclude by summarizing what I have tried to frame. I have tried to outline what I mean by a progressive LGBT movement, and I have outlined my belief that it is possible for us to forge a coalition on certain issues and in certain contexts.

Several months ago, Rich Tafel and I actually attempted to write a joint Op-Ed piece about why we could—across our serious ideological divisions—find ways to work together. We wrote about the possibilities of such an unusual coalition. Work and perhaps the difficulties inherent in the task prevented the completion of the project we began, but I'd like to close with some lines we wrote together about what this coalition could mean. "We champion a dangerous kind of coalition politics—a politics of the unlikely and unpredictable, the libertarian and the liberationist, the populist and the unpopular, the independent and the radical.... What is the glue that holds our dangerous coalition together? Mutual respect... Let us model the respect for difference that we demand from straight society. This coalition may be our secret weapon and it's been here all the time."

SOME WOMEN ARE LESBIANS AND WE ARE PART OF THE WOMEN'S MOVEMENT[148]

The Fourth World Conference on Women, held in 1995 in Beijing, is remembered for the Platform of Action committed to by the countries that attended, and for an historic speech that then First Lady Hillary Rodham Clinton gave declaring "human rights are women's rights and women's rights are human rights once and for all."[149] The fact that such a declaration needed to be made less than two decades ago attests to the unfinished business of women's economic, political, and personal freedom.

Thousands of women and men from every country gathered in China, which was at the time a great deal more closed than it is today. Official delegations were present, but were outnumbered by the grassroots activists who came for the Non Governmental Organization (NGO) Forum that accompanies the official U.N. deliberations at such global gatherings. The Chinese Government was nervous to have so many activists enter, and it sought to keep control by building a convention site that was over thirty miles outside of Beijing in Huairou. They kept us busy with logistics—the only way to get to the site was by buses; and so we left our assigned hotels early in the morning and came back at the end of the day. It rained a lot during that conference, and the NGO Forum site, which consisted of a bunch of hastily built tents pitched outside, and largely incomplete buildings, quickly became a messy, muddy trudge. But the experience was exceptional, especially for lesbian-rights activism.

I found myself there through factors that had little to do with me, and everything to do with the right wing's anti-lesbian attacks leveled against this conference. Bella Abzug had founded a global women's rights organization called the Women's Environment and Development Organization (WEDO), and its then-executive director asked me to be a member of WEDO's delegation to the NGO Forum. She wanted an expert on lesbian and gay rights, she said, because the right-wing was targeting all U.N. resolutions that had the word "gender" in them for rejection: they argued that the use of the word "gender" was a radical lesbian feminist plot to destroy the idea of male and female and replace it with five genders (male, female, homosexual, lesbian, and transgender). WEDO was planning advocacy with the government delegations, public forums, testimony, and receptions to connect women's activists around the world, and it wanted to make sure a lesbian voice was part of its presence.

The lesbian activist voice at Beijing was indeed represented in large numbers. As a result of the global organizing of feminist and lesbian activists from the International Lesbian and Gay Association, the Center for Women's Global Leadership, the Ms. Foundation for Women, the Astraea Lesbian Foundation for Justice, and the International Lesbian and Gay Human Rights Commission (IGLHRC), led at the time by its brilliant founder Julie Dorf, among others, a global lesbian presence had been mobilized to attend. A lesbian tent was constructed at the NGO Forum. The brave Chinese gay activists threw an amazing underground lesbian dance party from Chinese Rainbow. To attend, one had to walk the gauntlet between armed members of the Chinese military and undercover police merely to get inside a modern three-story disco in downtown Beijing filled with more police, military, and several hundred Chinese young people and several hundred lesbians from around the world. The party was shut down mid-way, and one of the organizers was detained after the conference ended.

In the end, the Platform for Action from Beijing included the terms "gender" throughout and also included an explicit recognition of and calls for protection of "sexual rights" for women. This simple term was a huge advance.

In December of 2011, Secretary of State Hillary Rodham Clinton presented another global address on human rights, this time focusing on LGBT rights, and once again setting a new standard for the U.S. government's engagement. Secretary Clinton's comprehensive, detailed, and brave challenge to the U.N. Human Rights Council focused on the importance of incorporating sexual orientation and gender identity (SOGI) issues fully into the international human rights framework. It was a remarkable step forward for U.S. foreign policy. Not only were the analyses and policies announced by Secretary Clinton substantive and helpful, they exceeded the commitments that the largest domestic (U.S.) LGBT organizations have made thus far to the global sphere of activism.

The foundation for this incredible step forward was laid by a handful of LGBT and non-LGBT organizations (Council for Global Equality, IGLHRC, the Arcus Foundation, Open Society Foundations, Astraea, and others who choose to remain anonymous), a core of individuals on the State Department and White House staff, and supportive leaders (like Secretary Clinton, senior State Department officials, and President Obama) many who worked diligently on these issues for years.

Secretary Clinton's remarks put the full force of the U.S. government's authority behind the full inclusion of SOGI in the global human rights framework. And they systematically took apart the key arguments used to oppose the inclusion of SOGI into the human rights framework.

Echoing her 1995 remarks, she affirmed with all the power of her office that "gay rights are human rights and human rights are gay rights," and then proceeded to detail what that meant (and I edit a long paragraph):

> *It is a violation of human rights when people are beaten or killed because of their sexual orientation, or because they do not conform to cultural norms about how men and women should look or behave...*

> *It is a violation of human rights when lesbian or transgendered women are subjected to so-called corrective rape, or forcibly subjected to hormone treatments, or when people are murdered after public calls for violence toward gays...*

> *And it is a violation of human rights when...public spaces are out of bounds to people because they are gay. No matter what we look like, where we come from, or who we are, we are all equally entitled to our human rights and dignity.[150]*

Secretary Clinton also addressed resistance to rights based on SOGI directly and honestly. "Some seem to believe [homosexuality] is a Western phenomenon," she notes, and goes on to detail how being LGBT is in fact "a human reality. And protecting the human rights of all people, gay or straight, is not something that only Western governments do." Noting that cultural and religious traditions are often cited as obstacles, her talk brilliantly reinterpreted those traditions as inclusive. "Indeed, our religion and our culture are sources of compassion and inspiration toward our fellow human beings..." She noted that the same commitment to human rights and freedom protects people of faith, arguing, "[L]et us keep in mind that our commitments to protect the freedom of religion and to defend the dignity of LGBT people emanate from a common source..." And she stated, "It is because the human experience is universal that human rights are universal and cut across all religions and cultures."

The Clinton speech was noteworthy because it named the role that ideas of cultural tradition play in blocking LGBT human rights. The impact of tradition is indeed mixed as Secretary Clinton suggests, and her highlighting of the inclusive roots to such traditions was quite strategic. Notable also was the way that the talk reframed harsh traditions that harm women under the rubric of tradition. She argued that violence in any form was wrong –"it's not cultural, it's criminal." Ultimately, it is social justice movements, like the women's movements, and the global SOGI movements, that provide the inspiration, the courage, and the muscle to change repressive cultural traditions around gender and sexual orientation. Secretary Clinton affirmed this truth and noted the vital need for allies and LGBT advocates to continue and press the struggle forward: "[L]eadership by definition means being out in front of your people when it is called for."

My remarks below were presented at a modest forum hosted by WEDO, in another time when comments like Secretary Clinton's on SOGI seemed far beyond the reach of the LGBT movement. I include them here as a marker of progress, to mark how far the conversation and arguments about LGBT rights as human rights have moved in these past seventeen years. Interestingly, today a reverse-version of this talk needs to be given to mainstream LGBT organizations to explain why feminism should be a central part of their work.

With hearts full of hope and an abiding faith in justice, we have traveled to this Fourth U.N. International Conference on the Status of Women to bear witness to the lives, dreams, and struggles of women. We have come to Beijing to call for an end to all forms of discrimination against women. We have come to build a Platform for Action whose goal is nothing less than social justice and meaningful improvement in the status of women.

Most fundamentally, we have come here united—across national, religious, economic, cultural, or sexual difference—united by our love for women and for the human family of which we are such an integral part. It is this spirit of social justice, hope, and love which I invoke as we broach the topic of sexual orientation and gender identity, which antagonizes women who otherwise agree on much.

I am an Indian woman, born in New Delhi. I am an

immigrant woman, who came with my family to America as an eight-year-old child and became a United States citizen. I am a lesbian—a woman who loves other women—by virtue of my natural sexual orientation. For twenty years, I have worked as a community organizer, attorney, and writer to advance lesbian and women's equality in the feminist and gay-rights movements in the United States. My identity is bicultural, and my sexuality is fully integrated into my identity. When I struggle for equality as a woman, against racism or ethnic prejudice, these struggles are indivisible; indeed to me they are one.

Women's Right to Sexual Autonomy

This afternoon I am here to ask this Congress for its support of one principle: the principle that every woman must be free to determine for herself the conduct of her sexual and reproductive life. That each woman, in whatever country or family and of whatever marital status, is accorded the freedom to make decisions about her sexual life to the same extent, and with the same kind of power and autonomy, that men the world over have for so long enjoyed. I am here to ask that the question of lesbian and gay equality be addressed in its proper and true context—as a question of human freedom and sexual expression, and not as a matter of shame, sickness, immorality, sin, or prejudice, labels, which disallow the possibility of genuine dialogue on this matter.

The right to sexual self-determination which lesbian women seek is a subset of the broader battle for sexual freedom and power over our lives, in which all women are engaged.[151] Others at this Forum will focus on the debate on reproductive health and abortion. My focus is on the possibility that every woman one day will be able to live her life as she chooses, without fear or persecution—whether that leads her to be married or single, lesbian or heterosexual, childless or a mother.

Framed in this way, is it any wonder that discussions of sexuality and reproduction are so explosive? The fact is—as every woman in this room knows—it remains a profoundly radical act for a woman to assert her right to individual autonomy, and to assert her "right to attain the highest standard of sexual and reproductive health."[152] Violence greets women who assert such autonomy or seek such rights. Governments try to censor and contain women's sexuality. Some religions condemn women who disagree with their dictates as dirty, shameful, and immoral. Some families resist women's autonomy. And through it all, corporate profiteers make fortunes on the repression and controlled marketing of sexuality.

When lesbian rights are considered in the context of women's power to determine their sexual and reproductive lives, it becomes apparent that such freedom is far from within every woman's reach. Instead, women and girls face coercion, stigmatization, criminalization, and terrible social condemnation simply for being what we are: sexual human beings. Such social repression is evident in the attempts by governments to restrict and regulate our reproduction; it is evident in laws which outlaw women's relationships to one another; it is evident in the dangerous and violent movement to compel women to bear children; and perhaps most painfully for many women, it is evident in the energy our spiritual leaders expend to maintain a sexual double standard for women and men—a double standard endorsed by every religion which promotes the idea that women's sexuality and biology ought to be under the control of the state, the church, and the community, rather than under the control of each woman herself.

Those who oppose women's rights fear most the idea of women's sexual and reproductive autonomy—this is why the Cairo conference[153] on Population and Development was so explosive. Their fears are based in a fearful fantasy of what they think might happen should women be allowed to live without the centuries of sexual shame and sexist repression we have endured. The conservative fantasy imagines this: that women and men are incapable of being moral sexual beings without the repressive intervention of the state and organized religion; that families themselves and all moral order would crumble if homosexuality is accepted; that all societies will decay and social cohesion splinter if sexual freedom is allowed to women. This fantasy rests on fear as its chief and most effective weapon. Like all fear, the fear of women's sexual freedom and the fear of homosexuality are emotional, powerful, and deeply held. The opposite of fear is trust. And one question that the women's movement must ask itself is do we trust the fantasy of what our opponents tell us or do we trust the real-life truth of our own hearts, minds, and lives?

If we turn to our experience and turn away from fear, we will see that morality and decency have little to do with a person's sex, sexual orientation, family background, race, nationality, or economic status. We will readily see that to argue that women must have individual autonomy and sexual agency to the same extent that men enjoy is not to argue that women are the same as men, nor is it to argue that women want to be like men. It is merely to argue that women are human beings and must be allowed to be full and free people. When we seek equality in our ability to be sexual agents, we seek to empower every woman at the most fundamental level—individually and in her family. To argue for sexual liberty is to argue that we believe no stigma should be attached to a woman who is a mother, or to the woman who is single and chooses not to have children. It is to say that we believe there should be no violence against any woman who engages in her God-given sexuality or gender identity—be it heterosexual, bisexual, transgender, or homosexual. And it is to say that we have great faith in the ability of women and men, girls and boys, to achieve new kinds of partnerships, friendships, and relationships once the second-class status of women is eliminated in every form.

I ask this Congress and the international women's movement to take a stand for women's sexual freedom by speaking out forcefully against homophobia. Homophobia has been defined as the "fear and hatred of those who love and sexually desire those of the same sex."[154] Not only is anti-gay sentiment or homophobia present in some form in every nation and culture, it also exits within feminist and women's organizations the world over. Evidence of both forms of homophobia is eloquently gathered in a document, which I submit to this tribunal as part of my testimony. Titled *Unspoken Rules: Sexual Orientation and Women's Human Rights*,[155] and prepared by the International Gay & Lesbian Human Rights Commission (IGLHRC) based in the United States, the report documents the status of lesbians in thirty-one countries. As international human rights activist Charlotte Bunch writes in the introduction to *Unspoken Rules*, "Lesbians, both in and out of the 'closet,' are vital participants in all kinds of struggles for human rights, seeking to end violence against women as well as racial violence and the violence of wars and militarism. But all too often the price of acceptance in this activism has been silence about their own human rights as lesbians…The vision suggested by this book is that as more women and men of all sexual identities better understand human rights violations and discrimination based on sexual orientation, they will join forces to end these abuses just as many lesbians are participating in struggles for the human rights of others. The only hope for the future realization of human rights for all is in acting on our understanding that human rights are indeed universal, indivisible and inalienable."[156]

Lesbian Rights Are Human Rights

Human rights are indeed indivisible: all people are covered by the scope and ideals set forth in international human rights documents. When exceptions or limits on these rights are made, the progress of human freedom is slowed. Although the United Nations Charter, the Universal Declaration of Human Rights, the Vienna Declaration and Programme for Action, the Convention on the Elimination of All Forms of Discrimination Against Women, and other documents do not yet specifically mention sexual orientation or gender identity, each of these conventions contain a framework that can protect the human rights of lesbians and gay men.

Late last year, the Regional Preparatory Conference of the U.N. Economic Commission for Europe explicitly included the term sexual orientation in the ECE Regional Platform for Action.[157] In addition, thousands of women from more than sixty countries around the world have signed a petition to this International Conference asking that this conference recognize women's rights to determine our sexual identity, to control our body, to establish intimate relations, whether and how to bear and raise our children.[158] The Draft Platform for Action at this Fourth U.N. Conference on Women in Beijing, which will be debated these next two weeks, contains several paragraphs,[159] which would formally include sexual orientation for the first time. On behalf of many lesbian and heterosexual women attending this Forum, I urge all who can hear me to lobby vigorously for the inclusion of sexual orientation.

Lesbian rights activists at this conference seek the legal and cultural recognition that human sexual difference should not be a basis for the persecution of women, for discrimination or stigmatization of women, or for violence against women. The specific human rights that lesbian activists seek can be summarized in five categories: (1) the right to life, liberty, and security of person or what might be defined as the right to be free from torture, violence, and ill-treatment; (2) the right to enjoy basic freedom of association, expression, information, and personal liberty; (3) the right to nondiscrimination and equal protection under the law; (4) the right to form family; and (5) the right to work, health, and education. Let me speak to these briefly in turn.

The Universal Declaration of Human Rights (UDHR), Article 3, states, " [e]very one has the right to life, liberty and the security of person." These human rights ideals have been further endorsed in Article 5 of the UDHR, which states,

"No one shall be subjected to torture or to cruel, inhuman or degrading treatment or punishment." The right to life, liberty, and security of person, and the interrelated right to be free from violence, torture, and ill-treatment are denied to lesbians and gay men in nearly all countries as we face high incidence of violence, physical intimidation and harassment, extrajudicial execution and disappearances, forced "medical" treatment and hospitalization to change sexual orientation, rape and sexual abuse, and high rates of suicide. Time does not permit me to detail the stories of lesbians persecuted and terrorized by violence and government repression. I refer this tribunal to two reports that detail these kinds of abuses—the *Unspoken Rules* report and a document prepared in 1994 by Amnesty International USA entitled, *Breaking The Silence: Human Rights Violations Based on Sexual Orientation.* [160] The Amnesty Report details examples of each of these human rights violations in countries as diverse as Costa Rica, the United States, Turkey, Britain, and Romania.[161] The *Unspoken Rules* report discusses cases of such violence against lesbians from Zimbabwe, Brazil, Great Britain, India, Thailand, and the United States.[162] Lesbian rights include a commitment to freedom of association, expression, and information. UDHR Article 20 states, "everyone has the right to freedom of peaceful assembly and association." Yet, these freedoms are routinely denied as police raid lesbians meeting places and bars (as they have recently in Peru and Argentina, and they have historically in the United States); as lesbian books and periodicals are banned in some countries (most recently in Zimbabwe, but also in Canada); and attempts are made the world over to outlaw expressions of support for lesbian equality (a local school board in the U.S. in the state of New Hampshire just last month banned any talk about homosexuality in the classroom, and individual reports detailed in *Unspoken Rules* from Jordan, India, South Africa, Romania suggest that such suppression is widespread).

The International Covenant on Civil and Political Rights

(ICCPR), Articles 2.1 and 26 set forth principles of non-discrimination and equal protection under the law. Lesbians, however, encounter discriminatory laws, which target us and which outlaw lesbian expression, behavior, and relationships. We face rejection by courts of law when claims of discrimination are pursued. We often receive prejudicial treatment by the criminal justice system and prison systems. And we experience widespread discrimination in private and public employment. Nondiscrimination laws are critically important to lesbians as we strive to challenge our second-class social, economic, and cultural status.

The ICCPR at Article 23 states that the "right of men and women of marriageable age to marry and found a family shall be recognized . . . No marriage shall be entered without the free and full consent of the intending spouse." This freedom to form family is a principle that lesbian activists seek to extend to our families. As this tribunal no doubt knows, this area is among the most controversial in the entire spectrum of lesbian rights. Some are deeply threatened by the desire of lesbians and gay men to form committed relationships and to have that status recognized as the marriages that they are. Others object to our capacity to bear and rear children. The facts of lesbian lives expose such fears as stemming from prejudice, misinformation, and mistrust rather than accurate knowledge of the capacity and ability of lesbians to parent or form committed relationships. The desire for family is a human one that women and men share, regardless of their sexual orientation, and one that sound social policy should support.

Finally, basic human rights to health, education, and work are guaranteed by Article 23 of the UDHR, and Articles 12.1 and 13.1 of the International Covenant on Economic, Social, and Cultural Rights (ICESCR). The IGLHRC report details the ways in which sexual orientation serves as a barrier to the attainment of adequate health care, education, or employment in many parts of the world. Lesbian-rights activism seeks the opportunity for all lesbians to live their lives, work, and to receive basic social services without persecution or prejudice.

This brief overview suggests several concrete ways in which lesbian rights are part of the existing human rights framework being constructed by women and men at conferences such as this. Yet, this recitation does not adequately convey to this tribunal, nor can any one person convey, the complex, dangerous, and oppressive conditions under which lesbians must live, work, and survive. An international movement for women's equality must oppose this kind of persecution of women.

Opponents of Lesbian Rights

Opposition to the recognition of lesbian rights falls into three overlapping categories: those in denial and misinformed about homosexuality; those who fundamentally oppose women's equality and use homophobia as the vehicle through which they organize; and those who genuinely harbor religious or moral opposition. Denial and misinformation are at work when some in the international community base their opposition to lesbian rights on the theory that lesbians and gay men are a "western" phenomenon. Such thinking is epitomized in the recent attacks on lesbians and gay men voiced by President Robert Mugabe of Zimbabwe. In early August of 1995, Mr. Mugabe's government banned the Gay & Lesbian Association of Zimbabwe from displaying an exhibit at a book fair in Harare. According to recent newspaper articles, Mr. Mugabe said that he was "extremely outraged that homosexual rights advocates live in Zimbabwe." In a speech given August 18, 1995 in Harare, Mr. Mugabe characterized homosexuality as a foreign "madness we shall never accept here in Zimbabwe."[163] Mr. Mugabe's opposition is in large part based on a rather sad denial of reality. In fact, those asserting the right to participate openly in their nation are gay and lesbian people who live in Zimbabwe. The truth is that a Zimbabwean gay and lesbian movement is emerging in that country and is being actively suppressed by the

Mugabe government.

I urge this Congress not to dismiss the lesbian and gay rights issue as a North American concern. Such a characterization demeans the battle for human rights in which sexuality plays such a critical role, and it renders the lives of millions of gay and lesbian citizens of every country invisible. The truth about lesbians and our movement for political rights and cultural freedom is far more global. Women who love women live in every corner of the world and are members of every family and culture—they are not acknowledged, silenced, suppressed, or otherwise rendered invisible. The visibility of gay and lesbian citizens of the world is growing as an international gay and lesbian movement has emerged to combat homophobia in nearly every global region and nation—from Japan to Southeast Asia, from India to South Africa, from the Middle East to Latin America, and from the United States to Russia and to nearly all countries across Europe.

In large part, the attack on lesbian rights is leveled by those who are opposed to women's full equality and autonomy overall. For example, at this Conference the same U.S. organizations that have long opposed women's equality—by fighting to defeat an Amendment to the United States Constitution that would have guaranteed equal rights for women (the Equal Rights Amendment), by opposing government policies which help working mothers, by actively opposing aid for single mothers—are here today claiming to support women's equality. We cannot be deluded by their false representations, nor can we be seduced by the appeal of words like pro-family. Their distorted characterizations of the women's movement are designed to do three things: to divide our strength, to stall the momentum for women's equality, and to boost the political power of conservatives intent on preserving the traditional status quo for women.

All of us must be cautious and have the wisdom to see through the divisive rhetoric of those who have come to this Conference to stall women's equality. A principal vehicle these anti-women forces are using at this conference is homophobia. They argue that the involvement of lesbians in this Conference is proof that the Platform for Action is anti-family. To that argument, I can only repeat this truth: some women are lesbian, and as women we have are a part of an international community of women. Furthermore, this international Conference on women, as all the others before it, needs no one to tell it that it is pro-family: we know we are pro-family whenever we are pro-woman.

When these conservative forces claim that terms like "gender" are over-inclusive, what they are really saying is that they would like to limit women's options only to traditional female roles of mother and heterosexual spouse and to traditional roles of subservience and inequality. When they call all who disagree with them "anti-family," they expose their disdain for the lived experience of millions of people who make family in diverse ways. When they attack all women whose views differ from tradition as "radical feminist" or "anti-family," they are trying to marginalize the work of women's organizations around the world. We must not be silent about or complicit in these divisive tactics.

The anti-lesbian agenda of these conservative forces actually uses "homophobia as a weapon of sexism" and by doing so, bolsters sexism. By advocating the ideal that all women must be heterosexual and married in order to be "real," legitimate, complete, or truly women, conservative organizations, like the U.S.-based Concerned Women For America or the Holy See, campaign against the idea that a woman's rights ought to depend on her humanity, not on her relationship to husbands or children. As writer Suzanne Pharr observes, "The central focus of the right wing attack against women's liberation is that women's equality, women's self-determination, women's control of our own bodies and lives will damage what they see as the crucial societal institution, the nuclear family... To resist marriage and/or heterosexuality is to risk severe punishment and loss."[164] I believe that the women's movement stands against the forced marriage of women, as it stands against force of all kinds.

We stand instead for the principle that women and men are human beings, entitled as such to certain fundamental human rights, which should be equally available to women and to men. We believe that every woman is a complete and total human being in her own self. And we have created a detailed Platform for Action, the enactment of which will support all women and men in forming families, caring for children, building healthy relationships with their partners, and participating fully in the world. This agenda is not anti-family—it is pro-woman. This agenda is not anti-male, it is pro-human rights. And it is radical to the extent that it is honest and attempts to pull out the roots of the oppression of women.

A third type of argument against the full recognition of lesbian and gay sexuality is religious opposition. Notably, it is only the most orthodox, fundamentalist, and rigid proponents of the world's religions who perpetuate such opposition. A growing number of moderate religious denominations and leaders have endorsed full human and civil rights for lesbian, gay, bisexual and transgender people. These moderate voices represent the voice of balance and wisdom, yet are often drowned out by the larger, better-financed voices of conservative opponents. The fact is that a vigorous discussion about sexual orientation exists within every religion, and the debate is far from over.

Arguments that associate the full acceptance of lesbians and gay people with damage to the moral fiber of society betray a deep disregard for the humanity of LGBT people. Lesbians, bisexuals, transgender people and gay men are fully moral human beings—with all the capacity for goodness and evil which is a possibility in every human being. To demonize all lesbians as perverts is as wrong as it is to demonize all women who are unmarried as whores. To argue that social tolerance and human rights will undermine the moral fabric of a nation is to hold too little faith in that moral fabric's ability to withstand honesty. The dynamic of defamation, demonization, and suppression must be replaced by a new dynamic of social and cultural honesty, and recognition of human rights.

In conclusion, I urge this Congress and tribunal to consider carefully and closely the importance of this International Conference to lesbian women from every country in the world. The human rights we seek to achieve for women affect all women and ought not be circumscribed.

WE'RE DYKES, DON'T TOUCH US, WE'LL HURT YOU[165]

Throughout the modern queer movement's history, there have been moments where lesbians have felt the need to challenge something that seems inevitably to happen to dykes—our invisibility. The Lesbian Avengers and the Dyke March emerged as grassroots strategies to assert the presence of lesbians and to claim an anti-corporate politics within an increasingly corporatized and bought-and-sold LGBT movement. The first U.S Dyke March (labeled as such) was held on April 24, 1993, the night before the third National March on Washington for Lesbian, Gay, Bi Rights and Liberation. I was there and the wonderfully dry chant that the organizers used to step off that March gave me the title for this chapter.

Dyke marches are generally held the night before a city's LGBT Pride march and they vary in style and presentation. Some (like San Francisco and Boston) feature music and speakers; others (like New York) prefer to remain unpermitted and less formal in their production. The remarks below were given at the Boston Dyke March on June 10, 2011.

This and the following essay come out of my interest in encouraging lesbians to be more politically engaged and the broader movement to be more aware of women's liberation as an integral concern. I love dykes and feel deeply challenged by our present-day political assimilation. Feminist issues are urgently in play in both domestic and global politics. Matters as basic as contraception, as fundamental as who makes the decision to have a child (lawmakers or a woman herself), and the freedom of women to have sexual agency are contested. Lesbians, bisexual women, transgender women are all implicated in these arguments, as are men who seek transformation of patriarchal notions of manhood. A new wave of dyke political engagement is crucial to the reintegration of feminism into the LGBT movement.

The great American poet Muriel Rukeyser wrote,

Give my regards to the well–protected woman,
I knew the ice-cream girl, we went to school together.
There's something to bury, people, when you begin to bury.
When your women are ready and rich in their wish for the world
Destroy the leaden heart
We've a new race to start.
                    "More of a Corpse Than a Woman"[166]

Four decades of organizing as a dyke boil down to one question for me: for what do dykes stand? Whether we are bisexual, transgender, queer, intersex, corporate, femme, butch, or whatever kind of dyke—for what kind of political and cultural order, for what kind of society are we fighting? Do dykes "wish for the world"—do we still envision ourselves engaged in a world-building project?

Are dykes ready to bury the myth of the "well–protected woman" or are we simply building new "protections" around our particular form of femaleness?

Do dykes dare to believe that we can start this new race, be part of a new social justice coalition that takes and exercises power?

Or have we settled ourselves comfortably into domesticity, a complacent acceptance of the fenced–in form of liberal equality, sold to us by capital and consisting of a slightly renovated, yet still intact, old-world-order, with its traditions preserved and virulent? At least this form of equality promises to us what it in fact delivers: a private zone of formal equality within a larger public sphere in which inequality, injustice, misery, fear, and repression get worse every year.

To answer the question of "what do dykes stand for" requires us to know something of what dykes have stood for in previous decades.

In the historic and brave play that Larry Kramer wrote about the AIDS epidemic, titled *The Normal Heart*, which recently was revived on Broadway, the lead character says at one point, "I belong to a culture that includes Marcel Proust, Walt Whitman, Tennessee Williams, James Baldwin, Herman Melville…Tchaikovsky, Auden, Forster, Byron, Plato, Socrates, Aristotle, Alexander the Great, Cole Porter, Michelangelo, Leonardo da Vinci…"[167]

A comparable dyke genealogy can be claimed. We come from a culture that includes Sappho, Emma Goldman, Gertrude Stein, Virginia Woolf, Georgia O'Keefe, Agnes Martin, Judith Butler, Angela Davis, Monique Wittig, Mary Daly, Romaine Brooks, Susan Sontag, Bessie Smith, Colette, Marlene Dietrich, Alice Walker, Willa Cather, Bernice Reagon, Ethel Waters, Moms Mabley, Adrienne Rich, and June Jordan, to name just a few! It is an amazing and radical herstory, and one I can trace in each of the past four decades of dyke action.

In the '70s, dyke politics and culture were about discovery and self-definition. We were preoccupied with the question of what did it mean to be a dyke? How did lesbian experience connect to women's experience? How was it similar to and different from gay male experience?

We spent a lot of time defining, and ultimately policing, our boundaries. The "Woman Identified Woman" manifesto, written in 1970 by Radical Lesbians, opened with this line: "What is a lesbian? A lesbian is the rage of all women condensed to the point of explosion. She is the woman who, often beginning at an extremely early age, acts in accordance with her inner compulsion to be a more complete and freer human being than her society...cares to allow her."[168] The manifesto goes on to say: "'Dyke' is a different kind of put-down from 'faggot,' although both imply you are not playing your socially-assigned sex role . . . are not therefore a 'real woman' or a 'real man.' The grudging admiration felt for the tomboy, and the queasiness felt around a sissy boy point to the same thing: the contempt in which women—or those who play a female role-are held. And the investment in keeping women in that contemptuous role is very great."[169]

Dyke politics in the 1970s was overtly feminist. It sought to build separate space and institutions, to define itself against the dominant patriarchal ways of seeing, organizing, imagining, and living. Groups like Lesbian Feminist Liberation, the Furies Collective, early bisexual organizations and newsletters, the explosion of feminist bookstores, the dyke emergence into separatism, the presence of transsexuals and transvestites in the leadership of GLF, a critical rethinking about gender itself.

All of these were part of a dyke strategy to transform the three options that had previously been available to us—wife/mother, heterosexual consort, or spinster—into a world of possibilities.

Lesbian and bisexual women of color and artists (writers, painters, musicians) were at the heart of the intellectual work being done to define what dykes wanted and stood for. Writers like Audre Lorde, organizers like Barbara Smith, and the Combahee River Collective articulated connections between systems of oppression in a way that made you want to storm the barricades in solidarity with all sorts of movements!

Dykes and bi women were at the heart of the black feminist movement—its analysis, its thinking. Dykes and bi women were at the heart of a publishing boom—*Lesbian Connection*, *Sinister Wisdom*, *Connections*, *Hysteria*, *Off Our Backs*, *Gay Community News*, Persephone Press, and Kitchen Table Press, to name a few. Dykes decided to build our own music industry and made today's taken-for-granted status of women in the music business possible. The roots of the riot grrrrl explosion of the 1990s can be traced to Olivia and Redwood Records.

The 1980s saw the emergence of a dyke politics that was more out of the closet and integrated with the previously largely gay male movement. The resulting queer politics of the 1980s was explicitly anti-racist, feminist, and critical of the right wing ideas gaining prominence in that decade. The bisexual movement flourished in the 1980s, led by bi-dykes, as new networks were founded—BIPAC, BIPol.

Dykes co-founded, led and worked through social justice movements, but did not necessarily do that work as out lesbians. What movements did we birth and lead? The violence against women movement, the prisoner's rights movement, the international women's rights movement, the welfare rights movement, the reproductive rights movement, and the movement for reform inside religious institutions in their treatment of women. And there are more.

The 1980s marked the emergence of a truly co-gender queer politics—large numbers of dykes dropped separatism and embraced coalition with gay men to fight HIV and the right wing. This coming together of dykes, bisexuals, transgender people, and gay men created an amazing array of institutions that survive to this day: centers, health clinics, political organizations, softball leagues, choruses, and business guilds.

Dykes led in the anti-nuclear movement—the biggest demonstration in American history in New York has been the 1982 anti-nuke march organized by Leslie Cagan. The Seneca

Women's Peace Encampment, the Women's Pentagon Action, Greenham Common in the United Kingdom were all dyke-led anti-war and anti-nuke actions.

Dykes exposed the secret war the CIA was waging in Central America and organized to end U.S. intervention in Nicaragua and El Salvador.

Dykes helped build ACT UP, expanded its focus to include prevention and health care reform, flocked to care for and help to create the HIV/AIDS organizations and guided national HIV policy in D.C.

The transgender movement's current forms began to emerge in the 1980s, although the leadership of early drag and transgender people had long been a founding force in our movement. New groups like FTM International, creative work and writing by transgender artists, and calls for transgender inclusion and representation in the legal and political agendas of the movement began to be made to national LGBT organizations.

But as much as the co-gender LGBT movement flourished, the dyke-specific movement faltered. The end of the 1980s also saw the withering of the dyke cultural movement. Lesbian bookstores struggled for survival and closed; fewer publications existed; while gay male visibility increased, lesbian, bisexual, and transgender women's lives and politics receded again into the background.

The 1990s marked the emergence of a mainstream gay movement united around the shared demand of equal rights. The Clinton Administration embraced us but left us with DADT and the Defense of Marriage Act (DOMA). The 1993 March on Washington was our largest to date, and yet the mainstream access achieved did not translate into laws passed or violence reduced.

The bisexual and transgender movements also took great leaps forward in the 1990s. More local bisexual organizing and advocacy groups were founded, as was a national magazine called *Anything That Moves*, and a stronger national network among local groups. Transgender activists and transgender dykes have played a powerful and under-acknowledged role in the progressive history of national LGBT movement politics, especially since the 1980s. Working with determination and few resources, transgender leaders educated and articulated a political and legal advocacy agenda. NGLTF shocked its peers by opposing a trans-exclusive Employment Non-Discrimination Act (ENDA) in the late 1990s. A trans-inclusive ENDA is now the dominant position of the movement, but in 1997 and 1998, this was treated as heresy. Transgender political theory and new ideas about gender also exploded in the 1990s through the leadership of transgender academics and queer activists. This process grew yet again in the 2000s with the founding of new transgender leadership and advocacy organizations like the Sylvia Rivera Law Project, the National Center for Transgender Equality and the Transgender Law Center.

At the same time, what lesbians stood for became more muddied in the 1990s and 2000s. Our politics got diffuse and unanchored. A national lesbian conference held in 1991 in Atlanta attended by more than 3,000 women was a disaster. LGBT people have always had children, but in the 1990s lesbians consciously started to have them as out dykes, starting the so-called gay baby boom. Choosing children changed our lives, the politics of our movement, and the shape of our communities. Our new horizons as dyke activists included schools, partnership recognition, access to health care, and much more.

The juxtaposition of a greater cultural visibility with a decreased and shrinking community was another hallmark of the mid to late 1990s. We got distracted by the media-created lesbian chic moment of mid-1990s, when celebrity coming-outs became stand-ins for actual grassroots engagement and a consciously feminist lesbian politics.

By the mid-1990s, Republican gay male politics was ascendant in the LGBT movement. And by the late 1990s, feminist demands for reproductive justice, sexual freedom, legal protection for non-traditional families, universal health care, and childcare had been removed from the LGBT agenda. By the new millennium, these demands were largely displaced by a narrower consensus agenda that included demands for equal treatment but retreated from the ambitious feminist demands of redistributive justice made by an earlier movement.

It was clearly in response to this shocking disappearance of progressive and lesbian visibility that new action groups like Lesbian Avengers and the Dyke March itself came into being in the 1990s. These new groups challenged the complacency of assimilationist politics. They engaged an intergenerational group of dykes: women (lesbian, bisexual, transgender) who took for granted the value of dyke power led this movement. But they did not articulate an ideology for the movement, nor did they create a coherent set of actions, interventions, or critiques of the mainstream LGBT agenda. As a result, I would suggest that neither the Dyke March nor the Lesbian Avengers led to the development of a new lesbian politics.

In the first decade of the 21st century, the mainstream LGBT political movement has made greater gains than ever before, as the culture catches up to our existence and our families and friends stand up for our equality.

But in this same time, there is a decrease in the cultural and political influence of lesbians. There is one simple reason for this: the L-word was no substitute for the F-word. Lifestyle lesbianism is not the same as feminism.

Indeed, it is interesting to see that the places where gender analysis is taking place in the dyke and queer world—the progressive transgender movement—are the places where there is the most excitement and energy today. Feminist analysis and a critique of heterosexism have virtually disappeared from the mainstream LGBT agenda. What is left is a movement focused on dating and relationships, love and marriage, horse and carriage. We have gone from being a social movement seeking to change who holds power in the world and how they wield it to being a movement fighting for our right to a picket fence.

Yes, the world now has Ellen DeGeneres and Wanda Sykes; yes, there are dyke political leaders like New York City Council Speaker Christine Quinn and Mayor of Houston Annise Parker. But because we no longer have a political movement that is focused on changing gender inequality, ending racism, achieving socially responsible capitalism and greater social justice, we are losing ground as women and as dykes.

Look at the reality of today's LGBT and progressive politics:

- The political agendas of LGBT organizations are *not* feminist; indeed, these agendas are often actively anti-feminist. This fact should be unacceptable to every person at this March. How can the institutions we created through our sweat and tears be anti-choice? The freedom to control our sexual and reproductive lives is a non-negotiable human right. It is a non-negotiable woman's bodily right. And insuring it should be an LGBT movement priority.

- Similarly, the political agendas of progressive organizations are still too often silent on issues facing dykes and transgender people in particular, and LGBT folks in general. This fact should be unacceptable to every person at this March. How can the peace and social justice movement be silent on insuring full equality for LGBT people?

- The weakness of dyke politics today can be seen in the absence of racial diversity in the leadership of our community-based institutions and the absence of racial justice in the agenda of our major movement organizations. This fact should be unacceptable to every dyke at this March. Lesbian-feminists are why the LGBT movement once prioritized gender parity in queer organizations. We are the ones who demanded there be racial parity in the movement.

We must do so again. Sexism and racism structures exclusion and disparate treatment in many parts of our lives—and our movement must commit to work against all systems of racial and gender exclusion and bias.

- Dyke politics always focused on issues of economic justice. Yet, today our movement does not work at all on poverty or confront its class biases. After all these years, men as a whole still make 25% more ($1.22 for every $1 a woman earns) for the same work. The way our current economic system perpetuates and expands inequality should be unacceptable to every person at this March. The economic disempowerment of women, dykes, transgender people, and working people of all colors is massive and evident everywhere.

- In a country obsessed with financial assets—where wealth is seen as genius and it alone buys influence and respect, where financial deals are still made by white men in all-male golf clubs like that hideous enclave in Augusta, GA where the Masters play, where data show that the boards of Fortune 500 companies are nearly 80% male—we still have a long way to go, baby.

- Ending violence remains a central issue on the dyke political agenda—violence against women, violence of poverty and racism, violence in prisons, violence in the home. And we are not making enough of a difference on this issue. The tolerance of misogyny and gender-based violence all over the world should be unacceptable to every person who can hear me at this March. The singer Rihanna was criticized for her video depicting a man who pays the ultimate consequence for his violent action, while the TV and movie business depicts atrocity after atrocity against women (in the name of entertainment) with barely a peep being raised in critique. No feminist condones violence. Rihanna is trying to end it. She made a work of art and a provocation to make people think. If it has made some people nervous, well, then even better.

- The very few (count them on one hand) national lesbian-identified organizations that exist today do amazing work and are fantastic groups, but they are tiny and unsupported by the majority of dykes, not to mention even a fraction of gay men. Astraea Lesbian Foundation for Justice has a budget under $3 million for national and international funding; the National Center for Lesbian Rights has a budget under $4 million; the Lesbian Herstory Archives has a budget of probably well under $500,000. Every dyke at this March should be a member of these groups and others at the local level.

The great poet Audre Lorde wrote, "Our childhood wars have aged us/but it is the absence of change/which will destroy us."[170]

We have to get to work to make another wave of feminist-based change inside and outside the LGBT movement.

The Dyke March is a symbol of resistance to conformity. So in the next year, let us remember this and act upon this fact. Let us not conform.

Dykes disturb nature. We upend gender hierarchies. We stand for gender equality, racial equality, and social justice. We do not conform to the female script of subservience to men.

Let us make dykes really loud, non-conforming, and visible as voters.

Let us emerge from our silence and never stop coming out.

Let us insist that the LGBT movement live up to our progressive and feminist expectations. And let us continue to make history!

ENDING PATRIARCHY

Political Legacies of the 1970s
Lesbian Feminist Movement[171]

In 2010, I worked with a small group of volunteers at the Center for Lesbian and Gay Studies (CLAGS) at the City University of New York (CUNY) Graduate Center to produce a conference focused on the impact of the lesbian feminist movement of the 1970s. The conference was titled, "In Amerika They Call Us Dykes: Lesbian Lives in the 1970s." The response was surprising: more than 500 women and men attended. Every session was packed, political conversation was lively, and disagreements abounded.

Lesbian feminism was not the only kind of lesbian politics in the community, but it was the political movement within queer activism that focused on producing an explicitly lesbian-supportive infrastructure. Lesbian feminism gave us women's bookstores, production companies, record labels, publishing houses, festivals, farm cooperatives, and a host of small businesses, a few of which last to this day. But its separatist inclinations and its radically decentered politics of social justice led many lesbians in directions very different from gay and lesbian rights activists. As a consequence, much of the mainstream

LGBT movement has no connection or grounding in the formative impact that lesbian feminism played in ideas and practices it takes for granted. These include ideas as diverse as the feminist articulation of the politics of difference, inclusion and intersection, a commitment to accessibility despite any disability, the idea of consensus decision-making as a norm, and the value placed on healing and spiritual renewal. This talk on a plenary panel elaborates some of these contributions. A critical appraisal of the past, in turn, suggests the relevance of seeing sexism as a structural system of social control and gender-based privileges.

For me the 1970s were not about gay liberation. They were about believing that I could bring down capitalist patriarchy and build a radically egalitarian society.

They were about discovering the brilliance of 1970s feminist theorists (like Shulamith Firestone, Sheila Rowbotham, Simone de Beauvoir, Monique Wittig, and Susan Brownmiller, among others), and they were about discovering the vapidity of left politics.

They were about identifying with the Situationist International and the manifesto *The Poverty of Student Life*. They were about organizing against apartheid in South Africa, organizing against violence against women, organizing for prisoners' rights (post-Attica), organizing against the military, discovering women's bookstores and feminist newsprint manifestos, and listening to punk rock and Patti Smith, while producing women's music.

Those years were so infused with radical ideas that when I came out to my parents in the '80s, my father joked that he was a little relieved because he knew something was up, but he worried that I was in the Weather Underground—which surprised me to no end, since I critiqued my own work as reformist, at best.

I started the decade in junior high school, a very nerdy Indian girl with long hair to my waist and Coke-bottle glasses, and I ended the decade still a nerdy girl, moving to Boston at the age of twenty in September of 1979 into a macrobiotic group lesbian house with eight other women, a chore chart, and designated cooking nights.

Along the way I organized: feminist coffeehouses on campus, poetry readings, conferences with titles like "Feminist Union Socialist Symposium" or "Anger and the Rebirth of Woman Power," Holly Near concerts, and bringing the Olivia Records and Roadwork sponsored tour titled "Varied Voices of Black Women" to my campus.

And I learned new things—how to strip wallpaper and paint houses, how to spackle and build things, how to play a bass (badly), how to write a leaflet, how to use a French press to make coffee, how to create a budget for an event, how to put together a publication, how to fundraise and make things happen with no money, how to burn sage and use crystals, how to run a food co-op, how to be a secretary, how to live on food stamps, how to line up buses for demonstrations in Washington, D.C., how to put brewers yeast in my popcorn to get B12 vitamins.

Our moderator for today's panel, Sarah Schulman, asked us to talk about what we think took hold from the lesbian ideas and movements we were part of in the 1970s. This is a great question because I think today's activism inherited many things from the lesbian-feminist movement of the 1970s. Among these ideas were the following.

- Lesbian visibility accompanied by inspired definitions of what a lesbian is—from the Furies, to Radical Lesbians, to poets and artists.
- Ideas about accountability and transparency in organizing (another form of process-consciousness)—e.g., publishing the budgets and salaries of everyone in programs for events so there was no mystery.
- A self-help health movement—which became the prototype for the People with AIDS (PWA) and treatment action movements in the HIV/AIDS epidemic during the next decade.

- A lot of second-wave feminist institutions that were started and run by lesbians who did not necessarily do their work as out lesbians.
- A critique of the structures of all institutions, not just laws.
- Spirituality and new age culture—crystals and woo-woo.
- Grunge clothing and style—flannel way before Nirvana in the '90s.
- Women's rock-and-roll bands and technical skills.
- The first openly lesbian or gay political leaders (Elaine Noble, 1974; Karen Clark; Gwen Craig).
- The idea that sexuality could be a choice and not just a biological imperative.

In addition, I would cite four significant political contributions made by lesbian, bisexual, and transgender dykes from the '70s to feminism, LGBT liberation, and to the world of progressive activism generally. First, while lesbians did not invent feminism, the lesbian contribution to feminism certainly toughened it up and strengthened it by making it more inclusive. Betty Friedan, Simone de Beauvoir, Susan Brownmiller, or Gloria Steinem are to be credited with early analysis, but it was Audre Lorde, Adrienne Rich, Barbara Smith, Charlotte Bunch, Rita Mae Brown, June Jordan, Leslie Feinberg, Riki Anne Wilchins, and other lesbian, bisexual, and transgender feminists who proposed and embedded the ideas of the multiplicity and interconnectedness of race, class, sexuality, and gender oppression. From the publication of *Motive* (the United Methodist publication) on Lesbian Feminism in 1971, to the Combahee River Collective statement of 1977, to the speech Audre Lorde gave at the October 1979 March on Washington, we created a new and inclusive consciousness. We all were, as Lorde said in her speech, "committed to struggle for a world where all our children can grow free from the diseases of racism, of sexism, of classism, and of homophobia. For those oppressions are inseparable."[172]

I took a picture of a big banner at the 1995 U.N. International Conference on Women held in Beijing that said "Lesbians Free Everyone." This commitment to intersecting identities and interconnected struggle has been part of lesbian feminism for decades and of progressive wings of all social justice movements since the '70s. In the progressive world, however, those who hold such intersectional politics have not—until very, very recently—been in power within mainstream movements for social justice. This has changed and today leaders with a commitment to intersectional practice are in leadership positions in the labor movement, Planned Parenthood, the National Association for the Advancement of Colored People (NAACP), the Center for American Progress (CAP), the National Council of La Raza (NCLR), and NGLTF to name just a few groups. This is a political achievement we ought to celebrate as lesbian feminists because where these organizations all started out was pretty conservative.

Related to our demand for inclusion was the idea of accessibility due to economic status, race, ability, childcare, and every other factor. This was an insistent demand of lesbian feminist activism. It meant that concerts were signed for the hearing-impaired. I had never seen or heard of such a thing—like most of us, I suspect—until I went to my earliest women's music shows. Seeing the interpreters Susan Freundlich or Shirley Childress Saxton dancing out the songs and signing in ASL are among my most vivid, life-shifting memories. Today, what distinguishes feminist spaces is their consciousness about and commitment to accessibility.

Our commitment to inclusion was double-edged, however. It led us to expect absolutely perfect inclusion at all times in all ways, and that was simply not possible. We beat ourselves, and each other, up a lot over our failure to achieve our ideal of perfect inclusion and safe space. And we willfully ignored the ways in which our own language and rhetoric was exclusionary of some women because we saw gender in such a narrow and biological manner. I am thinking of the whole idea of "woman-born-woman." I cannot begin to tell you how many hours I spent talking and trying to define and understand that term. In the same way, we spent hundreds of hours talking about what "woman-identified woman" meant. What I see now is that these were boundary-setting words that some women felt were needed to protect and discipline a space and a fledgling culture they had fought so hard to carve out; women felt under siege and vulnerable. I remember the change in my own politics from unquestioned acceptance of the idea that women-only space meant literally that—limited to biologically born women—to seeing gender and woman as a socially-constructed notion, and being fully comfortable allowing all sorts of people to identify into "my" space. The Michigan Womyn's Music Festival still operates on this biological determinism and it is to me an example of how the radical inclusivity we professed broke down on the shoals of our acceptance of gender as primarily biological.

A second political idea that we brought forward that has "taken hold" in progressive movements is our insistence on the importance of process to the outcome. Now I suspect this was a Maoist hangover from the ultra-leftists of the anti-war movement, but I was too young to experience them, so I will tell you how I experienced it. Process meant that you did every meeting, planned every event, and ran every gathering with an eye toward how power imbalances were implicated in whatever we were doing. Process meant we made no decision without full consensus, and we would discuss and discuss until everyone in the room agreed. Any one person could block consensus and we could not move forward. (Sounds like a Republican filibuster.) Process meant that we rotated chairs, allowed everyone to speak, and sought to question every hierarchy from alphabetical order to right-handed domination. Process meant that my Feminist Union meetings on campus were three-and-a-half hours long each week. It meant that we made an effort to ensure that everyone spoke and that we urged the loudest to speak less; that we turned leadership over to whoever volunteered with no regard to skills or competencies; that we had criticism and self-criticism as core values throughout every darn step of the way, so there was always someone raising a concern and feeling unsafe or wanting something to change to widen the circle. My partner, Kate, and I often say that our most vivid sound memory from lesbian feminist meetings in that decade is the sound of folding chairs moving backwards as we perpetually widened the circle to include people who came in late for the meeting. What a radical departure from Robert's Rules of Order!

Related to the idea of process was the importance we placed on the link between culture and politics—our third important contribution. Michelle Parkerson made a great point at the opening plenary of this conference about how culture was critical because so much of our effort in our early years as out lesbians was to create visibility. Lesbian communities were built through cultural organizing; coffeehouses, poetry readings, dances, potlucks, women's music and comedy concerts, documentaries, photography, lesbian and feminist theater companies, and performances just flourished in this decade. You could be living in Poughkeepsie, New York and hear that Holly Near was coming to perform in town and a crowd of 600 lesbians would gather, pre-Internet, with no mainstream advertising, just face-to-face outreach through bookstores, bars, flyers, ads, mailing lists, and phone calls.

Culture helped us get together and build a shared set of values. Because of cultural workers like Sweet Honey in the Rock founder Bernice Johnson Reagon, Olivia Records artists Holly Near, Cris Williamson, and Meg Christian, because of Robin Tyler, Linda Tillery, Maxine Feldman, and Alix Dobkin, we had a shared set of jokes, like the words to Meg's song, "Ode to a Gym Teacher," a shared consciousness about Central America (pro-Sandinista and anti-junta in Chile and Salvador), a shared

Amazon Alphabet, and amazing songs to challenge Anita Bryant with when she came campaigning against gay men and lesbians in late 1977–78.

This cultural consciousness extended to the idea that we needed to create women-owned businesses—record companies, bookstores, bars, theaters, newspapers, construction companies, lesbian printers, stores that sold groovy New Age crystals and patchouli oil, and lots of purple and lavender clothing. It was expressed in the many and varied kinds of collectives, women's communes, and land that women inhabited in communities designed as countervailing strategies to take back power over our lives. This culture continues to this day, but it is smaller and struggles financially.

Finally, I believe the fourth lasting contribution from lesbian feminist politics of the '70s came from radical feminism and its critique of heterosexism, of the patriarchy, and of the nuclear family. We all spent a great deal of energy (in consciousness-raising groups and in our early political writing) naming and talking about how to dismantle the systems of male domination that held women down and that held racial and economic hierarchies intact. Gay men who were feminists were important contributors to a critique of patriarchy in the late '70s and '80s, as Bryant and the Moral Majority started crusading for the so-called Family Protection Act, which would have codified a hetero-only form for the family. Today, the idea that a majority of the gay male leadership of the LGBT movement would be feminist is so shocking because many of the current male leaders in that movement seem to not even be aware of women's existence separate from theirs, much less to be questioning their own privileges within patriarchal structures.

A note that was raised yesterday bears some further consideration. What happened to sexual liberation, which was such a large priority for the lesbian movement of the '70s? It is important to remind each other that sex still matters to us and our sexual desire for each other has not disappeared or magically mutated into spooning or desiring sex with men with the advent of age, longevity in our relationships, or a few wrinkles. What we all loved about the '70s was how hot it was. It was a lot about the sex, at least in my age group and in the political world. Many lesbians were heavily influenced by gay male culture in the '70s and longed for the "zipless sex" culture they had created. While ours always had to have more process, and romance, it was less U-Haul than today's satires suggest. Instead, our communities were literally an army of ex-lovers. We were consciously non-monogamous. We questioned the whole idea of coupling in nuclear family units—my friends and I used to plan the collectives we would live in when we got older.

What happens to sexual liberation movements when they are attacked as they were in 1950s, '60s, and the '70s by Joe McCarthy, Anita Bryant, Jerry Falwell, and many others? They hide. We lived under the radar, as gay male sexuality did pre-AIDS, a flourishing but relatively insiders' network known to each other, but not the straight world. Lesbians have not been taken seriously enough as sexual people to be noticed, so we always were under the radar. But what happens to a sexual liberation movement when it is outed—as we were in the 1980s—by the anti-AIDS right wing response, and by the backlash to feminism? We put on straight drag and became the very things that lesbian feminism critiqued in the '70s—coupled, married, with children, living in nuclear families, isolated from and no longer building our communities.

Our moderator also asked us to think about our disappointments from the 1970s. The biggest disappointment to me is the decrease in the spaces for lesbian communities—oddly, there are now fewer publicly lesbian events, spaces, political statements, and writers focused on lesbian lives, culture, and ideas. There are many more lesbians who are out and visible and indeed powerful in many spheres (Ellen, Rosie, Melissa, Wanda, Billie Jean, and so on). Lesbians are still leaders in every social justice movement—and now often as *out* dykes. Women are still doing great organizing work and writing amazing literature and creating music and art—often with little mainstream support. But, strangely, the space for lesbian life on the ground has shrunk; there are fewer bookstores, bards, newspapers, 'zines, and even not that many lesbian-aimed political websites. Our sense of community with each other has decreased.

Where else did we fall short? In my view, we fell short with our:

- Rather rigid notions of identity—the split between separatists and non-separatists, between gay women and dykes, between political in the mainstream and political in the back-to-the-land sense, between transgender people and biological separatists. For an inclusive people whose politics encompassed every oppression, we spent a lot of time excluding.
- Inability to build an economically viable basis for our culture, our businesses, and our institutions.
- Weakness at cross-generational translation to embrace and engender successive versions of dykeness. We did not have *the* definition of lesbian feminist politics in the '70s, just the one for our times. We have failed in connecting to those who came up after us.
- Struggles to balance the competing demands of political and public life with motherhood and its necessary domesticity and time requirements. The fact that so many of us are and were even then mothers remains a very under-discussed aspect of lesbian lives.
- Rejection and dislike of femaleness itself, expressed in rejection of the affiliation with the term lesbian for many years until Lesbian Avengers brought it back into vogue among some younger women in the 1990s.
- Purity politics that promised an impossible and

never realized (therefore always criticized) perfectly
safe space.

- Avoidance of the mainstream, which meant that the
  LGBT movement grew without feminist politics
  being embedded anywhere except in the radical
  parts.

In addition, a splintering from feminism by lesbians over
the homophobia of the feminist movement, coupled with a
virulent backlash against women, has left the women's liberation
movement so weak today that as Susan Faludi noted in her terrific
article in 2010 in *Harper's*, "[O]ver the course of their prime
earning years, women make 38 percent of what men make."
Faludi also notes that "men occupy 80 to 95-plus percent of the
top decision-making positions in American politics, business,
the military, religion, media, culture, and entertainment; sexual
and domestic violence remain at epidemic levels (nearly 20%
of American women report having been sexually assaulted or
raped, and 25% of women are physically or sexually attacked by
their current or former husbands and lovers); and fundamental
reproductive freedom is perpetually imperiled...no abortion
services in 85% of U.S. counties."[173]

Back in the '70s, I really wanted to destroy the patriarchy
and smash imperialism in all its forms. You know what, I still do.
In many ways the patriarchal order today has discredited itself
and is in complete disarray. Although its lack of solutions and
lack of concern for the lives of millions of poor and ordinary
people, the lion's share of whom are women and children, are
obvious to anyone looking at the news.

What can we do now to hasten its demise, before its dying
convulsions consume us all?

POLITICS AS AN ACT OF FAITH
Ten Lessons From LGBT Activism[174]

The faith-based sectors of the LGBT movement are often the most neglected by the political and legal sides of the movement. They operate, after all, in domains where lawyers, lobbyists, and politicians on the left rarely tread—in the realm of social service, spiritual ministry, community creation, and family support. The LGBT movement still acts as if people of faith are obstacles, rather than beneficiaries and leaders of movements for gender and sexual freedom. In part, this is because major religious orders (Catholicism, Evangelical Christianity, Islam, Mormonism, Orthodox Judaism, to name just some) campaign so vigorously against movements for gender and sexual justice. It is hard to cut through the anti-gay noise to identify the dissident voices that support LGBT and women's freedom within each of these faith traditions.

In 1990, I made a conscious commitment to strengthen pro-LGBT faith-based movements. Initially, I did so out of pragmatic considerations. At that time, the ultra-right within each faith tradition was actively manipulating gender and sexuality to move previously justice-oriented faith communities to support narrow political agendas. Their goal was political and cultural power. Their strategy was to link social conservatism and economic conservatism, to energize evangelical pastors, and to build a powerful voting bloc that would influence and dominate the Republican Party, and the country, for decades.[175] I wanted to organize and network faith-based advocates in tangible ways. In the course of two decades of engagement with a segment of the movement I had largely avoided before, my politics changed. I cannot claim a spiritual awakening, but more of a shift in values and a greater cultural understanding for my activism. The shared language of faith-based activists (literally a shared Book, in many instances) was a marked change from the intellectual dissonance of progressive queers. This common language of values, spiritual engagement, and how it affected ones intimate relationships and interactions with the world was eye-opening for an Indian, lesbian-feminist activist, who came up in the grassroots left of the 1970s. Because I had not experienced the homophobic and sexist damage done by the Christian right personally, I think I was able to engage with its adherents more openly. In the process, I learned a great deal. I was moved by the testimony and experience of LGBT clergy dealing with excommunication, harassment, and significant marginalization within their faith traditions. I learned from studying the systematic way that organizers on the Christian Right built an infrastructure, invested in leadership training programs, created policy and advocacy institutions, used media and communications networks, and leveraged funding streams to build a powerful political force. It was clear that secular voices like mine were no match for this movement's claim to religious authority.

As executive director of NGLTF, I began to reach out to LGBT faith-based activists. In 1992, I convened the first gathering of pro-LGBT faith-based advocates at the national level at the NGLTF Creating Change Conference. Many years later, I initiated a Religious Leadership Roundtable to network LGBT faith denominations to assert a more powerful public voice. Throughout the past two decades, I urged mainstream and LGBT philanthropic efforts to strengthen the leadership of pro-LGBT advocates working inside religious denominations and organizations. This work assumed new significance in the past few years as the extent of the U.S.-based religious right wing groups promotion of anti-gay prejudice through their missions in Africa has been exposed: Uganda's waves of anti-gay legislation have been directly encouraged and enabled by the intervention of U.S. anti-gay activists.[176]

Pro-LGBT faith based activism flourishes today in a wide range of denominations in the U.S.—Episcopal, Methodist, Lutherans, Reform and Conservative Judaism, American Baptists, and many progressive Catholics have joined longstanding leaders like the Unitarian Universalists, Quakers, the Metropolitan Community Church, and the United Church of Christ to stand openly for LGBT rights in the U.S. and around the world. In addition, increased organizing within Muslim, Hindu, and Buddhist traditions has begun. Yet, this work remains under-resourced and regarded with skepticism by hard-boiled gay activists. Still, it is work that is meaningful to the daily lives of millions of people, and that I believe can enrich the LGBT movement's practice. And so, it is work in which I continue to engage, as a secular advocate, and a firm believer in the separation of church and state.

I've given several versions of the talk shared below at denominational meetings and interfaith gatherings of leaders. One occasion was at a gathering of the welcoming Christian congregations organized by the group Reconciling Ministries, in August of 2000, called "Witness Our Welcome," held in Arizona. Another version was shared in June of 2002 at the Presbyterian Church's Annual convention (that version is published on my website). The following talk was given at the Unitarian Universalist Association's Intergenerational Seminar, held in April 2009 in New York City.

I want to offer some reflections on activism and share ten key lessons gleaned through the trial-and-error process of my own organizing in social movements. My work has been in social justice movements at the grassroots level, particularly movements for LGBT rights, gender, and racial justice. I've worked on campaigns for prisoner's rights, reproductive choice, economic justice, anti-violence, same-sex marriage, women's liberation, affirmative action, HIV/AIDS action, and more. In the course of this work, I have been lucky enough to see enormous advances and equally devastating setbacks.

From all of these experiences, I have learned that social change is never linear, nor inevitable, but that it is always faith-based.

The idea that activism—or as my generation used to call it, our politics—is an act of faith is both dangerous and fitting to contemplate. It is dangerous because political practice and religious, or faith-based, practice are not the same. To conflate them leads to theocracy. Dr. Martin Luther King Jr. argued that the church was the conscience of the state, not the monarch itself. This message bears repeating today as the idea of secularism and secular states is challenged around the world by those seeking to impose their own particular version of state-sponsored religion upon all others.

Yet despite this caveat, my experience with politics leads me to see it as an act of faith. The very act of being an advocate for justice is an act fueled by a belief in political and social change, a belief in the idea that we can make a better world. As an activist, you have got to believe. This belief in the possibility of social change not only fuels people's willingness to engage in activism, but it is, in itself, the first lesson for social activists of any kind. The philosopher William James wrote that, "Faith means belief in something concerning which doubt is still theoretically possible; and as the test of belief is the willingness to act, one may say that faith is the readiness to act in a cause the prosperous issue of which is not certified in advance."[177]

You have to be able to imagine the impossible to be able to believe in change.

I wonder about the kind of imagination it took my predecessors, like Harry Hay, Del Martin, and Phyllis Lyon— gay activists in the 1950s who founded the modern LGBT movement in the United States. They lived in a time when being gay was totally stigmatized. It was a time when lesbians and gay men were clinically diagnosed as mentally ill, denigrated as morally depraved, legally banned as criminals, and socially shunned as perverts. What other than sheer faith in the human capacity to grow and change could have emboldened these pioneers to found gay and lesbian organizations in an era when the only publicly supported spaces for gay people were prisons and mental institutions? In this hostile context, groups like the Mattachine Society and Daughters of Bilitis published journals, organized self-help support groups, presented public education seminars, and even held public protests like the first gay rights picket in front of the White House in 1964.

These leaders of the early LGBT movement embodied the second lesson of LGBT activism, the lesson that knowledge is power. People who are outside of the power structure or disempowered or marginalized in some way must first organize to understand themselves, to build their own self-awareness in order to change the awareness of others. The early LGBT movement activists put their time and energy into this kind of knowledge building. They worked tirelessly to create support groups, challenge derogatory claims about homosexuality, challenge public forms of homophobia, create publications to promote positive messages, founded hotlines to break through the isolation and negativity LGBT people grew up hearing. They organized to challenge and correct misinformation and distortion about LGBT people with more balanced and factual data. Through information tables at professional conferences, they networked with scholars working to prepare and produce factual and unbiased research. They brought lawsuits arguing that fairness, the Bill of Rights, and equal protection under the law applied to all citizens, not just to heterosexuals. As a result, the early gay rights movement won its first huge victory—a vote by the American Psychiatric Association removing homosexuality from its list of mental disorders in 1973. This was a win with great legislative consequence, because the laws of the time codified this defamatory characterization of gay people in all sorts of statutes. And it was a huge cultural victory as well, as it enabled gay people to begin the difficult task of confronting the internalized shame and self-hatred so many of us grew up with.

But the early gay liberationists also knew that knowledge would not be transformational if it was limited to self-awareness. They believed in changing public consciousness, and the gay liberation movement of the 1960s and 1970s prioritized a simple form of knowledge-building about LGBT people borrowed from the women's movement: the women's movement slogan of the "personal is political" was transformed into "come out, come out, wherever you are." The coming-out strategy, a process of self-determination, of going public with something you were told should be kept shameful and private, was a huge and brilliant success. As people came out about their sexual orientation, and, more recently, about their gender identities, to their loved ones, families, workplaces, and churches, these family members realized we were not aliens, not at all the *other*, but simply their siblings, their children, and their friends. We began to be seen as part of the diversity that constitutes *human* being. People are still coming out every day, and still facing some of the stigma and shame encountered by activists in earlier decades. Yet, millions of us who are out can also lay claim to the changes in attitudes and public opinion achieved over the past several decades.

LGBT politics bears witness to many moments in which acts of faith were committed. Another early act of faith in the history of the movement was the formation of national LGBT organizations like Lambda Legal Defense and Education Fund and the National Gay and Lesbian Task Force, both founded in 1973. Could any of Lambda Legal's founders have envisioned then that, nearly four decades later, Lambda would win the freedom to marry for gay men and lesbians in Iowa? Did the founders of the Task Force imagine that in 1989, it would win the first federal bill to include sexual orientation, the Federal Hate Crime Statistics Act? I think they did imagine these changes because they understood the third critical lesson of activism: you have to get organized if you want to win change.

We got organized as lawyers, as voters and grassroots organizers, in our workplaces and unions, in our churches, in the media, in universities, schools, and in political campaigns. We formed all sorts of local, state, and national organizations. We began to reach out to allies and ask for help. LGBT activism became broad and deep. Gay people organized wherever they found resistance and as a result there are gay sports leagues and gay choruses; LGBT synagogues and seminarians; LGBT media and gay rodeos. It is hard to remember that just three short decades ago, the community behind these flourishing entities had practically no public visibility, few cultural spaces in which to meet or connect, barely a political presence in state capitols across the country, and very few political friends.

Of course, the past several years have also taught the LGBT community and other social justice movements that there is nothing unidirectional about social change. It goes forward and backward, and while we sometimes have the power to win, we also have shown we lack the power to preserve those gains. So we won equal marriage rights in California by legislation, only to see then-Governor Schwarzenegger veto the bill. We won the same rights through the courts, only to see the voters overturn them in 2008. And while we have won marriage equality in some states so far, we have also seen more than thirty states enact anti-marriage amendments to their constitutions, which will take years to overturn through the ballot box.

This brings me to the fourth lesson for activists working for social justice and LGBT rights to remember: working for social justice is a marathon, not a sprint. The long view is not something I held onto when I was twenty years old. My motto was embodied in a great punk anthem I often played, by the band Television: "What I want, I want now, and that's a whole lot more than 'anyhow.'"[178] In my fifties, I have realized there is no contradiction between wanting it all *now* and committing to disciplined organizing. How do you win ballot initiatives? Through door knocking to identify voters positions, through tireless efforts to talk to people at every community gathering place, through grassroots get-out-the-vote drives, through field and district leaders who encourage their friends and neighbors to vote, and through effective and focused messages that are repeated by every level of a campaign. There is no shortcut to that kind of process. Indeed, the process of organizing is as important as the outcome of a win because it builds leadership and a lasting organizational infrastructure that can be mobilized again. One of the reasons we lost the marriage vote in California was that there was not enough of this kind of grassroots organizing done in parts of the state that did not have large LGBT communities and populations. We did not effectively reach out to our allies inside progressive faith communities, or even within our own extended families. But we will change that, because this is a marathon and not a short race.

A fifth important lesson to being an activist is to know your enemies. This is a deceptive axiom. While there are opponents to the goals of the LGBT movement, and we must understand and refute their arguments, the truth is that you have to be prepared as an activist to have all your assumptions about the enemy blown away by experience.

Let me share a story to illustrate this lesson. I spoke at a university near Richmond, VA many years ago and the day after my talk I had an early morning flight. It was still dark outside at 4:30 A.M. when a taxi picked me up at the hotel to drive me the thirty minutes to the airport. My driver was my stereotype of a Southern homophobe, and he eyed me warily from the rear-view mirror. He asked whether this was my first trip to Richmond, and I said no, indeed it was not. What had I been doing here? He asked. I told him I had given a talk.

"You spoke at the university?"

"Yes, I did."

"About what?"

So I took a deep breath and said, "Well, I spoke about the lesbian, gay, bisexual, and transgender rights movement, because I am a gay activist and I work for the National Gay and Lesbian Task Force."

He squinted at me in the mirror and said, "You a lesbian?"

I thought to myself, here goes, and said, "Yes, I am."

And without missing a beat, he started to tell me about the most prominent lesbian mother custody case in Virginia, the Sharon Bottoms case, with which I was very familiar. He said, "You know, we got a case here, where this lesbian is being sued by her own mother for custody of her children because her own mother says she is not a suitable parent." He paused dramatically and eyed me in the mirror before adding, "Hell, she raised a lesbian; what makes her think she's going to be such a good parent!" And he laughed hard, as did I.

Then he proceeded to tell me how appalling he found that case, because if one of his own kids were to tell him they were gay, and he had four of them, mind you, he would never disown any of them.

Lesson learned about my own wrong-headed assumptions. That taxi driver was not my enemy. The ordinary people whom we encounter in our lives are often extraordinarily sensible and fair, especially if they can put themselves in our shoes. But while ordinary people who may disagree, or even organize against us, are not the enemy of social justice advocates, the values and policies for which they organize are indeed anathema to the LGBT movement's view of social and economic justice, specifically the values of the anti-democratic, authoritarian, and theocratic right wing. The authoritarian right wing is not dead, and it is still dangerous. Yet, LGBT people are among a minority for whom the cultural and political defeat of the right wing globally remains a top priority.

Issues like transgender inclusion, which challenge fundamental assumptions about gender as an either/or, or issues like same-sex marriage, challenge and broaden the moral assumptions underlying ideas about human rights. This is the sixth lesson I wanted to share with you, that rights have a moral basis and this framework must be addressed in order for the notion of human rights to be expanded to include gender and sexual justice. Battles for justice are often fought on the moral plain, and not just the legal and political realm. Indeed, some faith-based advocates are pushing back against today's limitations on public support for human needs like food, shelter, and security from a moral lens.

Morality is about ethical choices. What do we value? What do we not value? Which threats do we prioritize and which ones ignore? When do we turn to tradition and when should we turn away? The morality we need at this crucial time is not the "faith of our fathers" nor the "traditional values" of our mothers. It will not be found in the exclusionary forms of fundamentalist religions dividing the world today, even when it is disguised in the rhetoric of community and love. The moral values we need today can be found emerging from people who are creating movements for social justice around the world—accountability, pluralism, democratic participation, human rights, rule of law, caring, and environmental sustainability. These movements put their faith in imagination, not tradition. Their leaders are the visionaries who are creating solutions to all sorts of threats and risks. Social justice movements remind us that our care and stewardship of the environment must shift toward sustainability away from mere profit. And they challenge us to affirm the moral worth, and basic goodness, of LGBT people.

This is a lesson that the LGBT movement has struggled to learn. The evidence of our history is clear that the precondition to the achievement of our full human rights is both cultural and legal change. LGBT people will continue to lose at the polls if we fail to contest the denigration of our lives by religious leaders and by those who believe they are interpreting the great moral codes. California, Arizona, and Arkansas revealed that the movement for civil and political equality for LGBT people has run into the buzz saw of moral condemnation—the famous "millennia of moral teachings," which the U.S. Supreme Court invoked in the *Bowers v. Hardwick* case in 1986, when it upheld Georgia's sodomy law. LGBT people have to engage with religion and engage the anti-gay arguments made against them on terms of moral equality and fundamental human rights, rather than avoiding these issues.

A perspective that grounds our aspirations in the moral basis of human rights leads to a seventh lesson from years of LGBT activism: that social justice in the U.S. cannot be achieved unless we challenge and end racism. America's history of slavery created structures and residues that continue to affect our society to this day. The history of American racial prejudice is littered with examples of how government regulations engineered the families of immigrants, African Americans, and other low-income people. From calls for sterilization of people of color or low-income women, to Moynihan's 1964 report on how to address decline in the black family, to the welfare policies of the 1990s welfare reform that punish certain kinds of family and reward others—all are deeply racist measures promoted by the U.S. government to regulate low-income families in general, and families of color in particular. These efforts to constrain and contain family forms in communities of color through government policy are linked to the efforts to ban our access to the institutions of family formation and protection. Not only are they linked by the same forces being behind them, namely the right wing, but they are also linked in policy terms: when government can mandate one form of family as its sole desirable form, we all suffer.

Today's racism pretends to be colorblind and it has colored tokens like Condoleezza Rice and Ward Connerly as its spokespersons. It is embodied in cartoons, talk-radio rants, and racist imagery denigrating President Obama and the First Lady. Today's racism blames the immigrant for taking jobs and argues for a closing of the borders for some, while offering an open door to anyone with money. For LGBT people, the lesson of the importance of racism was driven home again in the aftermath of the 2008 elections. LGBT leaders and institutions that build meaningful relationships with allies in communities of color will be able to win at the ballot box and in the streets. This in turn will happen only when LGBT people of color leaders have greater power, voice, and visibility of LGBT people of color within both communities of color and within the LGBT movement.

I think the experience of LGBT people with family issues leads me to an eighth lesson learned: social justice advocates need to have vision, which is in key ways faith-based. Politics at its most inspired is about organizing with a vision. Vision is present every time an activist imagines some goal, institution, or idea that goes against the dominant grain. Both vision and faith are qualities that advocates for social justice and LGBT activists urgently need today. To claim that we want equality and that we are mainstream is not to articulate a vision, it is to state an extremely obvious fact. To seek to move the moveable middle is not a vision, it is an electoral strategy to get to 51%. Vision is found in the work that activists have done to change school systems. It is found in the creative policies that seek to expand family forms and extend them to a larger number of families. Vision is found in the creative advocacy to educate and counter homophobia within religious denominations. It is found in the thriving cultural work of LGBT artists and poets and writers.

Vision requires a clear-headed assessment of the political landscape in which we find ourselves. Several years ago, LGBT grassroots activists were grappling with the fact that the legitimacy and power of the federal state had eroded. Local governments (city, county, and state) were increasingly the sites of new power and opportunity. In addition, we recognized that the arenas of engagement in our ongoing battle against homophobia were not limited to legislatures or courts. The media, the church, the synagogue, the school, the family, the neighborhood, the workplace were all places in which great change was needed. The old paradigm of politics as primarily focused on law making and rule shifting at the federal level needed to change to accommodate the new paradigm of politics as rule and culture shifting taking place at the state and local level. This is why the LGBT movement refocused at the state and local level, and I would argue became more effective: because it has the vision to understand the importance of the local.

Vision often requires courage because it can take you against the grain. And this is a ninth lesson I have learned: to be effective as a political activist, *you have to have courage*. In a classic sermon at the Ebenezer Baptist Church entitled "Antidotes for Fear," Dr. King wrote that courage, love, and faith were the chief antidotes to fear. He described how faith could help overcome the spiritual fear that one has *"deficient resources and…a consequent inadequacy for life."* [179] He went on to credit the importance of psychiatry in dealing with fears arising from damaged self-esteem but argued that faith, and in this instance he was speaking of religious faith or a faith in God, was itself essential to overcoming fear, to finding courage and finding the motivation to carry on a sustained political struggle.

Fear mediates and governs the lives of ordinary LGBT people. We encounter that fear in a million ways: the cultural fear of our open homosexuality or bisexuality or transgender nature is present everywhere; we live in a culture that is terrified of the consequences that our open lives will have on its values, its way of life, its peace of mind. Gay people to this day must confront fear at every step as they decide how out to be: Will I be understood? Will I be happy? Will the ones I respect and love accept me? Will my parents understand? Will my boss understand? Will my employees accept me? Will I experience violence and be attacked? Will I lose my children? New generations of LGBT people still come to awareness of their sexuality inside this context of fear. Another kind of fear we face is the fear of disclosure. Most of our community fears disclosure more than it fears eternal damnation. These personal experiences of fear are the places where your ministry and your loud and proud affirmation of LGBT people are most needed! We need the Reconciling Ministries movement and all pro-LGBT faith-based groups to be militant and loud in their love and affirmation of LGBT people and in their advocacy for equal rights.

But to me the most paralyzing fear that LGBT people face as a movement today is found in the failure of progressive LGBT people to articulate their values and vision. We are a movement afraid of owning our unique queerness, our roots in feminism, our challenge to gender roles and gender rigidity. We are a movement that believes that sexuality is human and divinely given and not bad, yet we are a movement running away from these issues when it comes to arguments about women's sexual and reproductive autonomy, desire and pleasure, or the goodness of a healthy sexuality. This is a fear of what they will say about and think about us. This is a self–censoring fear that is paralyzing us from truly rebutting the outrageous untruths and defamatory lies that the right puts out about our sexuality.

This avoidance stems from our fear of and our lack of faith in straight people. It stems from our fear of the right wing. And ultimately, it reflects a lack of faith in ourselves—in our own goodness and decency and integrity. Our sexual selves are nothing to be ashamed of.

I find great courage in the leadership of grassroots activists. I saw it in the 1980s during the struggle to get the government to respond to HIV/AIDS. People engaged in amazing acts of daily heroism, in the care that volunteers provided to complete strangers living with HIV long before we knew that there was any chance of treatments. I can see courage in the eyes of a gay leader from Nepal named Sunil Pant. Sunil's quiet and effective leadership has brought him to the national assembly of Nepal as an elected official and brought that country to the opportunity of becoming the sixth nation to include homosexuality in its national constitution. Nepal is about to do something that the United States remains far from doing.

Sunil has guts. But you know, so does that straight young person who organizes a Day of Silence against homophobia at her school. Courage is in the heart of the pastor who stands up and condemns anti-gay violence in a fundamentalist church. It can be found in the Unitarian Universalist Association's steady and growing support of LGBT equality over the years.

And this brings me to the final lesson I wanted to share with you from years of LGBT organizing, the lesson that *justice means intersectional practice*. Progressive politics is an optimistic politics that believes that through democratic participation, debate, and innovation, the institutions that reproduce inequality can be transformed. Progressives are people who believe, that justice is not severable: we cannot get ours without standing up for and beside others seeking theirs. Justice implies remedies, redress for wrongs done, a fair standard by which claims are evaluated. Any sober assessment of the status of LGBT people, of women, of people of color, of poor people, of immigrants, of those dispossessed of economic power reveals that justice is an ideal we have not achieved. And it is a harder and harder idea for us to believe in. It takes a lot of faith to believe in the possibility of achieving a more just economic system as banks merge, and microchips reign, and those of us with assets and homes and jobs worry about our security and the future that many of our fellow citizens have given up on ever seeing. It is in fact only blind and raw faith in the idea that justice exists beyond nation or law or police state, that something called a spiritual justice does exist, that keeps me believing that I can in my lifetime achieve a society where all people have affordable health care, food, work, shelter, access to education, and freedom.

But here is where faith is not enough and where we need the action that politics represents. We stand at a crossroads as a movement. Down one road lies the pursuit of narrow self-interest, single identity, and the old paradigm of LGBT politics as we have been practicing it for the past three decades. Down the other road lies the pursuit of a just society. Both roads are legitimate but they do represent a clear choice in tactics and strategy and goal.

Standing against us on either road is the same enemy: the theocratic right and supremacists of all kinds (racial, sexual, gender, religious, as well as powerful forces that place profit above human lives). Against these opponents, a politics of cooptation, adaptation, and friendship is not plausible. We need a practical politics of cultural engagement and resistance: organized both locally and at the state level, premised on the idea of alliance, and committed to transformation. We need to commit an act of faith.

To advance we must never forget the connection we each have as people committed to human rights, we must put our bodies and hearts on the line and into the struggle for racial justice, women's equality, and rights of all people on the margins to fair and just treatment.

To advance, we must support each other across our political divides, because we are ourselves a coalition. We must in short take a leap of faith.

BEYOND THE WEDDING RING
LGBT Politics in the Age of Obama[180]

This talk represented my attempt to make sense of the Obama Administration, one year into the first term. It was written after the economic collapse of 2008, but before the 2010 elections further consolidated the power of the far right at the national level, and it was given at Washington University St. Louis in October of 2009. At the time it was given, critical advances made by the LGBT movement at the national level on military repeal, in the Administration's eventual opposition to the federal Defense of Marriage Act (DOMA), in U.S. foreign policy and U.S. foreign assistance, and within a range of federal agencies had not occurred and seemed far from assured. The talk traced lessons from LGBT history and sought to place that experience within the larger context of economic volatility and xenophobia.

In the two years since this was originally written, President Obama has proved himself to be a staunch ally to LGBT people. Curiously, many in the community cite his caution and equivocation on LGBT issues (like marriage) more than they credit the unprecedented progress that the LGBT equality movement has made under his leadership.

This is attributable to the style of leadership the President embraces—a detached, third party-intermediary approach that allows others to lead while allowing him to maintain some plausible deniability. It is leadership guided more by branding (image, appearance, symbols) rather than values (insistence on progressive values, direct engagement with policy). It is a cousin of the destructive democratic centrism popularized by former President Bill Clinton, who so often compromised core values to win a few points at the polls. But politics in the age of Obama has failed even more abjectly than the Clinton-era centrism for one reason: the right wing is stronger, bolder, and richer today than it was then. Centrist compromises cannot be won if opponents have no interest in reaching an accommodation. Like Clinton, or Jimmy Carter for that matter, President Obama mystified many of his supporters by refusing to nurture and sustain the base that elected him. As a result, his re-election in 2012 is more imperiled than his performance warrants.

This talk also reflects my long-standing interest in strengthening social justice infrastructure to counteract the impact of the massive right-wing idea machine that dominates public discourse today—through its corporate-oriented think tanks, hydra-headed media organs all repeating the same message, carefully built pseudo-scholarship, political activist training programs, get-out-the-vote mechanisms, and attack-dog mindset. The left in this country began to counter this ruthless and authoritarian movement for corporate domination only in the late 1990s, through investments by a handful of donors in a competing infrastructure. I pushed hard inside progressive philanthropy for such investments to build institutions that could advance social justice. But, until the grassroots emergence of the Occupy Wall Street movement, the progressive movement and fledgling infrastructure had little visibility or emotional traction with ordinary Americans. This may be changing, but nothing about the future of progressive outcomes is guaranteed. The left faces a disciplined opposition that has a simple and primal objective: to preserve the wealth and power of its financiers. What is a progressive LGBT movement to do?

In 2009, I attended a meeting of foundations that work in

or are based in Europe. At the start of the meeting, Giorgio Napolitano, then President of Italy welcomed the group. In a particularly pointed statement widely reported in the Italian press, President Napolitano spoke about the danger of the rising wave of xenophobia sweeping Europe. Xenophobia—the fear of the stranger. He noted that Italy itself had just enacted strict new laws criminalizing many immigrants and that this was a dangerous trend with echoes of Italy's chauvinistic past. As I thought about his remarks, I read in the paper about a range of laws being proposed across Italy, which range from restricting social services only to Italian citizens, to restricting the right to sit on a subway seat to national-born residents of Milan.

History is replete with the violent legacy of manipulated xenophobia. Fascist regimes in Europe from the '20s and '30s to the regime in Serbia in the '80s have ridden to power on the brilliant exploitation of the fear or hatred of the foreigner, the other, the outsider, the pariah, the weak, and the one who is different. Schoolyard bullies and masculinist social movements all thrive on the exploitation of each of our desire to fit in, to belong, and to be safe and secure. They count on our own fear of insecurity for their success.

If you think I overstate the case, just look at the laws passed by 20th century fascist regimes. A claim to an idealized notion of national identity that must be preserved from dilution or purified lies at the root of every authoritarian movement, from the KKK to the Nationalist parties gaining ground in Europe, lies at the root of every genocidal regime, from Bosnia to Darfur to Rwanda.

From Rome to Grand Rapids, from Texas to London, the world is facing an anxious time. The old order is crumbling. The old ways are threatened. Dead-end systems of domination like the violent repression of women and the exploitation of race, gender, sexuality, or other natural human difference to divide us from each other are no longer succeeding in keeping women silent, in preventing America from electing an African American

President, in keeping fair- minded people from seeing gayness as part of the spectrum of human being.

The old systems of economic and social control—where wealth and jobs and the economy are manipulated to enforce the power of some over the power of many—are collapsing under the weight of their fraud and fundamental dishonesty.

The power of violence and terror to keep us all in fear is diminishing as ordinary people stand up and say no more violence. We want to live in peace and dignity. The dividing lines are blurring and that is threatening the powers that have had control of wealth this whole time.

This collapsing of the old order is the most hopeful of signs and it is the reason that the blame game is all that opponents of social and economic justice have to offer. They are engaging in blaming and hateful actions in earnest and they must be called out and challenged.

The thing about blaming immigrants for all sorts of social ills is how crazy the logic is behind such arguments. As if the guest workers who came to Europe to work—at the urging of European governments—are to blame for anything more than wanting to improve their lives. As if the guest workers who came to Michigan to work in the asparagus fields are the cause of the demise of the auto industry. As if the Indian doctors and professionals who came here in the 1960s, like my parents, who paid their taxes and raised their kids to be citizens who loved this country, as if they are alien to the ideal of America instead of the embodiment of that very ideal.

Why do I start with this meditation on migration and racism? Why draw connections between the global battle underway to recognize that migrants—documented or undocumented—deserve to be seen as people and not as demons, and the global battle underway to recognize the humanity and full political and moral equality of LGBT people? I do so because there are such deep connections to our two struggles.

If xenophobia prevails, you and I are endangered. The

online Merriam-Webster's dictionary defines xenophobia as "the fear or hatred of strangers or foreigners or of anything that is strange or foreign." It is an intimate cousin to homophobia—the irrational fear and anxiety and even hatred of homosexuality; to racism (the systems that structurally exclude and create barriers to opportunity and participation for people of certain races and backgrounds because of a notion that they are inferior to others); and to sexism (the systems that structurally enforce women's subordination to men).

Whenever racism masquerades as the rule of law, every person is threatened with the immorality of that act. When women are violated brutally, as we are being every day in every country from the U.S. to the Congo, when we are regarded as less important or less equal, men are damaged and harmed as well. And when gay, lesbian, bisexual, and transgender people are treated as second-class citizens in a society that is not a theocratic state, our very liberty and most-cherished values are endangered.

At the time my family came to the U.S. in 1966, my visa was called the "green card" and it designated my status as "Permanent Resident Alien." I became a naturalized citizen when I turned eighteen but I have often reflected that gay people in America essentially live on a green card—we are Permanent Resident Aliens. LGBT people have the burdens but not the benefits of full citizenship. We pay taxes, but transgender people still cannot serve in the military. We vote heavily in elections and were a significant part of the majority that elected President Obama, but are shunned by some Democrats and even moderate Republicans who seem more afraid of our opponents than they are interested in our support. We are law-abiding, follow the rules, and try to do the right thing, but we are routinely rounded up, turned in and turned over to the authorities for persecution, as we are whenever our most fundamental, personal, and basic rights—to be free, to work, to form family—are put up for a popular vote.

We come out in schools only to be assaulted by the bullies and thugs who cannot handle the truth. We make families only to risk having them destroyed by legal attacks that prevent us from parenting, strip us of the right to be recognized as domestic partners, deny us equal marriage rights, and defame us as sinners. And we live in communities like this one—all across America, we take care of our neighbors, we sing in our church choirs, we give our time and love to our civic and political institutions, only to be told that we are bad people, that we should be ashamed, that we should not come out, that we are doing something horrible—by simply saying we want to live our lives in peace.

Arguments Against Homosexuality

In the more than forty years since the Stonewall Rebellion, LGBT people have won many key cultural, legal and political victories as a movement. Essentially four anti-gay arguments have been used against LGBT people for decades. They have said we are sick, that we are criminal, that we are sinful, and that we are immoral. These same four arguments are still deployed against LGBT people in the U.S. and around the world, and they still seem to carry weight. It is worth exploring the resonance of each of these arguments as a threshold matter to understand the true status of LGBT equality.

You may know that in the U.S., the de-stigmatization of gayness as a mental illness was achieved quite recently in 1973. The American Psychiatric Association's removal of homosexuality from the list of mental disorders paved the way for legal and social attitudes to change. Until then, homosexuality was categorized as a mental illness; LGBT persons were routinely "treated" with shock therapy, drugs, and incarceration. This notion of illness was codified in scores of statutes banning gay people from immigrating to the US among other things, a barrier itself removed only in 1991. And the fight still continues. Categories like gender identity disorder remain contested and biased. Around the world, LGBT people are still regarded as sick, characterized as ill, and forcibly imprisoned. In the U.S., there is still a large domestic movement that proposes that gay people are ill, need to be treated and converted from their homosexuality through so-called reparative therapy. The idea that LGBT people are sick and pathological is at the heart of many anti-gay electoral campaigns. And most shocking to me is that I still meet people, young and old, who tell me stories of being sent to mental hospitals to get shock therapy and other "treatments" to cure them of their homosexuality.

Similarly, the argument that LGBT people are criminals still has resonance today. Efforts to decriminalize sexual behavior remain a main political goal of the LGBT movement globally—because seventy-six countries still criminalize same-sex sexuality. In the U.S., most forms of private same-sex behavior were decriminalized in 2003, through the U.S. Supreme Court ruling in *Lawrence v. Texas*. The Indian Supreme Court ruled in 2009 that India's sodomy law was unconstitutional (and of course there is an effort to reinstate it). An estimated seven nations still have the death penalty for homosexuality—and in recent years, a sweeping bill has been proposed in Uganda that would, among other things, criminalize any support for LGBT human rights and put a death penalty provision into the Ugandan law.

The argument that LGBT people are sinful is leveled against gay people in every country, and from every faith tradition, no matter how differently that faith's version of sin might be expressed. The good news is that there is a vigorous fight about this characterization of gayness in every faith tradition, with advocates who are spiritually based challenging the underlying premise that god's love is not available to LGBT people. All religious traditions speak of love as a force for transformation, as the source for meaning in our life, as a force for wholeness and peace in the world. And given the centrality of love to every religious tradition, there is a profound irony to the demonization of a movement based on a right to love and be loved. Reconciling this injunction to love with their practice of preaching intolerance has led religious leaders to contortions like "love the sinner/hate the sin." Yet, if we believe that love is not a sin, then offering an act of love cannot be a sin. If we are of God and sex is of God then the reduction of same-sex love to an "abomination" is an act of selective condemnation, rendered to enhance the secular power of those making this argument.

The hostility towards LGBT people by religious institutions has another direct and practical secular result—data show that those who attend anti-gay houses of worship are themselves less supportive of LGBT human rights than those who attend houses of worship that are more supportive and welcoming. Yet, in the face of this hostility there is a vibrant and growing minority movement that is striving to become the majoritarian voice in denominations like the Episcopal and Methodist churches. The United Church of Christ (UCC), the Unitarians, the Metropolitan Community Church (MCC), some Quakers, Reform Judaism, and now a growing number of conservative Jewish institutions are among those leading this movement. The argument is being carried inside the conventions and regulatory bodies of many religious denominations. Congregations across the country are striving to be more welcoming of their LGBT members, coalitions of clergy and faith leaders are lending their voices to anti-violence measures and nondiscrimination laws, while seminaries and houses of religious training and religious scholars are enlivening our understanding of religious traditions by countering fundamentalist interpretations with other, sound, theological frameworks. This vital and growing pro-LGBT faith movement in this country needs much more energy, visibility, support, and resourcing.

Closely related to the sinfulness argument is the final anti-gay argument made against LGBT people—the claim that LGBT people are immoral. Several years ago, then-Chairman of the Joint Chiefs of Staff, General Peter Pace, made a fascinating set of remarks about the immorality of gay behavior, and he seemed to cite this as a reason not to change the military policy of discrimination. He said: "I believe homosexual acts between two individuals are immoral and that we should not condone immoral act... I do not believe the United States is well served by a policy that says it is OK to be immoral in any way. As an individual, I would not want [acceptance of gay behavior] to be our policy, just like I would not want it to be our policy that if we were to find out that so-and-so was sleeping with somebody else's wife, that we would just look the other way, which we do not. We prosecute that kind of immoral behavior."[181]

Pace expressed an individual opinion and a larger cultural attitude. The view that gayness itself is somehow wrong, dangerous to social order, and bad is the most significant barrier facing LGBT people. It lies at the root of every anti-gay policy or position. Moral disapproval against us has, until very recently, stayed fairly constant over time, as data from the National Opinion Research Center at the University of Chicago and the General Social Survey shows. Since 1972, participants have been asked, "What about sexual relations between two adults of the same sex—do you think it is always wrong, almost always wrong, wrong only sometimes, or not wrong at all?" In 2004, 56% of those surveyed said homosexuality was always wrong, in 2006 that number was 53%, and by 2010, it had dropped to 44%. Another 41% of those surveyed agreed with the statement that same sex sexual relations were "not wrong at all" a gain of nearly 27% since 1991. But, as the researchers from the University of Chicago's National Opinion Research Center observed, public opinion on homosexuality remains "highly polarized."[182]

The moral denigration of homosexuality prevents LGBT people from being seen as the great parents, neighbors, citizens, and family members they often are. It allows straight voters to bifurcate their views. How often have you heard, "I got nothing against gays, I just don't think it's right." The notion that there is something wrong with gayness, and that it would be dangerous to allow it to be openly accepted, in turn sanctions the high and intolerable levels of violence that LGBT people experience.

The moral condemnation of homosexuality transcends particular religions, countries, ideologies, skin color, and even deep-seated nationalist or fundamentalist hatreds. For example, when the little gay community center in Jerusalem (Jerusalem Open House) sought to produce the World LGBT Pride celebration in 2006, *all* religions in Jerusalem came together despite centuries of animosity towards each other to condemn the event. Somewhere I saved the photo of all these religions leaders united only by their condemnation of the lovely gay community in Jerusalem. The Pride celebration happened in 2007, and it was indeed marred by violence, when an orthodox individual stabbed several marchers. But Jerusalem Open House perseveres, and has expanded its work to include an overt focus on religious organizing.

Anti-gay moral arguments derive primarily from religious interpretations that characterize our desire as a violation of the divine code. It arises from an association of sex with something dirty and bad. And it also derives from the effort to control sexuality and women's autonomy—a driving objective and underpinning of every religious tradition. It's worth thinking a lot about how the fear of women's independence and the leveling of arguments about immorality against women who are sexually active is related to the use of the same arguments against gay people. Sex and gender, indeed the body, are key battlegrounds for arguments over morality. LGBT people have to engage with religion and engage the anti-gay arguments made against them on terms of moral equality and fundamental human rights, rather than avoiding these issues. Until LGBT people confront and challenge the moral opposition to gayness, until gay activists demand and command the respect of straight families, colleagues, and friends, until LGBT people come out and claim their rightful place everywhere, until allies and gay people themselves stop believing those who defame, denigrate and deny the humanity and goodness of LGBT people, the

LGBT social justice movement cannot win full human rights.

State of LGBT Rights

Overall, two curious things happened in 2008 on LGBT specific issues: first, LGBT people continued to constitute a large portion of the progressive electorate and contributed heavily to progressive wins; and second, LGBT rights lost heavily on several ballot measures.

The lesbian, gay, and bisexual (LGB) vote was a significant segment of the overall vote in 2008 elections—constituting 4% of the national electorate (a number gathered via self-identification at exit polls).[183] Data on transgender people continued not to be gathered in exit polls. A total of 4% of all votes cast in 2008 would mean that out of 122,698,661 million voters in the national election, 4,907,946 were LGB. Seventy percent of those LGB votes went to Barack Obama, making gay voters second only to black voters in their support for President Obama. It must also be noted that 27% of the LGB vote in 2008 went to John McCain—confirming what exit polls and political analysts have shown since 1990—that at least one-fourth to one-third of the LGB vote supports Republicans, depending on the candidate and the positions of the Party at the time.[184]

Yet, the 2008 elections also exposed the weakness of LGBT political power as key ballot initiatives lost in California, Arkansas, and Arizona. Overall in 2008, as the Ballot Initiative Strategy Center (BISC) documented, voters rejected right wing ballot measures. According to BISC, there were one hundred fifty-three total ballot measures in thirty-five states in 2008, and twenty-six were right wing backed. But "only 6 of the 26 rightwing or conservative backed initiatives were approved by voters—a passage rate of 23%." Another twenty-nine measures promoted by conservatives failed to quality for the ballot, "an early indication that much of the extreme ideas put forth in 2008 via initiative were out of sync with voter's priorities," according to BISC.[185]

The bad news was that same sex marriage rights in California were defeated by a margin of about six hundred thousand votes, or 4.6% percent of the overall vote. (Support for the anti-gay measure garnered seven million votes, or 52.3% of the total while opposition to the measure secured about six million and four hundred thousand votes, 47.7%). The anti-same-sex marriage amendment passed in Arizona by 12% points, or by two hundred and forty eight thousand votes. The anti-same-sex marriage amendment passed more emphatically in Florida by 24% points, or by more than 1.6 million votes. And a measure in Arkansas that banned unmarried couples and single people from being adoptive parents won by 14% points, or by nearly one hundred and forty-two thousand votes.[186]

The LGBT community lost each of these issues because of the active and deeply funded organizing clout of the anti-gay religious right and the anti-gay conservative movement. Two major churches made an alliance to fund the anti-marriage ban—the Mormon Church and the Catholic Church. According to the Los Angeles Times, the Mormon Church alone was estimated to have raised more than 40% of the $31 million reported raised as of the last pre-initiative filing deadline on October of 2008.[187] They were joined by the grassroots mobilization of evangelical protestant denominations and leaders, many of whom have long made a career out of condemning homosexuality. The conservative right represented by groups like Focus on the Family, Concerned Women for America, the American Family Association, and the National Republican Party—all of whom used homophobic messages and tactics to scare voters into voting against gay people's lives—piled on to the homophobia bandwagon.

Interestingly, LGBT rights also lost because of racism. The New York Times noted that many polls had expected the Arkansas anti-gay adoption measure to fail, but it passed in large part because potential moderate voters stayed away because they did not like Obama and because "conservatives mounted a grassroots campaign, mainly through church groups that framed the state's case-by-case approach to adoption requests as an affront to traditional values."[188]

A closer analysis of the key losses and the way certain communities and age groups within them voted on these measures suggest several lessons to be gleaned from these defeats.

For one, fear and the exploitation of fear remain successful tools in ballot measure campaigns and electoral efforts that put gay rights on the ballot box. More precisely, a hysteria about kids and homosexuality as a danger to children underlies a number of these anti-gay messaging campaigns. Support for gay rights is always characterized as being bad for children. This was a huge part of the right's anti-gay marriage campaign in California. This was clearly the message of the Arkansas measure. And this is a huge part of the right's strategy in the local anti-discrimination fights it has brought in Gainesville, FL and in Kalamazoo, MI; in both instances opponents of LGBT rights focused on the idea that transgender people could use the same bathrooms as non-gay folks. (Voters defeated both anti-gay efforts in 2009.)

This is an old trope—from Anita Bryant in 1977 to today, the danger-to-children argument is designed to scare and silence and distract. It comes from the reality of pedophilia, but instead of being directed at getting people to avoid the Catholic Church or avoid being parented by straight men, who are the largest perpetrators of child abuse, it is redirected at gay people. One of the key challenges facing the movement is how effectively it counters this homophobic set of arguments.

A second lesson to learn from 2008 elections is that the LGBT movement must not be silent or inactive on issues of racial and economic justice. These issues impact our own communities. But even more importantly, social justice is the ground for which LGBT people are fighting and from which this movement emerges. Economic and racial justice is integral to LGBT equality and these issues are essential to the justice coalition of which the movement is a member. We must work for social and racial justice in order to secure our own freedom. The 2008 elections in California revealed that when LGBT people avoided engaging with communities of color or issues of racial justice as a movement, it would lose. Interestingly, some activists characterized the loss of Proposition 8 as a symptom of "black homophobia." But it would have been just as accurate to say this loss was a consequence of "white homophobia"— after all, 63% of the electorate in California was white and 49% voted against LGBT rights. In addition, 64% of white Catholic voters voted overwhelmingly against the measure—as did 65% of white Protestants. Indeed, neither characterization is correct. Same-sex marriage in California lost because the movement did not do a good enough job in organizing, and because it failed to refute a key argument made by opponents: that same-sex marriage would be harmful to children. The LGBT movement did not effectively mobilize its allies, did not organize people of faith well, and wrongly assumed that more people of color would support LGBT rights. This is in marked contrast to the right, which attended to each of these arenas.

A third lesson from the past several decades and election lesson from the defeat of the ballot initiatives is that defeats of gay rights create growth in the LGBT movement. This happened in 1986 when the Supreme Court upheld the Georgia sodomy law in *Bowers v. Hardwick*; or when the government's hostile response to the emergence of HIV/AIDS spurred the formation of the ACT UP in 1987; or when anti-gay violence rose to the national agenda with the murder of Matthew Shepard. A new LGBT and allied mobilization was born out of the defeats of 2008.

A fourth lesson from the elections is that an agenda that focuses only on marriage is too limited and damages the full range of what LGBT need and want. It would certainly be easy for me to simply stand here and talk about the LGBT agenda in the language of marriage equality alone—that is a part of what the movement seeks. However, to do so would give an incomplete picture of the agenda of this movement and the needs of LGBT people. There is a fuller equality agenda in the LGBT movement that remains to be won. It includes:

1. Workplace equality—reflected in things like the enactment of a federal executive order banning discrimination based on sexual orientation and gender identity in employment and the conduct of federal contracts; and ultimately the passage of a federal nondiscrimination law that is comprehensive, covers employment, housing, and other areas of our lives and that includes sexual orientation and gender identity.

2. Military equality—reflected in the repeal of "Don't Ask, Don't Tell" and inclusion of transgender service.

3. Family equality to recognize the myriad ways that LGBT families are denied federal benefits they have earned and deserve; a repeal of DOMA so that states that have enacted same-sex marriages can have their marriages recognized.

4. Fair treatment for People with HIV and adequate funding for the demands of this global epidemic— the Department of Health and Human Services (HHS) should lift its ban on federal dollars going to support HIV prevention aimed at gay men and men who have sex with men; the global HIV/AIDS commitment the U.S. has made should be robust and not cut.

5. Increased attention and resources for LGBT homeless youth, LGBT seniors, African-American gay men who are HIV-positive or at risk, and LGBT health and social service institutions on the front lines.

6. Family reunification and immigration equality—to allow partners of same-sex couples the right to be united with their families.
7. Safety and security—reflected in support for all victims of crime and a focus on organizing to challenge the roots of violence.
8. Promotion of human rights around the world, starting with strong leadership from the State Department to promote LGBT human rights around the world.

This agenda is not pie in the sky and provides lots of opportunities for activism and involvement. But even this basic equality agenda does not do justice to the range of desires for freedom in the LGBT movement, to the dreams we have of a really different world.

The LGBT movement has different histories that often get collapsed into or captured by the dominant groups that represent the movement in the public eye. The mainstream legal and political organizations in the LGBT community are very important and credible. They have my support. But they are not the full representation of the LGBT community or its views. On each issue I mentioned on the equality agenda, there are arguments and disagreements within the LGBT movement about its priority, its ultimate value, and its validity. On "Don't Ask, Don't Tell," for example, many LGBT people who push for military equality are against the wars in which the US is engaged. Many LGBT people are gravely worried about the outsourcing of military and defense capacities to private mercenary armies. LGBT poverty activists are troubled by a system that requires poor people to enter armed service to gain access to educational and health care opportunities, literally sacrificing their lives while rich people can volunteer not to do so by not signing up. LGBT people of color, homeless advocates, and transgender advocates are alarmed at the ways that national security is used to justify increased surveillance and incarceration of immigrants, poor people, and people of color. LGBT feminists are troubled at the high rate of rape and sexual assault in the military—a byproduct of a misogynist and homophobic training culture and outdated views of masculinity and religiosity.

Or take the issue of marriage equality as another example. There has long been a very broad family protection agenda in the LGBT movement. For decades in the LGBT health movement, in the HIV movement, and in gay communities of color, we have argued and fought for full health care access for all people as a right—not as something tied to a person's marital or family status. The argument for marriage equality should not be a substitute for this larger goal of health care for all regardless of marital status, yet the larger goal has gotten obscured and the more tactical goal of marriage has risen to the foreground.

Similarly, the LGBT movement for many years fought against the ability of the state or the church to control our reproductive or sexual lives. That is why the movement was for so many years strongly pro-choice—it believed that individuals should have that bodily liberty, to determine their lives, not the state and not the church. Yet, today the mainstream movement uncritically embraces state power over our intimate lives when it acts as if all gay people want to get married and have the state bless our relationships. As a recent manifesto by Queer Kids Say No To The Gay Marriage Agenda expressed: "We reject the idea that any relationship based on love should have to register with the state." The manifesto goes on to argue that the movement's objectives should aim to protect a wider range of straight families and not just gain access to a narrow form of marital relationship or family.[189]

My point is that the equality agenda is what it always has been: a consensus agenda of basic rights that are needed. But it does not capture the full spirit or energy or social justice heart of the LGBT progressive movement. Looking ahead, several interesting opportunities are available to LGBT and progressive activists in the age of Obama. These opportunities include: organizing through networks instead of through the traditional organization form; focusing on communication (or message building); concentrating on cultural transformation; and building political power as a progressive majority.

Networks vs. Organizations

The model of civil rights infrastructure built by the LGBT movement was inherited from the historic social movements on which we modeled ourselves—the black civil rights struggle, the antiwar movement of the '60s, the women's movement, the environmental movement. That model has essentially been to create national organizations built around strategies and identities: legal groups that do litigation, lobbying groups that do advocacy, education groups that do organizing, and groups for every gay identity under the sun that provide support, make us visible and create change in a wide range of contexts (employment, religion, sports). The organization form is valuable and useful—infrastructure matters. However, it has also been limiting and classist.

On the one hand, it is precisely the existence of the old organization-based infrastructure (not merely the existence of technology) that has facilitated queer and queer supportive mobilization today. The organized infrastructure has done the unsexy work, day in and day out, of building support in state capitols to get LGBT people to the point where, as of this date, nineteen states have some form of anti-gay discrimination law. This infrastructure, which includes LGBT community centers, the HIV/AIDS organizations, the youth groups or the Gay-Straight Alliances, campus LGBT program offices, statewide LGBT advocacy groups, is a vital resource for future activism and to sustaining the pressure in the fallow times.

On the other hand, the institutionalization of social movements always carries a down side—a bureaucratization, the professionalization of activism, a more conservative politics than street action affords, even a shrinking of leadership as ordinary folks just let others do the work and become checkbook activists.[190] Most damaging is the way that lobbying organizations can become closed domains, essentially trade associations rather than vehicles for the engagement of all sorts of individuals in common purpose. They must pay attention to fundraising, to their major donors, to the image they project. And they lose the courage and firepower that made them valuable and necessary in the first place.

Perhaps most damning is the fact that after five decades of organizing for LGBT liberation, the movement has been able to mobilize only a small number of LGBT people, and an even smaller fraction of straight allies. There are fewer than three million unique names of people in all the databases of these forty largest domestic national organizations. We have access to only a fraction of our people and only tiny minorities of these participate as members.

The National Equality March in October of 2009 was a revelation to many. It demonstrated that tens of thousands, by some count more than 250,000 people, could be mobilized outside of the traditional infrastructure of LGBT movement organizations. This march had virtually no mainstream publicity until its last week, tepid support from the largest LGBT organizations, and it faced opposition from many gay political and grassroots leaders. It also had no money. Yet, its organizers reached thousands of people and created a beautiful and important historic gathering. How did they do that? They used new technologies, and excited thousands of individuals who were not in the purview of the mainstream LGBT organizations.

This is an example of new forms of organizing, mobilizing technology to build networks or relationships, rather than organizations. The next wave of LGBT liberation will need to create new and powerful networks that are not limited by organizational forms, but that link people who share values of sexuality and social justice to each other and allow us to engage in coordinated local and global action. It will need to create such networks without regard to a person's identity but rather organized around values, goals, and broad change agendas. It will need to create new structures that do not require money from people for their participation (although there will always be a financing element to these structures—they cannot exist without some resourcing). If it does this kind of organizing, it may end up re-engineering the existing national political organizations, which will have to adapt to compete.

Technology creates exciting new opportunities for networks to be formed across vast distances and types of issue. MoveOn. org's success in organizing is extraordinary—a small (fewer than thirty people) staff, dedicated Internet-based group now reaches more than 1.6 million subscribers, and has proven it can generate hundreds of thousands of letters to members of Congress, raise millions of dollars, and put bodies on the street. Other examples of how technology enables organizing can be seen in the work of the Independent Media Center movement to provide progressive perspectives and reporting on major events; in the organizing of the Global Justice Movement against IMF and World Bank policies; and in the efforts of a number of transnational social movements such as the movement to ban land mines, to stop dam construction, and to protect the environment.[191]

Still, I am old fashioned. I believe that there is no substitute for actual bodies in the streets and in the suites; no change without pressure and real engagement by lots of people. That is why I believe we need new structures either to supplement or transform the organizational forms we have been working with for the past forty years.

Message Building

A second reality confronting LGBT activists in the age of Obama is the need for better, attractive, and winning messages. This is a vexing task. I have long argued that one of the critical weaknesses of the LGBT infrastructure lies in its disconnect between our big aspirations for equality and our narrow framing of these issues to the general public. The challenge of distilling a digestible, sometimes sound-bite-sized message out of an agenda that challenges the core of American moral and religious thinking is daunting. LGBT people rarely speak to America in universal language. When we do, it is achieved by dumbing ourselves down, by pretending to be who we are not, rather than honestly addressing the anxieties and fears of heterosexist society. A new values-based message could offer the inspiration to solve common problems in fresh ways, something I believe many in this country long to hear. The moral values and vision that ground LGBT liberation are appealing and healing to the world. If we only talk about the particulars of the Employment Non-Discrimination Act (ENDA) or the destructive impact of the Defense of Marriage Act (DOMA) as matters that affect LGBT people alone, we miss the opportunity to transform the very idea of national identity, and the meaning of Constitutional freedom.

The LGBT movement must engage the public debate on a much deeper level and on a broader level: deeper in the sense of not letting the moral argument go unanswered, and broader in the sense that we have to take positions in this moment on the broad challenges that face our world—economic opportunity, the balance between liberty and security, the value of equality for all, and the value of a plural and diverse society. An economic message to counter the market fundamentalism of the day with an appeal that revives a role for the public sector is essential.

The core faith of progressivism has always been that prosperity can be more widely shared –through systems that deliver education, health care, jobs, training, housing, and other forms of social support to a wider array of people. The U.N. Human Development Report for 2003 noted that estimates for how much aid is needed to achieve the Millennium Development Goals aimed at halving the world's poor by 2015 range from

$50-$100 billion dollars in new aid; a figure that represents less than a .5% of the gross annual income of the 23 members of the Organization for Economic Cooperation and Development (OECD).[192] The lower of those figures could be achieved by a less than 10% reduction in the annual U.S. defense budget alone. These figures demonstrate that a drastic reduction in poverty is achievable.

The messages of equality, justice, and plurality are equally relevant and important. Our parent's generation fought battles against communism or against fascism. I think our generational battle is the struggle between pluralism and fundamentalism. Pluralism is the notion that there are many voices and views in civil society and that these can coexist and flourish; the hallmark of democratic government is that it allows dissent to flourish with the least regulation. People who work for social justice are people who believe in justice for all, under one standard of law. We believe that human rights are vital, essential, and that they include racial justice, women's reproductive freedom, sexual freedom, and accessibility, along with the basic rights to food, clothing, shelter, and other aspects of life articulated in the Universal Declaration of Human Rights.

In the end, visionary messages matter for the reason that the gay political leader Harvey Milk identified" "You gotta give them hope." We must be aspirational and not just pragmatic to inspire people to join together in building a really different world.

Progressives must tap into accessible cultural language and different cultural strategies to reach new supporters and to make ourselves better understood. People engage in civic action to find community and experience belonging, as much as they engage to vote or express a position. The right has been masterful at using pre-existing communities and turning them into ideological training grounds: churches and the infrastructure they offer are one clear example. The use of spaces like NASCAR, patriotic moments (July 4th, Memorial Day) are less visible as ideologically organized sites for the transmission of a world view. Cultural messages from a progressive perspective must also emerge from and utilize our own communities of belonging. These include non-profit and social service organizations, welcoming and liberal denominations, progressive churches, synagogues, and other places of worship, cultural festivals, direct action movements, online communities, and any other site of civic action that engages or brings together people to tackle shared problems. These are spaces in which democratic values can be developed, and new language for change formed.[193]

Culture Matters

Social movements in America have thus far won as much or more culturally as they have politically and legally. This is certainly true for LGBT folks, and it is true for issues like support for and belief in women's equality, cultural respect and recognition of African Americans, and an understanding that immigration has made this country both diverse and strong. Yet, each of these cultural gains and the movements that achieved them is the target of a backlash campaign. What should we make of the existence of cultural progress and cultural backlash?

For one, cultural gains need to be defended and preserved in a conscious and thoughtful manner by social justice movements—there is nothing permanent about their achievement. Today, the bulwark against erosion of the cultural space that LGBT people have won lies in two sources: progressive religion and the constitutional guarantees of freedom of expression (freedom of speech, association, press, and assembly). The work ahead requires LGBT people and progressives to target these arenas as inviolable lines of defense. It will not be easy. Worldwide and in the U.S., religious fundamentalism is ascendant. Similarly, worldwide and in the U.S., demands for security and safety are trumping commitments to liberty: with many advocates from the latter side now arguing vehemently for the erosion of the very guarantees that have created America's wealth and power.

Second, the right wing's ascendancy and its multi-pronged attacks in the age of Obama challenge LGBT people and progressives to prioritize the defeat of the chauvinistic and hostile cultural vision of the right. What was striking about the Glenn Beck rally titled "Restoring Honor" and held on August 28, 2010, was its familiarity, not its strangeness.[194] Everything about it was a repetition of messages and ideas reinforcing the version of American tradition that "imaginers" on the right have promoted for decades. A national identity erased of color or class or gender or religious plurality; a restoration fantasy of "taking this country back" (to the pre-Civil War 1850s at least, if not the 1760s); the banal invocation to "do good" while acting really badly against anyone defined outside of the Christian nation. In a similar vein, Jane Mayer's expose of the Koch brothers in *The New Yorker*[195] was also eerily familiar—another excellent analysis of the strategic funding and ideological commitment of right wing donors.

How many times have we read this story? Yet, each decade it seems that mainstream and even progressive-minded people newly "discover" the right. We are reminded (again) that they have built a comprehensive totalitarian infrastructure (from ideas to action to communication). Liberals are shocked to realize how much money the ideological right commits to consolidating its political power. People bemoan the collapse of a moderate wing of the Republican Party. Alarms are sounded and then everyone goes on as usual.

Sadly, there is a shortage of ideas about how to respond to and how to defeat the right wing culturally and politically. Leaving aside the liberal denialist response of those, including the President, who act on the deluded belief that it is possible to work rationally with an opposition that is armed to destroy, not debate, progressives have tried at least three approaches to defeat the right over the last four decades: 1) research and document the enemy, 2) build infrastructure to challenge their influence on a wide range of fronts, and 3) play hardball politics.

Each of these approaches remains necessary, but each strategy must go deeper and be supplemented with new ideas.

Research and analysis are critical to identify clearly the constituencies and the ideas our opponents represent. Research on the right has shown the effective ways that religious conservatives married cultural conservatism to economic conservatism; the links between the intelligence communities and the right; the links among hard right militias and racist elements in this country; funding trails between mainstream donors and fanatic shock jocks; and links between U.S. religious groups and global missionaries whose actions result in terror and violence against LGBT people to name just a few areas. The research shows us an ideologically broad coalition that effectively unites across class through its nationalism, racism, and misogyny.[196]

But our research has not enabled us to be brave or sophisticated enough to articulate a competing cultural vision of America that counters the right. Progressive think tanks generally do not communicate beyond a narrow elite base. We seem unable to face and answer the worries and anxieties of the rank and file followers of the right. The white working class feels blamed and burdened. It is resentful of elites because it feels looked down upon by them. It longs to be rich and buys up lots of lottery tickets to gain entry to the Land of Oz that capitalism promises. People of color who are working class or in the middle class are also not immune from racism or bias— they fear the loss of their hard-earned status. And LGBT people have also proved that we can be just as biased and narrow-minded about our interests as straight people—the experience of outsiderness does not necessarily make us understanding of other outsiders. To defeat the right culturally and politically, we are going to have to offer a new and inviting vision, a different kind of nationalism.

A second tool that progressives have (belatedly) deployed to fight the right is to build a countervailing policy and organizing infrastructure to generate and promote new ideas. As a result there has been great growth in the size and growth of mainstream and liberal think tanks (as well as growth in the libertarian and conservative ones).[197] Unfortunately, this effort is still too small and too weakly funded. Only a handful of think tanks monitor and study the right (Political Research Associates, People For the American Way, Southern Poverty Law Center, to name three). Liberal and progressive philanthropy has desperately underfunded this study because it fears that right-wing Congressmen will turn their regulatory ire upon them. The fear is warranted but cannot excuse cowardice. A lot more energy needs to be directed immediately to stem the growth of neo-fascist movements in the United States.

The progressive infrastructure being built cannot be limited only to Washington D.C., and a handful of other states. Until there is a progressive, anti-right wing infrastructure accessible to organizers in every region of the country, including the South and the Midwest, we will not reach down to the towns and suburbs where the right is gaining in strength. The local reality for progressives is that we lack visibility, coherence, and public presence; we lack champions who articulate a dissenting and inclusive voice in our local communities; and we are dispersed because we organize by issue, instead of by ideology. What structures should we create to address this weakness? This is a question that needs to be asked regionally and at the state level.

Finally, the progressive infrastructures being built must incorporate the valence of race, gender, sexuality, or religiosity in public opinion formation, in public policy making, and in political practice. They should not ignore what one could argue is a key reason for the left's weakness over the last forty years: its failure to take up issues of identity and knit them into a politics of pluralism. Instead of grabbing onto identities to define itself and to build power, the left has run away from the culture wars, splintered around the issues of racism, sexism, and homophobia, and resisted the leadership of women, people of color and LGBT people. As a result, there is actually a bifurcated progressive infrastructure. The mainstream corporate/civil rights/D.C.-based one (visible at gatherings like the Congressional Black Caucus weekend) and the more inclusive and diverse, grassroots one (visible at gatherings like the US Social Forum). How can a progressive movement win if it is so fundamentally divided?

The final strategy we have used against the right is surprisingly the newest and that is to play hardball politics. Progressives have waged successful campaigns to knock out (defeat) reactionary candidates and support progressives (in Colorado, Michigan, Iowa, for example), to defeat ballot measures, and to recruit great new candidates at the local and state level (the Center for Progressive Leadership, Progressive Majority, to name two). These efforts need to be put on steroids. Every social movement that considers itself progressive has to play hardball politics to defeat the right at the ballot box, in every election, at every opportunity, not just at the national-Presidential moment.

An unsolved problem for progressives around electoral work remains the fact that in many parts of the country, a key obstacle to our success is the weakness and dysfunction of local Democratic Party organizations. Despite every incentive to change, the Party remains flaccid and ineffectual because it has no energized base. It is so weak at the state level that it loses races it should win (for example, Republican Scott Brown's 2006 race in Massachusetts). The Democratic Party has a demoralized base because it keeps selling out its progressive values to appeal to supposedly moderate or swing voters. It is certainly true that campaigns need messages that broaden their appeal, but a political party needs to stand for a coherent and clear set of principles, and to defend these against all attacks. The President can be bipartisan. Congressional dealmakers may have to "reach out across the aisle." But a Democratic Party should be partisan and promote the policies for which it stands—offering a clear and contrasting set of values by which it is distinguishable.

These three approaches to defeating the right and winning the culture wars must be augmented by a greater investment in progressive media. Media is a critical tool in the battle of messages and votes. LGBT people have learned that our success requires us to be in the media, to create media of our own, and to participate actively in the public sphere. Progressives today lead efforts to insure that media and technology policy protects spaces for non-commercial public access, and non-partisan public discourse. Indeed, with hardly any backing, progressive media and journalism have been inspiring over the past thirty years: there is a vigorous and active blogosphere, brilliant researchers who ferret out information to draw attention to many issues (Box Turtle Bulletin, Media Matters), brave outlets (Grit TV, Democracy Now, Public News Service), excellent radio and TV journalists (many of them outstanding women like Amy Goodman, Laura Flanders, Rachel Maddow), and a loosely knit set of relationships among radio, TV, and Web-based outlets. What we do not have are national vehicles to promote messages and ideas. We lack deep-pocketed investors with an ideological commitment to teaching about and promoting progressive values. And we lack adequate opposition research and education capacities.

Political Power Building

To enact our equality agenda, we will have to join with straight allies and create a new powerful electoral majority in this country. For too long, we have done gay work primarily by ourselves. In part I think this has happened because we have had to engage in community building activities. So for example, most of the LGBT movement is involved in activities like individual support, social services, parties, the pursuit of recognition and respect, the creation of communities and institutions that will compensate in some way for the absence of government support for the community, and with the creation of spaces in which the community can exist with some measure of freedom.

Again, we follow the path laid down for us by previous social movements: the civil rights movement, the women's liberation movement, and the immigrant rights movement. Each has created community, worked for social and cultural integration and understanding, and pursued a political agenda that is fairly narrow: getting "our own" elected. Even other, more traditional social movements in this country, like labor and progressive religion, have been engaged in a more internally directed projects—organizing more union members, as opposed to organizing all supporters of unions into a political bloc.

For many decades, progressives have talked about the need to link up with each other beyond identity, around shared goals and values. That dream was partly realized in 2008 with President Obama's election. But progressives did not forge themselves into a coherent and organized political bloc after 2008, and the dream remains unfulfilled. Imagine the potential in the creation of such a local voting bloc of progressives in every state. Clearly, progressive voters would not be able to muster enough clout in every district, but given the reality of low-turnout elections, much can be achieved with well-mobilized minorities, a truth the anti-gay right has certainly proved. Through a systematic mapping of state districts to identify the progressive potential, strategic investment in the building of a progressive infrastructure, and the targeted organizing of women voters, LGBT voters, people of color voters, pro-labor households, and pro-choice voters into a political coalition, advocates for justice have created winning majorities in many states not at all considered liberal.

The motivation for this work could not be more urgent. All those marked as social outcasts are in dangerous territory when the economy plunges. Examples of scapegoating in harsh economic times abound, and such scapegoating has been rampant among the 2012 Republican candidates. Somehow immigrant workers are blamed for lost jobs and high unemployment, not the corporate leaders who moved factories overseas. Poor people are scapegoated as burdens on the "public" sector when, in fact, tax breaks and givebacks to industries overwhelm spending on poverty programs. Gays are blamed for the crisis of hopelessness in heterosexual marriages. Contraception and women's autonomy gets the rap for the moral dysfunction in the heteronormative family (not the horrible and mind boggling instances of sexual hypocrisy, domestic violence, child abuse, incest, and other forms of cruelty against women). We are told it is the cappuccino-drinking liberals who don't care about working people by rich mercenaries like Glen Beck and Rush Limbaugh, who are in turn hired by the rich to insure the general public's subsidization of the 1%'s lives through tax breaks and cuts. The harshness and irrationality of the resistance faced by advocates of social justice presents an opportunity for deeper understanding and demonstrates the wisdom of solidarity among progressive elements of the electorate.

Let me conclude by observing that like those who seek racial or gender justice, advocates working in the LGBT movement are often challenged with the charge that we work in isolation or in a "silo." This word, "silo" has become a the new spelling of the old epithet "politically correct," used to minimize or marginalize the impact of those working for change. We who have been working for LGBT liberation certainly do not see our goal as building a gay silo or living in one.

We see our work instead as building common ground—or cultivating soil. We see ourselves as part of an earth in which race, gender, sexuality, all of our identities are churned up in a rich and fertile soil.

And what we are trying to do is to create new institutions, new policies, new ways of imagining, creating a world out of this common soil of our identities and our experiences.

ACKNOWLEDGEMENTS

This book exists thanks to Don Weise's enthusiasm for critical thinking about the LGBT movement and his skillful editing. Thank you also to Kathleen Conkey, for legal support; Jurek Wajdowicz, for photography and design; and Jodi Solomon Associates, for lecture representation.

The organizations, colleges, and universities at which the original versions of these talks were given have my gratitude for providing venues to develop ideas. Thank you to Juan Battle, the Social Justice Sexuality Project, the Department of Sociology at the Graduate Center of the City University of New York (CUNY), and the H. Van Ameringen Foundation for their support of a Visiting Fellowship (2010-2011). Thanks to Sarah Chinn and the Center for Lesbian & Gay Studies (CLAGS) at CUNY Graduate Center, and to Barbara Warren and the Center for LGBT Social Science and Public Policy at Hunter College. For the opportunity to think more deeply about tradition and its impact on the feminist and LGBT movements, my sincere gratitude goes to the Center for Gender and Sexuality Law at Columbia Law School, to the Arcus Foundation, and to my colleagues at the law school, Katherine Franke, Suzanne

Goldberg, Kendall Thomas, and Vina Tran.

While the perspectives and limitations of this project are my own, the generous inspiration, challenge and teaching of many colleagues in the queer and feminist movements inform this work. Particular debts are owed to: Susan Allee, Virginia Apuzzo, Radhika Balakrishnan, John Barabino, Juan Battle, Michael Bennett, Chip Berlet, Jacqueline Brown, Richard Burns, Sean Cahill, Mandy Carter, Kevin Cathcart, Cathy Cohen, Matt Coles, Angela Davis, Trishala Deb, David Dechman, John D'Emilio, Michael Edwards, Eve Ensler, Ruth Eisenberg, Paula Ettelbrick (1955-2011), Chai Feldblum, Matt Foreman, Tim Gill, Patrick Guerriero, Letty Gomez, Lauren Gumbs, Catherine Hanssens, Jean Hardisty, Alan Hergott, Taryn Higashi, Jim Hormel, Amy Hoffman, Nan Hunter, Sue Hyde, Johnny Jenkins, Rev. Deborah Johnson, June Jordan (1936-2002), Joo Hyun Kang, Natalia Kanem, Linda Ketner, Rosa King, Sally Kohn, Karen Krahulik, Larry Kramer, Frances Kunreuther, Gara LaMarche, Geri Manion, Jennifer Manion, Manning Marable (1950-2011), Rodger McFarlane (1955-2009), Jade McGleughlin, Scott Miller, Katherine Pease, Suzanne Pharr, Nancy Polikoff, Bernice Reagon, Cindy Rizzo, Eric Rofes (1954-2006), Sarah Schulman, Rinku Sen, Curt Shepard, Bill Smith, Dean Spade, Gloria Steinem, Roberta Stone, Jon Stryker, Carla Sutherland, Vidhya Swaminathan, Tim Sweeney, Ted Trimpa, Judith Turkel, Carmen Vazquez, Darren Walker, Wayne Winborne, Evan Wolfson.

The unwavering support of my families of origin and choice are anchors at all times. Thank you to my parents, Krishna B. Vaid and Champa R. Vaid, to my siblings, Rachna Vaid and Jyotsna Vaid, my siblings-in-law, and to all of my nieces and nephews. My love and gratitude also goes to the following people for your sustenance: Jeff Arnstein and Michael Field, Nancy Asch and Beth Heinberg, Leslie Belzberg, Robert Berg, Robert Bloch and Barbara Kahn, Sandra Bolin and Cynthia Glott, Susan Coskey, Dave Ellner, Mary Farmer and Laura Flegel, Laura

Flanders and Elizabeth Streb, Eric Galloway and Henry Van Ameringen, Roslyn Garfield, Chris and Katie Grunden, Donald Huppert, Michael Liguori, Shelly Mars, Tracey Primavera, Mayo Schreiber, Ann Viitala, Trudy and Jesse Wood.

Finally and most importantly, I want to thank my partner and love, Kate Clinton, for the joy, laughter, creative pleasures, and happiness of our nearly twenty-five years together. This book comes out of, and attests to, the incredible life we share.

ENDNOTES

1. Esther Cooper Jackson with Constance Pohl, editors, *Freedomways Reader: Prophets In Their Own Countries* (Boulder, CO: Westview Press, 2000), p. 335, accessed on March 3, 2012 at http://books.google.com/books?id=-oivNmSJOfAC&pg=PA335&lpg=PA335&dq=Toni+Cade+Bambara+the+responsibility+of+an+artist+representing+an+oppressed+people+is&source=bl&ots=heypekNe7J&sig=J-qXmuq9YyZjtqlpvhsYo_4OEKU&hl=en&sa=X&ei=Q69TT5vjA6Hh0wH9k8jUCQ&ved=0CEUQ6AEwBw#v=onepage&q=Toni%20Cade%20Bambara%20the%20responsibility%20of%20an%20artist%20representing%20an%20oppressed%20people%20is&f=false.

2. *Perry v. Brown*, (9th Cir. February 7, 2012), p.5.

3. "Washington State Makes 7: Governor Signs Gay Marriage Law," *Los Angeles Times*, February 13, 2012 accessed on February 18 at http://latimesblogs.latimes.com/nationnow/2012/02/washington-governor-signs-law-legalizing-same-sex-marriage.html.

4. Kate Zernike, "Christie Keeps His Promise to Veto Gay Marriage Bill," *New York Times*, February 17, 2012,

accessed on February 18, 2012 at http://www.nytimes.
com/2012/02/18/nyregion/christie-vetoes-gay-
marriage-bill.html.

5. http://topics.nytimes.com/top/reference/timestopics/
    subjects/s/same_sex_marriage/index.html

6. Transgender Europe, "Sweden Will Remove the
    Sterilization Requirement After Strong Pressure from
    National and International Community," February
    18, 2012, accessed on February 8, 2012 at http://www.
    tgeu.org/Sweden_will_remove_the_sterilization_
    requirement.

7. *Perry v. Brown, supra at note 2*, p. 71.

8. Arvind Narrain, "Queering Democracy: The Politics
    of Erotic Love," in *Law Like Love: Queer Perspectives on
    Law*, edited by Arvind Narrain and Alok Gupta (New
    Delhi: Yoda Press, 2011), p. 4.

9. This chapter is based on a talk given on April 27, 2011
    at the Roosevelt Institute's Center for LGBT Social
    Science and Public Policy at Hunter College.

10. Red Star Singers, "Still Ain't Satisfied," *The Force of
    Life* (CD), (Pardon records, 1974), liner notes for the
    CD accessed on January 19, 2012 at http://media.
    smithsonianglobalsound.org/liner_notes/paredon/
    PAR01023.pdf.

11. Pew Research Center for People and The Press,
    "Attitudes Towards Social Issues," March 3, 2011,
    accessed on December 28, 2011 at-http://people-press.
    org/2011/03/03/section-3-attitudes-toward-social-
    issues.

12. ABC News/*Washington Post* Poll, "Support For
    Gay Marriage Reaches a Milestone," March 18,
    2011, accessed on February 28, 2012 at http://
    abcnews.go.com/Politics/support-gay-marriage-
    reaches-milestone-half-americans-support/
    story?id=13159608#.

13. United Nations High Commissioner for Human
    Rights, "Discriminatory laws and practices and
    acts of violence against individuals based on their
    sexual orientation and gender identity," November
    17, 2011, accessed on February 28, 2012 at http://
    thenewcivilrightsmovement.com/lgbt-rights-united-
    nations-report-finds-being-gay-illegal-in-76-
    countries-1/international/2011/12/16/31980.
14. "Historic Decision at the United Nations: Human
    Rights Council Passes First Ever Resolution on Sexual
    Orientation and Gender Identity," June 17, 2011
    accessed on December 28, 2011 at http://www.iglhrc.
    org/cgi–bin/iowa/article/pressroom/pressrelease/1417.
    html. The Council's resolution and the subsequent
    report by the Office of the U.N. High Commissioner
    for Human Rights followed a series of actions taken
    at the international level. In 2006, Norway introduced
    a resolution at the Human Rights Council that
    was supported by fifty-four states; in 2008, a joint
    statement initiated by Brazil and introduced by
    Argentina was signed by sixty-six states at the U.N.
    General Assembly; and in March 2011, Colombia
    delivered a Joint Statement at the Human Rights
    Council calling on all States to end violence, criminal
    sanctions and related human rights violations based
    on sexual orientation and gender identity, on behalf of
    eighty-five states.
15. See, Secretary Hillary Rodham Clinton, "Remarks
    in Recognition of International Human Rights Day,"
    December 6, 2011, accessed on December 28, 2011 at
    http://www.state.gov/secretary/rm/2011/12/178368.
    htm.
16. Michael Sean Winters, "New Report on Catholic
    Attitudes Toward LGBT Issues," *National Catholic
    Reporter*, March 22, 2011 accessed on February 21,

2012 at http://ncronline.org/blogs/distinctly-catholic/
new-report-catholic-attitudes-towards-lgbt-issues;
Public Religion Research Institute, "Majority of
Americans Say They Support Same-Sex Marriage,
Adoption by Gay and Lesbian Couples," May 9, 2011,
accessed on February 21, 2012 at http://publicreligion.
org/research/2011/05/majority-of-americans-say-they-
support-same-sex-marriage-adoption-by-gay-and-
lesbian-couples/.

17. Id.

18. Cathy J. Cohen, "The Attitudes and Behavior of
Young Black Americans: Research Summary," Black
Youth Project, University of Chicago, June 2007, at
p. 21, reporting that majority of black youth surveyed
believe homosexuality is always wrong, compared to
smaller numbers of Hispanic and white youth and that
there was a gender gap in these attitudes. Accessed on
February 25, 2012 at http://www.blackyouthproject.
com/wp-content/uploads/BYP-Research-Summary.
pdf.

19. See, Tom Smith, "Public Attitudes Towards
Homosexuality," National Opinion Research Center,
University of Chicago, September 11, 2011. William
Harms, "Americans Move Dramatically Towards
Acceptance of Homosexuality, Survey Finds,"
University of Chicago News, September 28, 2011,
at http://news.uchicago.edu/article/2011/09/28/
americans–move–dramatically–toward–acceptance–
homosexuality–survey–finds. See also, Tobin Grant,
"Poll: Majority of Americans Say Same-Sex Relations
Are O.K." *Christianity Today*, July 26, 2011, at http://
blog.christianitytoday.com/ctpolitics/2011/07/poll_
majority_o.html. All links accessed on December 28,
2011.

20. Robert Smith, *We Have No Leaders: African Americans in*

the Post Civil Rights Era (State University of New York Press, 1996), page. 17.

21. Government Accountability Office, "Gender Pay Differences: Progress Made But Women Still Overrepresented Among Low-Wage Workers," Report to Congressional Requesters, October 11, 2011, accessed on December 28, 2011 at http://graphics8. nytimes.com/packages/pdf/business/GAO-12-10.pdf.

22. Lisa Duggan, *The Twilight of Equality? Neoliberalism, Cultural Politics and the Attack on Democracy* (Beacon Press, 2004), p. xviii.

23. Id., p. 49.

24. U.S. Census Bureau, American Community Survey Data on Same-Sex Households, at http://www.census. gov/hhes/samesex/data/acs.html.

25. Id., "Table 1: Household Characteristics of Opposite-Sex and Same-Sex Couple Households (ACS 2010)."

26. Randy Albelda, M.V. Lee Badgett, Alyssa Schneebaum, Gary Gates, "Poverty In the Lesbian, Gay, Bisexual Community," (Williams Institute at UCLA, March 2009, p. ii, accessed on December 28, 2011 at http:// williamsinstitute.law.ucla.edu/research/census-lgbt-demographics-studies/poverty-in-the-lesbian-gay-and-bisexual-community/.

27. Id., p. ii.

28. Id.

29. Id., p. i.

30. Id., p. iii.

31. Zygmunt Bauman, "Happiness in A Society of Others," *Soundings*, Issue 38 (Spring 2008), p 20.

32. Id., p. 23.

33. Anthony Elliott, "The New Individualist Perspective: Identity Transformations in the Aftermath of the Global Financial Crisis," *Forum: University of Edinburgh Postgraduate Journal of Culture and Arts*,

Issue 11, accessed on February 21, 2012 at http://www.forumjournal.org/site/issue/11/professor-anthony-elliott.

34. Dean Spade, *Normal Life: Administrative Violence, Critical Trans Politics and the Limits of Law* (South End Press, 2011), p. 153.

35. Id., p. 102.

36. Id., Chapter 3 generally, and p. 123.

37. Duggan, *The Twilight of Equality*, *supra at note 22*, p.45.

38. The Movement Advancement Project notes, "we find that only 3% of LGBT adults have donated to a participating organization." "2011 LGBT Movement Report: A Financial Overview of Leading Advocacy Organizations in the U.S.," December 2011, p. 11 accessed on December 28, 2011 at http://www.lgbtmap.org/file/2011–national–lgbt–movement–report.pdf.

39. Dean Spade, *Normal Life*, *supra at note 34*, p. 137.

40. Gary Gates, "How Many People are Lesbian, Gay, Bisexual and Transgender?" Williams Institute, UCLA, April 2011, accessed on December 28, 2011 at http://williamsinstitute.law.ucla.edu/research/census-lgbt-demographics-studies/how-many-people-are-lesbian-gay-bisexual-and-transgender/.

41. Id., pp. 6–7.

42. *Lawrence v. Texas*, 539 U.S. 558 (2003).

43. This chapter is based on the Kessler Lecture, sponsored by the Center for Lesbian and Gay Studies at CUNY and given on November 18, 2010 at the City University Graduate Center in New York.

44. Kessler Award, http://web.gc.cuny.edu/clags/pages/kessler.html.

45. Charles Dickens, *A Tale of Two Cities*, (Penguin Classics, 2003), p. 1.

46. "Analysis by the Pew Research Center's Forum on

Religion & Public Life of National Election Pool (NEP) exit poll data reported by CNN shows that white Protestants, a group that has long been one of the key components of the GOP coalition, voted for Republicans over Democrats in their congressional districts by a 28%-69% margin." Pew Forum on Religion and Public Life, "Religion in the 2010 Elections: A Preliminary Look," November 3, 2011, accessed on December 28, 2011 at http://pewforum. org/Politics-and-Elections/Religion-in-the-2010-Election-A-Preliminary-Look.aspx.

47. Mark Bauerlein, "The Youth Vote 2010," accessed on December 28, 2011 at http://chronicle.com/blogs/ brainstorm/the-youth-vote-2010/28647. See generally Center for Information and Research on Civic Learning and Engagement (CIRCLE), "Youth Voting, Quick Facts," accessed December 28, 2011 at http:// www.civicyouth.org/quick-facts/youth-voting/.

48. Guidestar is a database created from the Form 990's that non-profit organizations with revenues over $25,000 in annual revenue are required to file with the Internal Revenue Service (IRS). www.guidestar.org. The MAP data was presented in its "2011 National LGBT Movement Report: A Financial Overview of Leading Advocacy Organizations in the LGBT Movement" (December 2011), pp.5-6 accessed on February 22, 2012 at http://lgbtmap.org/2011-national-lgbt-movement-report.

49. Id., p. 5.

50. Id., p. 5-6.

51. Id., at pp. 13-14.

52. Data accessed from Movement Advancement Project's research on individual organizational budgets, released only to participants and members.

53. Gabrial Arkels, Pooje Gehi, Elana Redfield, "The

Role of Lawyers in Trans Liberation: Building a Transformative Movement for Social Change," *Seattle Journal of Social Justice*, Volume 8, Issue Number 2, (2010), pp. 580-641.

54. A rare exception to this statement was Lambda Legal's state level organizing and community mobilization work in the late-2000's to secure a pro-civil union vote in New Jersey.

55. The work on sexual violence and sexual harassment is being led by a feminist ally organization, the Servicewomen's Action Network (SWAN), see www. servicewomen.org.

56. Sam Hananel, "Obama Appoints Record Number of Gay Officials," Associated Press, October 28, 2010, accessed on February 25, 2012 at http://www.thegrio. com/politics/obama-appoints-record-number-of-gay-officials.php.

57. *See*, "On The Family: A Rainbow Families Agenda," Keynote at the Rainbow Families Conference, Minneapolis, MN, available at www.urvashivaid.net.

58. For recent research on the relationship between Racial Justice Organizations and LGBT issues, see a report released by the Applied Research Center, "Better Together: Research Findings on the relationship Between Racial Justice Organizations and LGBT Communities," accessed February 28, 2012 at http:// www.arc.org/content/view/2169/201/.

59. Funders for Lesbian and Gay Issues, Racial Equity Campaign, at http://www.lgbtfunders.org/programs/ equity.cfm. *See also*, "Out For Change: Racial and Economic Justice Issues in LGBT Communities" (Funders for Lesbian and Gay Issues, 2005), accessed on February 25, 2012 at http://www.lgbtfunders.org/ files/LGBT-REJ.pdf.

60. "Bold Gathering—Nation's Largest Gathering

of LGBT People of Color—Aims to Increase
Political Power," press release from gathering, dated
December 2, 2011, accessed on December 28, 2011
at Steve Rothaus, Gay South Florida blog, http://
miamiherald.typepad.com/gaysouthflorida/2011/12/
bold-gathering-nations-largest-gathering-of-lgbt-
people-og-color-aims-to-increase-political-power.
html#ixzz1gXXfZRV3.

61. "Better Together: Research Findings on the
Relationship Between Racial Justice Organizations and
LGBT Communities," accessed December 28, 2011 at
http://www.arc.org/images/lgbt%20report_091710_
final.pdf

62. Tim Wise, "With Friends Like These, Who Needs
Glen Beck? Racism and White Privilege on the Liberal
Left," August 17, 2010 accessed on December 28, 2011
at http://www.timwise.org/2010/08/with–friends–like–
these–who–needs–glenn–beck–racism–and–white–
privilege–on–the–liberal–left/, p. 4.

63. Tim Wise, Id., p.4.

64. Peggy Noonan, "Obama's Gifts to the GOP," *Wall
Street Journal*, November 13, 2010.

65. http://www.perla.org/blog/previouspostings/RacePoll.
htm

66. Movement Advancement Project, "2011 National
LGBT Movement Report," *supra at note 48*, p. 14.

67. Movement Advancement Project, "2010 Community
Center Survey and Report: Assessing the Capacity and
Programs of LGBT Community Centers," September
2010, p. 15.

68. Vernetta L. Walker and Deborah J. Davidson, *Vital
Voices: Lessons Learned from Board Members of Color*,
(BoardSource, 2010), p. 2, accessed on February 25,
2012 at http://www.boardsource.org/dl.asp?document_
id=889.

69. Tim Wise, "With Friends Like These, Who Needs Glen Beck: Racism and White Privilege on the Liberal Left," accessed on December 29, 2011 at http://www.timwise.org/2010/08/with–friends–like–these–who–needs–glenn–beck–racism–and–white–privilege–on–the–liberal–left/.

70. Keith Lawrence, Stacey Sutton, Anne Kubisch, Gretchen Susi, and Karen Fullbright-Anderson, "Structural Racism and Community Building," Aspen Institute Roundtable on Community Change (Aspen Institute, 2004), available at http://www.aspeninstitute.org/sites/default/files/content/docs/roundtable%20on%20community%20change/aspen_structural_racism2.pdf.

71. Opportunity Agenda, "The State of Opportunity in the U.S.," 2009 Report and 2010 Update, accessed on December 29, 2011 at http://opportunityagenda.org/stateofopportunity/indicators/equality.

72. Id., *April 2010 update*, accessed on December 28, 2011 at http://opportunityagenda.org/files/field_file/State%20of%20Opportunity%202010%20Update.pdf.

73. Id., 2009 Report, accessed on December 28, 2011 at http://opportunityagenda.org/stateofopportunity/indicators/equality#education.

74. "State of Opportunity," April 2010 Update, p. 1.

75. "State of Opportunity," 2009 Report, accessed on December 29, 2011 at http://opportunityagenda.org/stateofopportunity/indicators/redemption.

76. American Correctional Association, Disproportionate Minority Contact/Confinement Task Force, "Fact Sheet," dated August 1, 2010, accessed on December 28, 2011 at http://www.asca.net/system/assets/attachments/970/ACA_DMC_Workshop_Materials_1_.pdf?1282052124.

77. Death Penalty Information Center, "Facts About the Death Penalty," February 16, 2012, accessed on February 25, 2012 at http://www.deathpenaltyinfo.org/documents/FactSheet.pdf.

78. Roderick Ferguson, "Racing Homo-Normativity: Citizenship, Sociology and Gay Identity," in *Black Queer Studies: A Critical Anthology* (Durham, NC: Duke University Press, 2005), pp.52–67; David Eng, *The Feeling of Kinship: Queer Liberalism and the Racialization of Intimacy* (Durham, NC: Duke University Press, 2010); Nancy Polikoff, *Beyond (Straight and Gay) Marriage: Valuing All Families Under the Law* (Boston, MA: Beacon Press, 2008); Jasbir Puar, *Terrorist Assemblages: Homonationalism in Queer Times* (Durham, NC: Duke University Press, 2007).

79. Administration for Children and Families, Region IV, "Grandparents Raising Children: A Call to Action," January 2007, p. 1, accessed on February 25, 2012 at http://www.acf.hhs.gov/opa/doc/grandparents.pdf. See also, Center for Community Health, University of North Texas Science Center, Fort Worth, "Grandparents Raising Grandchildren: The Skipped Generation," March 2008.

80. Movement Advancement Project, "2010 SAR Report," p.24.

81. Jeff Krehely, "How to Close the LGBT Health Disparities Gap: Disparities by Race and Ethnicity," (Center for American Progress, December 21, 2009) accessed on February 25, 2012 at http://www.americanprogress.org/issues/2009/12/pdf/lgbt_health_disparities_race.pdf

82. Human Rights Campaign, "At the Intersection: Race, Sexual Orientation and Gender," August 2009, p. 11–13. The link for the report does not appear to be valid online but a press release about the report was

accessed on December 29, 2011 at http://222.hrc.org/
issues/13246.htm.

83. Donna Victoria and Cornell Belcher, "LGBT Rights
and Advocacy: Messaging To the African American
Community" (Arcus Operating Foundation, 2010),
accessed on December 29, 2011 at http://www.
arcusfoundation.org/images/uploads/downloads/
Messaging_to_African_American_Communities_
Arcus_Belcher_Victoria_2009.pdf.

84. Zuna Institute, "Black Lesbians Matter," 2010.
Full report accessed December 28, 2011 at
http://zunainstitute.org/2010/research/blm/
blacklesbiansmatter.pdf. Executive Summary at
http://zunainstitute.org/2010/research/blm/ES_
blacklesbiansmatter.pdf

85. Tim Wise, "With Friends Like These, Who Needs
Glen Beck?" *supra at note 63.*

86. Funders for Lesbian and Gay Issues,
Racial Equity Campaign Update, 2008 and
2009, http://www.lgbtfunders.org/files/
RacialEquityCampaignUpdate2008.pdf

87. Tim Wise, "With Friends Like These, Who Needs
Glen Beck?" *supra, at note 85* p. 10.

88. See CNN National Exit Poll for 2010 Election,
accessed on December 28, 2011 at http://www.cnn.
com/ELECTION/2010/results/polls.main/#.

89. Randy Albelda, M.V. Lee Badgett, Alyssa Schneebaum,
Gary Gates, "Poverty in the Lesbian, Gay and Bisexual
Community," *Executive Summary*, pp. i–iv, Williams
Institute, March 2009), pp. i–ii, *supra at note 26.*

90. "Justice for All? A Report on LGBT Youth in the New
York Juvenile Justice System," 2001, p. 6, accessed on
December 28, 2011 at http://www.equityproject.org/
pdfs/justiceforallreport.pdf.

91. Gary Gates, Lee Badgett, Jennifer Macomber,

Kate Chambers, "Adoption and Foster Care by Gay and Lesbian Parents in the U.S.," Williams Institute/Urban Institute 2007, p. 1, 15–17, accessed December 28, 2011, at http://escholarship.org/uc/item/2v4528cx#page–7.

92. National Coalition for the Homeless, "Fact Sheet," accessed on December 28, 2011 at http://www.nationalhomeless.org/factsheets/lgbtq.html; "Justice For All: A Report on LGBT Youth in the New York Juvenile Justice System," supra, p. 6.

93. R. Bradley Sears, Gary J. Gates, and William B. Rubenstein, "Same-sex Couples and Same-ex Couples Raising Children in the United States: Data from Census 2000," The Williams Institute, UCLA School of Law, 2005. See also, Rachel Farr and Charlotte Patterson, "Transracial Adoption by Lesbian, Gay and Heterosexual Couples: Who Complete Transracial Adoptions and With What Results?" accessed on December 29, 2011 at http://williamsinstitute.law.ucla.edu/wp-content/uploads/Patterson-Farr-TransracialAdoption-Aug-20091.pdf.

94. Bianca D.M. Wilson, "Our Families: Attributes of Bay Area LGBT Parents and Their Children: A Needs Assessment of the GLBT Family Collaborative" (Our Family Coalition, San Francisco LGBT Center, California, October 2007), p. 5, accessed on December 28, 2011 at http://www.sfcenter.org/pdf/OurFamilyReport.pdf.

95. Gates, Badgett, Macomber, Chambers, "Adoption and Foster Care by Gay and Lesbian Parents in the U.S.," Williams Institute and Urban Institute, *supra*, pp. 11–15; Sabrina Tavernise, "Adoptions By Gay Couples Rise, Despite Barriers," *New York Times*, June 13, 2011 accessed on December 29, 2011 at http://www.nytimes.com/2011/06/14/us/14adoption.html?_r=2&h

p=&adxnnl=1&pagewanted=1&adxnnlx=1325176178–
p2N9J7k0VHgbTQ403ccrsA.

96. Evan Donaldson Adoption Institute, "Adoption by
Gays and Lesbians: A National Survey of Adoption
Agency Policies, Practices and Attitudes," (October
2003), accessed on December 29, 2011 at http://
www.adoptioninstitute.org/whowe/Gay%20and%20
Lesbian%20Adoption1.html.

97. "Tidal Wave: LGBT Poverty and Hardship in a
Time of Economic Crisis" (see at http://www.q4ej.
org/Documents/qejtidalwave.pdf) and "A Fabulous
Attitude: Low Income LGBTNC People Surviving
and Thriving on Love, Shelter, and Knowledge"
(Queers for Economic Justice, 2010), http://www.q4ej.
org/Documents/afabulousattitudefinalreport.pdf.

98. See full video of Melissa Harris-Perry (then Melissa
Harris-Lacewell), Keynote, Facing Race Conference,
Chicago, October 3, 2010, http://www.youtube.com/
watch?v=49ocDVphfRA.

99. June Jordan, *Affirmative Acts: Political Essays* (Anchor
Books, 1998), p. 177.

100. Paul Simon, "The Boy in The Bubble," *Graceland* (CD
released in 1986).

101. Sanford, David, "Back to the Future: One Man's AIDS
Tale Shows How Quickly Epidemic Has Turned," *Wall
Street Journal*, November 8, 1996.

102. Andrew Sullivan, "When AIDS Ends," *New York Times
Magazine*, November 14, 1996.

103. Movement Advancement Project, "2011 National
LGBT Movement Report," *supra at note 48*, pp. 13-14.

104. http://rootscoalition.wordpress.com/about–roots/
mission/

105. A new research initiative that recognizes this longer
term need is the Face Value Project. A paper on its web
site summarizes some of its aspirations. *See*, "Moving

Beyond Tolerance to Acceptance," accessed on January 20, 2012 at http://facevalueproject.org/wp–content/uploads/2010/03/3-Moving-Beyond-Tolerance-to-Acceptance.pdf.

106. Jordan, *Affirmative Acts, supra at note 99*, p. 175.

107. This chapter is based on a talk given at Vassar College on November 5, 2011 as part of the conference titled "Smashing History: 150 Years of LGBTQIA History at Vassar."

108. Anne MacKay, *Wolf Girls at Vassar: Lesbian and Gay Experiences 1930-1990* (New York: St. Martins Press, 1992).

109. Muriel Rukeyser, "Double Ode," *The Collected Poems of Muriel Rukeyser* (University of Pittsburgh Press, 2006), p. 534-537, at 537.

110. Patti Smith, "Privilege (Set Me Free)," *Easter*, Arista Records, 1979.

111. Julie Bolcer, "New York State Republicans Thanked for Marriage with $1.2 Million Dollars," *The Advocate*, October 14, 2011, accessed on December 29, 2011 at http://www.advocate.com/News/Daily_News/2011/10/13/New_York_Senate_Republicans_Thanked_for_Marriage_Vote_With_1_Million/.

112. Ed Walsh, "Gay Rights Groups Stir Flap With D'Amato Nod," *Washington Post*, October 23, 1998.

113. Kenyon Farrow, "Gay Marriage in New York: Progressive Victory or GOP Roadmap," Alternet, June 27, 2011, accessed on December 28, 2011 at http://www.alternet.org/vision/151444/gay_marriage_in_new_york%3A_progressive_victory_or_gop_roadmap/?page=1.

114. Will Kohler, "Former RNC Chair Ken Mehlman Helped Gay Marriage in NY But He Still Donates Heavily to Anti-Gay GOP Candidates," February 11, 2012, accessed on February 25, 2012 at http://www.

back2stonewall.com/2012/02/rnc-chair-ken-mehlman.
html; Ron Hill, "Working To Save The GOP From
Anti-Gay Extremists: Ken Mehlman Where Are You?"
February 26, 2012, accessed at http://pamshouseblend.
firedoglake.com/2012/02/26/ron-hill-working-to-
save-the-gop-from-anti-gay-extremists-ken-mehlman-
where-are-you/; Daniel Villareal, "Don't Bring Up
Ken Mehlman's Anti-Gay Past When He's Enjoying a
Victory Cocktail," June 29, 2011, accessed on February
25, 2012 at http://www.queerty.com/dont-bring-
up-ken-mehlmans-anti-gay-past-when-hes-enjoy-a-
victory-cocktail-20110629/.

115. Avi Zenilman, "Why Wall Street is Grudgingly
Supporting Obama," *The Daily Beast*, January 14,
2012, accessed on February 14, 2012 at http://www.
thedailybeast.com/articles/2012/01/14/why-wall-
street-is-grudgingly-supporting-obama.html.

116. Lee Fang, "Journalists Funded by 'Vulture Capitalist'
Paul Singer Campaign to Smear Wall Street
Protests," *Think Progress*, October 10, 2011, accessed
on December 28, 2011 at http://thinkprogress.org/
special/2011/10/10/339862/paul-singer-vulture-
capitalist-journalists/.

117. Tony Carrk, "The Koch Brothers: What You Need
to Know About the Financiers of the Radical
Right," Center for American Progress, April 2011,
accessed on January 24, 2012 at http://www.
americanprogressaction.org/issues/2011/04/pdf/koch_
brothers.pdf.

118. Williams Institute researchers found that more lesbians
than gay men lived in poverty, 24% of lesbians and
15% of gay men lived in poverty versus 19% of women
in the general population and 13% of men in general
population. When Census data on LGBT couples is
parsed by race, the rates grow even starker, especially

for African American LGBT same-sex couples (who have higher poverty rates than heterosexual African American same-sex couples). "Poverty in the Lesbian, Gay, and Bisexual Community," *supra at note 26.*

119. Jamie Grant, Lisa Mottet, and Justin Tanis, "Injustice at Every Turn: A Report on the National Transgender Discrimination Survey" (National Gay and Lesbian Task Force, 2011), accessed on December 28, 2011 at http://www.thetaskforce.org/reports_and_research/ntds.

120. Carl Siciliano, "Will the LGBT Community Protect Our Homeless Youth?" *Huffington Post,* October 24, 2011 http://www.huffingtonpost.com/carl–siciliano/homeless–gay–youth_b_1028509.html?ref=fb&src=sp&comm_ref=false; see also Nico Sifra Quintana, Josh Rosenthal, Jeff Krehely, "On The Streets: The Federal Response to Gay and Transgender Homeless Youth," Center for American Progress, June 2010, accessed on February 25, 2012 at http://www.americanprogress.org/issues/2010/06/pdf/lgbtyouthhomelessness.pdf.

121. Movement Advancement Project, "All Children Matter: How Legal and Social Inequalities Hurt LGBT Families," October 2011, accessed on December 29, 2011 at http://www.lgbtmap.org/file/all–children–matter–full–report.pdf.

122. Williams Institute, "Poverty in the Lesbian, Gay, and Bisexual Community," pp. 2-3, *supra at note 26.*

123. National Center for Transgender Equality and National Gay and Lesbian Task Force, "Injustice at Every Turn: Executive Summary, 2011," accessed on February 25, 2012 at http://www.thetaskforce.org/downloads/reports/reports/ntds_summary.pdf. In this report, 15% reported earning less than $10,000 while another 12% reported incomes of $10-20,000

a year. *See also*, Patrick Egan, Murray Edelman, Ken Sherrill, "Findings from the Hunter College Poll of Lesbians, Gays and Bisexuals: New Discoveries about Identities, Political Attitudes and Civic Engagement," CUNY, Hunter College, 2008. In this survey, 14% reported incomes less than $10,000 versus 5.9% of the comparable general population; and another 19% reported incomes of $10-25,000 (versus 15.8% of general population). In the 2009 HRC report, "At the Intersection: Race, Sexuality, and Gender," another 727 LGBT POC surveyed online, 46% reported incomes under $40,000, http://www.hrc.org/resources/entry/at–the–intersection–race–sexuality–and–gender.

124. Queers for Economic Justice, A Fabulous Attitude: Low Income LGBTGNC People Surviving and Thriving on Love, Shelter and Knowledge (2010)," http://www.q4ej.org/Documents/afabulousattitudefinalreport.pdf.

125. Id., p. 2.

126. Id., p. 17–18.

127. Frederick Rose, "Towards a Class-Cultural Theory of Social Movements: Reinterpreting New Social Movements," *Sociological Forum*, Volume 12, Number 3, (September 1997), pp. 461-494, at 467.

128. Gregory B. Lewis, Marc A. Rogers, Kenneth Sherrill, "Lesbian, Gay, and Bisexual Voters in the 200 Presidential Elections," *Politics and Policy*, Volume 39, Issue 5, pages 655–677 (October 2011).

129. Queers for Economic Justice, "Poverty, Public Assistance and Privatization: The Queer Case for a New Commitment to Economic Justice" (2009), accessed on December 29, 2011 at http://q4ej.org/wp–content/uploads/poverty-public-assistance-and-privatization.pdf.

130. Movement Advancement Project, 2011 National LGBT Movement Report, *supra at note 48*, pp. 5-6.

131. Id., p. 8.

132. Id., p. 9.

133. Id., p. 10.

134. *See*, data from the Williams Institute at UCLA; Randy Albeida, M.V. Lee Badgett, Alyssa Schneebaum and Gary Gates, "Poverty in the Lesbian, Gay and Bisexual Community" (March 2009); National Center for Transgender Equality and National Gay and Lesbian Task Force, "Injustice at Every Turn: Executive Summary," *supra*; Queers for Economic Justice, "Tidal Wave: LGBT Poverty and Injustice in a Time of Economic Crisis," http://www.q4ej.org/Documents/qejtidalwave.pdf; L. Michael Gipson, "Poverty, Race and LGBT Youth," *Poverty and Race Research and Action Council*, Volume 11, No. 2, March/April, 2002, accessed December 29, 2011 at http://www.nyacyouth.org/docs/PRRAC.pdf.

135. Despite the dependence on Medicaid and Medicare by so many in our communities (large numbers of gay men with HIV get health care through Medicaid; significant numbers of gay seniors need their Medicare or Medicaid to live; significant numbers of LGBT people report being on public assistance in surveys conducted in CA, NY, and MA), the mainstream LGBT movement has not been at the forefront of the broader debate on health care, access, or preservation of social entitlements. Grassroots racial and economic justice groups have prioritized these issues and are doing enormous education and organizing, but they lack resources for their work. HIV/AIDS continues to disproportionately affect poor people, gay and bisexual men and women of color, millions still need

drugs they cannot afford to access. Prevention still
is stymied by bias. Yet the place of AIDS research,
prevention, criminalization, Medicaid protection,
global access to retroviral therapies, and even health
care access itself have receded from the top priorities
of LGBT organizations. This is in large part because
the mainstream movement slackened its pressure to
distribute the gains and access it won more widely.
Grassroots HIV/AIDS groups like the Black AIDS
Institute, ACT UP, AIDS-service organizations, and
LGBT groups like QEJ and NBJC are campaigning
still for a range of HIV/AIDS interventions.
The earliest agenda item on the national movement's
agenda—the federal gay civil rights bill, as it was called
in 1975 when Bella Abzug and others introduced it—
reflected the sense of middle class gay Americans that
nondiscrimination in employment, access to housing,
public accommodations, and all other government
and private services should not be denied to them
because of sexual orientation (gender identity came
much later). Yet, access to jobs, access to job training,
promoting workplace policies that support working
families, participation in economic justice coalitions
focused on the challenge of de-industrialization and
loss of manufacturing jobs, active leadership in the
movement to provide expanded child care, leadership
in the efforts on health care reform, good schools, or
any of a number of issues that involve employment and
job-related benefits are objectives that the mainstream
LGBT movement has largely avoided.

136. Sylvia Allegretto, "The State of Working America's
Wealth, 2011" (Economic Policy Institute
Briefing Papers 292, March 23, 2011), accessed on
December 29, 2011 at http://www.epi.org/page/–/
BriefingPaper292.pdf.

137. Human Rights Campaign and Human Rights Campaign Foundation, "Demanding Equality Face to Face: 2010 Annual Report," accessed on February 25, 2012 at http://www.hrc.org/files/assets/resources/HRC_Annual_Report_2010.pdf.

138. Alexander Stille, "The Paradox of The New Elite," *New York Times*, October 22, 2011, accessed on December 29, 2011 at http://www.nytimes.com/2011/10/23/opinion/sunday/social–inequality-and-the-new-elite.html?pagewanted=all?src=tp.

139. Id., p. 2.

140. Lauren Berlant, *Cruel Optimism* (Durham, NC: Duke University Press, 2011), p. 3.

141. Id., p. 2.

142. Readers interested in the difference between equality-focused and liberty-focused arguments might read law review articles and books by law professors Kenji Yoshino and Nan Hunter, among others. See Kenji Yoshino, "The New Equal Protection," 124 *Harvard Law Review* 747 (2011); *Covering: The Hidden Assault on Our Civil Rights* (New York: Random House, 2006). See Nan D. Hunter, "Twenty-First Century Equal Protection: Making Law in an Interregnum [Eighth Annual Gender, Sexuality & Law Symposium]," 7 Geo. J. Gender & L. 141 (2006); and Nan D. Hunter and Lisa Duggan. *Sex Wars: Sexual Dissent and Political Culture* (10th anniversary ed.), (New York: Routledge, 2006).

143. Political Research Associates, "Who's Winning: Right Wing Responses to LGBT Gains," (October 2011); Cassandra Balchin, "Towards a Future Without Fundamentalisms: Analyzing Religious Fundamentalist Strategies and Feminist Responses" (Association of Women's Rights in Development, February 2011), accessed on December 29, 2011 at http://

www.awid.org/Library/Towards-a-Future-without-Fundamentalisms2.

144. Adrienne Rich, "Compulsory Heterosexuality and Lesbian Existence," *Signs*, Vol. 5, No. 4, *Women: Sex and Sexuality* (Summer, 1980), pp. 631-660 (The University of Chicago Press), http://www.jstor.org/stable/3173834

145. Lisa Duggan, *The Twilight of Equality: Neoliberalism, Cultural Politics and the Attack on Democracy* (Boston: Beacon Press, 2004); Jasbir Puar, *Terrorist Assemblages: Homonationalism in Queer Times* (Durham: Duke University Press, 2007).

146. This chapter is based on a talk given at the National Convention of Log Cabin Republican Clubs, August 28, 1999 in New York City.

147. Bernice Johnson Reagon, "Coalition Politics: Turning The Century," in Barbara Smith (Ed.), *Home Girls: A Black Feminist Anthology* (New York: Kitchen Table Press, 1983), pp. 356-368.

148. The remarks were given on September 1, 1995 at the Second World Women's Congress for a Healthy Planet, sponsored by Women's Environment and Development Organization (WEDO) at the NGO Forum, Fourth U.N. Conference on Women—Beijing, China.

149. First Lady Hillary Clinton's speech at Fourth World Conference on Women, September 5, 1995, transcript and audio accessed on January 20, 2012 at http://www.americanrhetoric.com/speeches/PDFFiles/Hillary%20Clinton%20-%20Womens%20Rights.pdf.

150. Secretary of State Hillary Clinton's Remarks in Recognition of International Human Rights Day, December 6, 2011, accessed on December 28, 2011 at http://www.state.gov/secretary/rm/2011/12/178368.htm.

151. The Programme of Action for Reproductive Rights, enacted at the 1994 U.N. International Conference on Population and Development (ICPD), called for such a broad right for all women. See paragraphs 7.2 and 7.3 in particular. *See also*, analysis of the Cairo Conference by the Center for Reproductive Law & Policy, New York, US accessed on February 25, 2012 at http:// books.google.com/books?id=OHhUcgAACAAJ&dq=i nauthor:%22Center+for+Reproductive+Law+%26+Pol icy.+International+Program%22&hl=en&sa=X&ei=eM dLT6WyCKTx0gHov7C5Dg&ved=0CEsQ6AEwAA; Urvashi Vaid, *Virtual Equality: The Mainstreaming of Gay & Lesbian Liberation* (New York: Anchor Books, 1995), Chapter 1.

152. ICPD, Programme of Action, Paragraph 7.3.

153. The International Conference on Population and Development was held in Cairo, Egypt from September 5–13, 1994. United Nations, Report of the International Conference on Population and Development Cairo, Egypt, 5-13 September 1994 at http://www.un.org/popin/icpd2.htm.

154. Suzanne Pharr, *Homophobia: A Weapon of Sexism* (Chardon Press, 1988), p. 1.

155. International Gay & Lesbian Human Rights Commission, *Unspoken Rules: Sexual Orientation & Women's Human Rights*, edited by Rachel Rosenbloom, 1995, available at http://www.iglhrc.org/cgi-bin/iowa/ article/publications/reportsandpublications/42.html.

156. Id., p. vii.

157. Id., p. xxv.

158. Id., pp. 243–246.

159. The bracketed language on sexual orientation was highlighted in a chart prepared by the Women's Environment & Development Organization, Women's Linkage Caucus Advocacy Chart. July 1, 1995, p. 14.

160. Amnesty International, "Breaking the Silence: Human Rights Violations Based on Sexual Orientation" (1994).

161. Id., pp. 14-18.

162. IGLHRC, "Unspoken Rules," *supra at note 156.* pp. ix, xiv-xv.

163. Angus Shaw, "Zimbabwe's Mugabe, at Book Fair, Assails Homosexuals as 'Perverts,'" *Boston Globe*, August 2, 1995, p. A2; "Zimbabwe President Steps Up Antigay Effort," *Boston Globe*, August 19, 1995, p. A7.

164. Suzanne Pharr, *Homophobia: A Weapon of Sexism*, p. 17.

165. This chapter is based on remarks given at the Boston Dyke March on June 10, 2011.

166. Muriel Rukeyser, "More of a Corpse than a Woman," *Selected Poems* (NY: New Directions, 1951), p.26.

167. Larry Kramer, *The Normal Heart and the Destiny of Me* (New York: Grove Press, 2000).

168. Radicalesbians, "The Woman Identified Woman," accessed December 28, 2011 at http://scriptorium.lib. duke.edu/wlm/womid/.

169. Id.

170. Audre Lorde, "Timing," *The Black Unicorn* (NY: W.W. Norton, 1978), p. 83.

171. A version of this chapter was presented on October 9, 2010 at the conference titled "In Amerika They Call Us Dykes," organized by the Center for Lesbian and Gay Studies at the City University of New York. A version of this talk was also edited by Lisa Weil, and published in *Trivia: Voices of Feminism*, in an issue titled "Are Lesbians Going Extinct," Volume 11, 2010, and available for order from http://www.triviavoices.net.

172. Audio Recording of Audre Lorde, Keynote Speech at the 1979 March on Washington for Lesbian and Gay Rights, accessed December 29, 2011 at http://www. rainbowhistory.org/audio/mow79_LordeKeynote. wma.

173. Susan Faludi, "American Electra," *Harper's*, October 2010, pp. 29–42, p. 30.

174. This talk was given on April 17, 2009 at the annual Intergenerational Seminar hosted by the Unitarian Universalist Association, and held at Hunter College in New York City. An earlier form of this talk was given at the "Witness Our Welcome" conference organized by Reconciling Ministries in Arizona on August 25, 2000. A later version was shared on June 15, 2002 at the Presbyterian Concerned gathering in Columbus, Ohio.

175. For more on the evangelical right and its growth see, Sara Diamond, *Spiritual Warfare: The Politics of The Christian Right* (South End Press, 1992); Sara Diamond, *Roads to Dominion: Right Wing Movements and Political Power in the U.S.* (Guilford Press, 2995); Daniel Williams, *God's Own Party: The Making of the Christian Right* (Oxford University Press, 2010).

176. Kapya Kaoma, "Globalizing the Culture Wars: U.S. Conservatives, African Churches and Homophobia" (Political Research Associates, 2009), accessed December 29, 2011 at http://www.publiceye.org/ publications/globalizing–the–culture–wars/pdf/ africa–full–report.pdf; Bruce Wilson, "Rick Warren's Dissertation Advisor Leads Network Promoting Anti-gay Uganda Bill," Talk 2 Action, December 4, 2009, available at http://www.talk2action.org/ story/2009/12/4/134435/084.

177. William James, *The Will to Believe and Other Essays in Moral Philosophy* (Courier Dover Publications, 1956), p. 90.

178. Television, "See No Evil," *Marquee Moon* (Elektra Records, 1977).

179. The Martin Luther King, Jr., Papers Project, "Draft of Chapter XIV: The Mystery of Fear or Antidotes For Fear," p. 542 at http://mlk–kpp01.stanford.edu/

primarydocuments/Vol6/July1962–March1963Draft
ofChapterXIV,TheMasteryofFearorAntidotesforFear.
pdf.

180. A version of this talk was given as part of the Assembly
Series at the invitation of the Washington University at
St. Louis on October 23, 2009.

181. Robert Mackey, "Top General Opposes Openly Gay
Troops," *New York Times*, March 13, 2007, accessed on
December 29, 2011 at http://thelede.blogs.nytimes.
com/2007/03/13/top–general–opposes–openly–gay–
troops/.

182. Tom Smith, "Public Attitudes Toward Homosexuality,"
University of Chicago/National Opinion Research
Center, September 2011, accessed on February 25,
2012 at http://www.norc.org/PDFs/2011%20GSS%20
Reports/GSS_Public%20Attitudes%20Toward%20
Homosexuality_Sept2011.pdf.

183. CNN Election Center 2008, accessed December 29,
2011 at http://www.cnn.com/ELECTION/2008/
results/polls/#val=USP00p3.

184. Robert Bailey, "Out and Voting II: The GLB Vote in
Congressional Elections 1990-1998," NGLTF Policy
Institute, 1999, accessed on December 29, 2011 at
http://www.thetaskforce.org/downloads/reports/
reports/OutAndVoting2.pdf; Gregory B. Lewis,
Marc A. Rogers, Kenneth Sherrill, "Lesbian, Gay and
Bisexual Voters in the 2000 Presidential Elections,"
Politics and Policy, Volume 39, Issue Number 5, pp. 655-
677, October 2011.

185. Ballot Initiative Strategy Center, "The 2008 Ballot
Initiative and Referenda Election Results," November
2008, p.2, accessed on December 29, 2011 http://
bisc.3cdn.net/f1e28b421d2db8cd37_3dm6y56ee.pdf.

186. CNN Election Center 2008. Final tally issued by
the CA Secretary of State at http://www.sos.ca.gov/

elections/sov/2008_general/sov_complete.pdf, p. 7.

187. http://articles.latimes.com/2008/oct/25/local/me-marriagemoney25

188. Robbie Brown, "Antipathy Toward Obama Seen as Helping Arkansas Limit Adoption," *New York Times*, November 9, 2008, p. 26.

189. *See*, www.queerkidssaynotomarriage.wordpress.com.

190. See for example, Robert Smith, *We Have No Leaders: African Americans in the Post Civil Rights Era* (SUNY Press, 1996); Debra Minkoff, "Bending With The Wind: Strategic Change and Adaptation by Women's and Racial Minority Organizations," *American Journal of Sociology*, Volume 104, Number 6 (May 1999), pp. 1666-1703; and Dean Spade, *Normal Life* (South End Press, 2011).

191. Since this talk was given, a new global web-based movement on LGBT rights has been launched through the web site www.allout.org.

192. U.N. Development Program, "Millennium Development Goals: A Compact Among Nations to End Poverty," Human Development Report 2003, (Oxford University Press, 2003), p. 146, accessed on February 25, 2012 at http://hdr.undp.org/en/media/hdr03_complete.pdf.

193. *See, e.g.* Francesca Polletta, *Freedom is an Endless Meeting: Democracy in American Social Movements* (University of Chicago Press, 2002).

194. Kate Zernike, Carl Hulse, Brian Knowlton, "At Lincon Memorial, a Call for Religious Rebirth, *New York Times*, August 29, 2010, accessed on February 25, 2012 at http://www.nytimes.com/2010/08/29/us/politics/29beck.html.

195. Jane Mayer, "Covert Operations: The Billionaire Brothers Who Are Waging a War Against Obama," *New Yorker*, August 30, 2010, accessed on

February 25, 2012 at http://www.newyorker.com/
reporting/2010/08/30/100830fa_fact_mayer.

196. Read, for example the work of Political Research
Associates, a think-tank devoted to the study of right
wing social movements, www.publiceye.org. Also
notable are recent books: Sara Diamond, *Roads to
Dominion: Right-wing Movements and Political Power
in the United States* (Guildford Press, 1995); Jean
Hardisty, *Mobilizing Resentment: Conservative Resurgence
from the John Birch Society to the Promise Keepers* (Beacon
Press, 2000); Rick Perlstein, *Nixonland: The Rise of
a President and the Fracturing of America* (Scribner,
2009); Chip Berlet and Matthew Lyons, *Right Wing
Populism in America: To Close For Comfort* (Guilford
Press, 2000); Chris Hedges, *American Fascists: The
Christian Right and the War on America* (Free Press,
2007); Michelle Goldberg, *Kingdom Coming: The Rise of
Christian Nationalism* (Norton, 2006); Max Blumenthal,
*Republican Gomorrah: Inside the Movement That Shattered
the Party* (Nation Books, 2009); Kevin Phillips,
*American Theocracy: The Perils and Politics of Radical
Religion, Oil, and Borrowed Money in the 21st Century*
(Penguin, 2007); Dan Gilgoff , *The Jesus Machine:
How James Dobson, Focus on the Family, and Evangelical
Americans Are Winning the Culture War* (St. Martin's
Press, 2007). These are just a handful of suggestions;
there are dozens more great books documenting the
roots, intersections, tensions, and ideologies of right
wing movements in the United States.

197. See for example, the 2008 article by Elizabeth
Bumiller, "Research Groups Boom in Washington,"
New York Times, January 30, 2008, at http://www.
nytimes.com/2008/01/30/washington/30tank.html.

ABOUT THE AUTHOR

Urvashi Vaid is a community organizer and attorney who has been a leader in the LGBT and social justice movement for thirty years. Currently the Director of the Engaging Tradition Project at Columbia Law School's Center for Gender and Sexuality Law, where she leads a multi-disciplinary project to examine the ways that notions of tradition affect and influence gender and sexual justice movements, Vaid was a Visiting Senior Fellow with the Department of Sociology at the Graduate Center of the City University of New York (CUNY) in 2010-2011.

She served as the executive director of the Arcus Foundation from 2005-2010; was formerly deputy director of the Governance and Civil Society Unit of the Ford Foundation, where she worked from 2001-2005; and held several leadership roles at the National Gay and Lesbian Task Force (NGLTF) from 1986-1993 and 1997-2000, including media director, executive director, and director of its think tank. She was a staff attorney for the National Prison Project of the American Civil

Liberties Union (ACLU), where she initiated the organization's work on HIV/AIDS in prisons.

Vaid is author of *Virtual Equality: The Mainstreaming of Gay & Lesbian Liberation* (Anchor, 1996) and co-edited, with John D'Emilio and William Turner, a ground-breaking anthology on public policy history, *Creating Change: Public Policy, Sexuality and Civil Rights* (St. Martin's Press, 2000). She was a columnist for *The Advocate*, the U.S. national gay and lesbian newsmagazine, and has contributed chapters to a number of books.

Vaid is a graduate of Vassar College, and Northeastern University School of Law. She lives in New York City with her partner of twenty-four years, the comedian, Kate Clinton.